Serving Those in Need

A Handbook for Managing Faith-Based Human Services Organizations

Edward L. Queen II

Editor

 JOSSEY-BASS
A Wiley Company
San Francisco

ECFA's Seven Standards of Responsible Stewardship (Exhibit 7.1) is used by permission of The Evangelical Council for Financial Accountability, P.O. Box 17456, Washington, DC 20041-0456, 1-800-323-9473.

Exhibit 7.2 (NRB Code of Ethics), Exhibit 7.3 (NRB Standards of Conduct), and Exhibit 7.4 (NRB Financial Accountability Requirements) are used by permission of The National Religious Broadcasters.

Manufactured in the United States of America on Lyons Falls Turin Book. This paper is acid-free and 100 percent totally chlorine-free.

Library of Congress Cataloging-in-Publication Data

Serving those in need: a handbook for managing faith-based human services organizations / Edward L. Queen II, editor.
     p.   cm.
   Includes bibliographical references and index.
   ISBN 0-7879-4296-0
      1. Human services—United States—Management. 2. Church charities—United States—Management. I. Queen, Edward L.
HV91.S37 2000
361.7'5'068—dc21   00-025342

FIRST EDITION
HB Printing   10 9 8 7 6 5 4 3 2 1

Contents

98940

Part Three: Moving Beyond Basic Needs

The Editor

Edward L. Queen II is director of the Islamic Society of North America's Fellowships in Nonprofit Management and Governance and principal investigator for the Project on Religion and Welfare Reform. Previously he directed the Religion and Philanthropy Project at the Indiana University Center on Philanthropy and served as a program officer at Lilly Endowment.

Queen received his B.A. degree (1976) from Birmingham-Southern College and his M.A. (1982) and Ph.D. (1986) degrees from the Divinity School of the University of Chicago, where he studied under Martin Marty.

A specialist in issues related to religion and culture, Queen's research interests are religions and nonprofits, democratization, and civil society. He has written, coauthored, or edited numerous books on these topics, including *Philanthropy in the World's Traditions* (1998) and *The Encyclopedia of American Religious History* (1992). Queen also serves as a consultant and adviser to numerous nonprofit organizations.

The Contributors

SANDRA C. BURGENER is associate professor of nursing at Indiana University School of Nursing. She received her Ph.D. degree (1989) in nursing from Wayne State University. Her research interests have centered on two major areas of concern: quality-of-life outcomes in persons with irreversible dementia and implementation and management of church-based, nurse-managed health centers. She has also conducted two large studies regarding the role of the church as a support element for caregivers and persons with dementia and has published over twenty articles and book chapters. She was awarded the George Pinnell Award for Outstanding Service for her work with church-based health centers and the Leadership Award for Excellence in Geriatric Care from the Midwest Alliance in Nursing for her work with older adults. The church-based health centers also have received a national award for excellence, the Trout Premier Care Award for Outstanding Health Service Provision to Underserved Minorities.

ERIC CLAY is a scholar and consultant in faith-based community economic development and an ordained minister in the Christian Church (Disciples of Christ). He received his Ph.D. degree in city and regional planning from Cornell University and is also a graduate of Union Theological Seminary in New York City.

CARL S. DUDLEY is professor of church and community and co-director of the Center for Social and Religious Research of Hartford Seminary, Hartford, Connecticut. He received his doctor of ministry degree from McCormick Theological Seminary in Chicago. His professional and personal interests focus on the application of the sociology of religion to the everyday needs of communities. He is nationally known for his work in mobilizing local churches for community ministries and is recognized for his long history of working for such causes as the peace movement, civil rights, and housing reform. He is president of the Religious Research Association, a fellow of the Case Study Institute, and a member of the Association for the Sociology of Religion and the Society for the Scientific Study of Religion. Dudley is the author of several books, including *Next Steps in Community Ministry: Hands on Leadership* (1996) and *Basic Steps Toward Community Ministry* (1991).

ARTHUR EMERY FARNSLEY III directs the research of the Project on Religion and Urban Culture for the Polis Center at Indiana University–Purdue University Indianapolis. He has received degrees from Wabash College, Yale Divinity School, and Emory University. While conducting research on Indianapolis, he has served as an adviser and proposal referee for the mayor's office, the Coalition for Homelessness Intervention and Prevention, and the juvenile court as each seeks to engage faith-based organizations in their programs. He is author of *Southern Baptist Politics* (1994) and contributing author, with Nancy Ammerman, of *Congregation and Community* (1997).

ERIC KNUEVE received his master's degree in public administration with a concentration in nonprofit management from Indiana University–Bloomington in 1998 and is pursuing a career in youth development in Seattle, Washington.

JOHN P. KRETZMANN is codirector of the Asset-Based Community Development Institute at the Institute for Policy Research at Northwestern University. The project locates, analyzes, and promotes neighborhood-based efforts that build on and strengthen local capacities to address issues and solve problems and develops policy recommendations aimed at supporting those efforts. This research resulted in the publication of *Building Communities from the Inside Out: A Path Toward Finding and Mobilizing a Community's Assets* (1993, with John McKnight). He has also been a community organizer on Chicago's West Side and served as a consultant to a wide range of neighborhood organizing and development groups. Among his publications are *Building the Bridge from Client to Citizen: A Commu-*

nity Toolbox for Welfare Reform (with Michael B. Green, 1998), and *A Guide to Capacity Inventories: Mobilizing the Community Skills of Local Residents* (with John L. McKnight and Geralyn Sheehan, 1997). He received his Ph.D. degree (1983) in sociology from Northwestern University.

JAMES B. LEMLER is dean and president of Seabury-Western Theological Seminary in Evanston, Illinois, and an ordained priest in the Episcopal Church. He received his B.A. degree at DePauw University, his M.A. at Nashotah House, and his D.Min. at Christian Theological Seminary. Prior to his appointment at Seabury-Western, Lemler was a parish priest, most recently at Trinity Episcopal Church in Indianapolis. There he also served as president of St. Richard's Academy. His publications include numerous articles and training materials, as well as *Trustee Education and the Congregational Board: Leadership in the Community of Faith* (1993).

STEPHEN V. MONSMA is a professor of political science and chair of the Social Science Division at Pepperdine University, Malibu, California. He received his Ph.D. degree from Michigan State University. Monsma served in the Michigan House of Representatives (1972–1978) and the Michigan Senate (1978–1982). He is the author of many books, including *The Challenge of Pluralism: Church and State in Five Democracies* (1997) and *When Sacred and Secular Mix: Religious Nonprofit Organizations and Public Money* (1996). In addition, he has contributed chapters to numerous books and has written articles for several journals, including the *Journal of Church and State, Policy Studies Review, Public Opinion Quarterly,* and *American Journal of Political Science.*

SARA ROBERTSON is retired as vice president of development at Pioneer Clubs in Wheaton, Illinois. She received her Ed.D. degree (1977) in education and communication from Northern Illinois University. She is also a Certified Fundraising Executive through the National Society of Fundraising Executives. Robertson is serving as a trustee at Northwestern College in St. Paul and is on the board of directors of Christians for Biblical Equality. As elder for endowment in the First Presbyterian Church of Glen Ellyn, Illinois, she directs the church's planned giving program. Robertson has published a variety of articles, as well as the book, *Helping the Hurting: A Guide to Financing Christian Social Service Ministries* (1996).

HAROLD DEAN TRULEAR is the director of church collaboration initiatives and vice president at Public/Private Ventures. He received his Ph.D. and M. Phil. degrees from Drew University and most recently served on the faculty of the New York Theological Seminary. A former urban missionary with Youth for Christ/Campus Life, Trulear has published more than thirty articles, essays, and sermons. He serves on the National Board of InterVarsity Christian Fellowship and Evangelicals for Social Action and the editorial boards of *Prism* and the *Living Pulpit*.

MARY TSCHIRHART is an associate professor of policy and administration at the School of Public and Environmental Affairs at Indiana University, Bloomington. She has an M.B.A., with a specialization in arts administration (1984), from the State University of New York, Binghamton. She received her Ph.D. degree in business administration from the University of Michigan in 1993. Her research addresses the relationships of organizations to their stakeholders and explores interactions among organizations in the public, nonprofit, and business sectors. She is the author of *Artful Leadership: Managing Stakeholder Problems in Nonprofit Arts Organizations* (1996). Her published articles include examinations of the AmeriCorps program and its stipended volunteers, use of information campaigns by nonprofit agencies, legitimation strategies, and corporate social responsibility.

ELLIOTT WRIGHT is an author, editor, and program design specialist in the area of American religion and society and an ordained United Methodist clergyman. He received his Ph.D. degree from Vanderbilt University. Since 1991, he has concentrated on faith-based community economic development. He helped to organize the Faith-Based Program of the National Congress for Community Economic Development and is a consultant to the United Methodist General Board of Global Ministries. He is the author or coauthor of seven books and scores of articles.

JOHN ZIETLOW is associate professor of finance at Mississippi College. He received his D.B.A. degree from the University of Memphis. In 1992 Zietlow received a grant from the Lilly Endowment to conduct a multiyear study of financial management in faith-based organizations, which culminated in his coauthorship of a treasury management manual, *Financial Management for Nonprofit Organizations* (1998, with Jo Ann Hankin and Alan Seidner). He recently developed three extensive financial management diagnostic instruments and an advanced financial ratio analysis model (with industry benchmarks).

Introduction

The Meaning of Faith-Based Human Services

Edward L. Queen II

Over the past several years, much has been written and said about the importance of religious organizations to the delivery of human and social services. Numerous commentators have pointed to the tremendous outpouring of money, time, and energy from congregations, denominational service agencies, and independent, faith-driven organizations as proof that the needs of the poor, the addicted, and the despairing can be met without government intervention and public monies. In addition, many have claimed that the nature of the service provision, of helping, from religious organizations is itself qualitatively better than that provided by secular agencies, particularly those directed by governmental bureaucrats. They view faith-based providers as more personal, more caring, and more engaged with the life of the suffering individual. Religious organizations, many have argued, do not view the individual as a case number to be processed, but rather as a human being, as a child of God for whom one should care as God cares for all of God's children.

Perhaps the most peculiar development regarding the delivery of faith-based human and social services is that something so old can appear so new and innovative. The first foundations or endowments for which we have records resulted from religious motivations. Dating from fifteenth-century-B.C.E. Egypt, these documents detail how the pharaohs provided monies to support, in perpetuity, a college of priests. In the ancient Mediterranean world, temples often became places of security and support for the outcast and weak. In the Greek-speaking world, temples dedicated to the god Aesculapius became the first hospitals. In India, the holy city of Benares early became known as a place where no one would starve. For Buddhism, the overwhelming concern for all sentient creatures and generosity as a mark of enlightenment made caring for others central to the tradition's essence. Within the three great monotheisms, the obligation to care for others is central, and from their beginnings, all have viewed the support of the poor and unprotected as an obligation incumbent on believers.

In the United States, the fruits of these beliefs are everywhere visible. In fact, they have become so ubiquitous that they go unnoticed and appear unremarkable. In the area of health alone, the names should alert one. Lutheran General Hospital, Presbyterian–St. Luke's, Jewish Children's Hospital, St. Vincent's: all attest to the role of religion in building the infrastructure of caring and concern that Americans have produced. Other entities—the Salvation Army, the YMCA-YWCA, the Damien centers—have become so ingrained in our psyche and so universalized that many remain unaware of their religious core. Such examples do not even reach the innumerable food pantries, clothes closets, tutoring programs, family counseling, shelters, and drug and alcohol rehabilitation programs that find their homes, volunteers, and funding from congregations and people of all faiths. From Buddhist temples in Chicago, to synagogues in New York, mosques in Dearborn, Catholic parishes in San Francisco, Baptist churches in Houston, and myriad other faiths, denominations, and mixtures of the two, women and men struggle from their faith commitments to aid, help, and redeem their sisters and brothers.

They attempt to fulfill what Aquinas called the acts of corporal mercy and the acts of spiritual mercy. The corporal, or physical, acts are "to feed the hungry, to give drink to the thirsty, to clothe the naked, to harbour the harbourless, to visit the sick, to ransom the captive, to bury the dead." The spiritual alms consist of instructing the ignorant, counseling the doubtful, comforting the sorrowful, reproving the sinner, forgiving injuries, bearing with those who trouble and annoy us, and praying for all (*Summa Theologica*, 2a2ae, 32, 2 ad 1).

The existence of this second list is what many would say separates religious services from others. The values embedded in that list take seriously the humanity of the other. They view each human being as not simply a mass of physical appetites, but as a being with value and abilities. A person is not to be left alone in her or his ignorance and failings but is to be called out of them. Simultaneously, each of us is commanded to bear much in our relationships with others, and forgiveness and forbearance remain as important as instructing and reproving. We are to live with others, to be in solidarity with them (to use the contemporary phrase) as we move along this path of life.

Although many individuals recognize these values mostly in the breach and that the vision of what ought to be does not correspond directly to what is, there are truths in that vision—truths that if ignored can result in a radically inadequate and false sense of the universe of service provision in the contemporary United States. The activities of religious organizations in the lives of people— in providing them with food and clothing, building homes, revitalizing neighborhoods, treating addictions, supplying health care, aiding abused women and children (the list could be extended infinitely)—are immense. From an organization as ubiquitous as the Salvation Army to a small, immigrant congregation, people and institutions are driven by their faiths to help and to serve others.

Unfortunately, while nearly everyone can see bits and pieces of this work—the food pantry at the church, the Salvation Army on the corner, the 12–Step Program downstairs in the synagogue, the job center in the mosque—overall we know very little about how much of this work currently takes place. We know that there is a lot, but how much of it, what is being done, how it is funded, and a host of other questions are lost completely to us. We also know very little about how successful many of these programs are. In many ways, this ignorance presents few problems, but in other ways it hinders our ability to do our work and do it well.

This lack of information often may lead to bad public policy decisions, especially when hope replaces reality. Ignorance of financing may lead to policies that produce increased demand at a time of declining revenues. Increased demand may lead to a loss of those characteristics that made these services so appealing—their deeply personal and engaged character. This book cannot address all of those issues, but it does attempt to provide some answers for those engaged in the delivery of human and social services. It looks at the work from a deep commitment to faith and a sense that religion has a powerfully important role in people's lives and in our public life. For those who view service to others as a means of realizing their faith, it tries to assist them in doing that. It hopes to be ecumenical, maybe even universalistic, while nevertheless recognizing that theology, context, and polity particularize all activities.

A small congregation serving new immigrants may choose to focus most of its activities on the immediate needs of its congregants: employment, housing, immigration issues, and the struggles of adjusting to a new life. Larger, more established congregations, especially those whose focus traditionally has been on providing services, will look at their work differently, as will congregations developing a new missional focus. This book has something to offer all of them, and everyone in between. The skills it addresses, as well as its argument for the centrality of faith, are readily transferable between organizations, although there will be activities and undertakings that may not be feasible for a particular situation. A small congregation with no support staff and an overworked pastor probably cannot take the lead in establishing a community development corporation. Such a congregation and its members can, and should, play a role in such a community-wide endeavor. Simultaneously, a large national organization should not undertake community-based work without a strong and respected local partner.

All readers may have to make translations for their own situation. At the same time, however, no one should be too quick to assume that their situation is unique and that the ideas and suggestions offered here will not work in their own community or city. The chapter authors have a breadth of experience in different locales, with different types and sizes of organizations. This book is designed to help those who want to address pressing community needs; it provides advice and information and suggests what experience has shown to be some of the most promising and successful ways of doing this work.

Although this book can be of use to everyone engaged in faith-based service provision, it is targeted primarily at certain groups of individuals. The first group are those who find themselves responsible for helping to lead such organizations: board members, clergy, volunteers, and employees. The second group are those committed people of faith who want to initiate a new service or expand the current services provided by a faith-based organization, or perhaps they feel called to establish a new organization designed to address a particular need or groups of needs in their community. Although this book does not set out step-by-step directions (some chapters often come close), it provides a strong sense of the issues, suggests how to avoid problems, offers important suggestions, and gives strong practical information that takes the religious component seriously and addresses the distinctiveness of the religious calling.

The importance of these latter elements are key presumptions of this book. We believe firmly that religious organizations, or those driven and run from a strong religious belief, should retain their religious character. They should not lose their distinctive nature and become indistinguishable from secular agencies. Their religious character, however, rather than exempting them from good practices and high standards, should drive them to higher levels of accountability, responsiveness, and commitment. Our faiths call us not to mediocrity and ease, but to perfection and striving. The service of God is not for those who are weak of will or of heart. If one sees service to one's fellow beings as part of service to God, then the quality of that service, the meaning of inadequate service, and the consequences, both theological and temporal, cannot be ignored. Inefficiencies mean that real individuals, children of God, go hungry, unclothed, and tormented by the demons of addiction. Our failings perpetuate suffering; our incompetence hurts people; our inadequacy damages.

Certainly we cannot do everything. We are limited by time, space, money, and ability. We can, however, strive to ensure that we do our work as well as possible. This requires reflection and discernment. Occasionally we might conclude that what we do is provide close personal support for a small group of troubled people: addicts, neglected children, those suffering from HIV/AIDS, and pregnant women. To do this work well, we might have to keep the numbers small. This requires a conscious decision, and often a heartrending one amid tremendous need. Often, however, to extend a program would be to sacrifice its essentials. In such cases, the reasons should be made clear and precise. It makes no sense to quit doing something well in order to begin doing something else badly.

Still other organizations may commit themselves to finding or creating the resources necessary to meet whatever demand arises. Those coming to the food kitchen may get only half a sandwich some days, as need exceeds supply. Everyone, however, will get something. Again, this decision should be a considered one and stated directly in the organization's materials.

In these instances, there might be no bad decisions. Both have potentially negative consequences and the threat of criticism and disparagement. Those who make them must be conscious of what they are doing and why, make the policies explicit, and be prepared to respond, when necessary, to public criticism. Not all criticisms need or deserve a reply, but when they begin to hinder the work, weaken fundraising, alienate supporters, and affect morale, they must be addressed. More important, when these criticisms reflect badly on the wider religious or denominational reality—when they become weapons in the hands of the despisers of religion—then response is demanded.

This point cannot be overemphasized. One of the burdens of being a religiously driven organization is that any failings or weaknesses—especially those having to deal with money, personnel, or sex—play into the hands of those who may look askance at the message. The hint of scandal also can damage the ability to generate the level of trust and support necessary to fulfill the mission of serving those in need. Passion and compassion are no excuse for lack of transparency and accountability. Doing good does not compensate for incompetence. Money squandered is money denied those in need. Those who undertake to deliver human and social services have assumed a tremendous burden and responsibility. In doing this work from a religious perspective, they have added another layer of burden. However, if it is truly from a deepseated faith commitment, then perhaps to speak of a burden is inappropriate. One could argue easily that such an activity is not something one can refuse, but is an integral part of the divine imperative. If such is the case, if one truly feels that one's activity is part of the Lord's work, then the magnitude of the obligation increases even more. For one finds oneself not only under the judgment of law and public opinion, but of the God whom one serves. One must therefore strive to hear God say, "Well done, my good and faithful servant."

We hope that this book will assist those who engage in the provision of services to be "good and faithful servants." The goal is to help them do their work better, avoid mistakes, and improve their skills. For that reason the book attempts to make the points as clear and concise as possible. Stories and illustrations drawn from actual situations bring to the fore the difficulties, struggles, and successes others have experienced. The chapters seek mightily to inform of the numerous variables that service providers must consider in doing their work. Certainly any situation will provide enough surprises; we hope that reading of this book will minimize them.

The book also points to sources of more information. Although the individual chapters provide important starter information and a useful review, they cannot answer all questions and meet all needs. Overall, the sources offer a variety of other books, videos, training programs, and organizations that can aid you greatly in this work. More important, these materials remind us that we are not alone. Innumerable other women and men of faith also struggle daily to address pressing needs: to feed the hungry, heal the sick, console the suffering, clothe the naked, and teach the ignorant. Others struggle to overcome the powers and principalities that lock children of God in prisons of poverty, oppression, and domination. Taken as a whole, this book focuses on building community and that, ultimately, is what we are about.

A Note on Terminology

The breadth and variety of religious organizations in the United States are tremendous. Structurally, theologically, administratively, and geographically, there exists a level of pluralism that beggars description. To ensure that every sentence and every thought encompassed this variety would have challenged even the most felicitous of pens, not to mention the patience of readers. For that reason, the chapters have focused on the congregation as the unit of description, as that structural component of the religious landscape from which these services will be undertaken. This choice, however, mainly is to allow for a consistency in language and to save the authors from the necessity of including multiple strings of descriptors. It does not detract from the book's application to other types of religiously based organizations. Interfaith groups, independent service providers, and even denominational agencies will find the skills ands tasks involved equally applicable to them.

Religious and theological diversity provide another troubling question. The focus on the individual congregation eases some of the language problems. Simply by using *congregation* instead of *church, mosque, synagogue, temple,* and so on, the chapter authors again are spared long strings of nouns that strive to be inclusive but are awkward. That choice, however, does not provide an answer to the fact that many of the contributors come from years of work in and commitment to a particular faith tradition. Their passion for this work has been driven by their faith. I have therefore decided that it would be preferable to allow them to speak eloquently out of their particularity rather than to "muzzle the ox which treads the grain."

Although all the contributors have a commitment to inclusiveness and ecumenism, which shines thorough the chapters, all equally have a higher level of knowledge and familiarity with a particular tradition. We ask readers' indulgence in this. You may have to construct the proof-texts most central to your tradition, but the skills, advice, commitment, and passion are readily portable.

PART 1

Preparing for Service

CHAPTER 1

Religion and the Emerging Context of Service Delivery

Edward L. Queen II

One of the underlying assumptions of this book is the belief that most of the world's faiths view human beings as more than just physical needs and appetites. They have abilities and strengths of mind and will; they suffer mentally and emotionally; they need to live in relationship with others. In those relationships people often fail us, yet those failures should, where possible, be borne and forgiven. We also will fail, and perhaps people also will forgive us. In nearly all of the world's major religious traditions, human beings are seen as sources of both strength and weakness. Often the weaknesses are to be forgiven; they are not, however, to be accepted and certainly not encouraged. Everyone, these traditions tell us, can be more or better than what they are. All are capable of realizing their essential nature. By being in community with others, we begin to understand this. Although articulated and actualized in various ways in different traditions, the dominant thrust of their teachings is that we realize our true humanity and highest nature in community with others. Even traditions that value wandering ascetics and eremitic holy men do so because those persons are able to manifest the values of the tradition and because of the element of holiness and religious enlightenment they impart to others.

The emphasis on the word *tradition,* however, should not mask the fact that religions must bring those traditions to bear on new and changing realities. This chapter surveys several of the emerging contexts with which faith-based providers must contend within the next decade or so. These contexts are grouped into three broad categories: political, social, and management.

Emerging Political Context

The perception that religious traditions combine a commitment to community with a commitment to the inherent worth of individuals provided a focal point for the increasing attention paid to the role of religiously based human and social services. This became a major issue during the debate over welfare reform that dominated political discourse in the early 1990s.

By that time, it had become evident to many throughout the political continuum, and a nagging suspicion to others, that the system of public welfare in the United States did not work or at least was not working. Regardless of whether the consensus was valid, and given the fact that many made this admission only with many caveats, it was widely shared. The evidence appeared overwhelming. The deepening of poverty, the collapse of families, increasing criminality, growing drug use, rising illegitimacy, and the establishment of an underclass all were used to illustrate this presumed fact. These "socially destructive" results as well as the development of a poverty mentality—"welfare dependency"—argued strongly in the minds of many for a massive overhaul of the system. This overhaul demanded not only a change in the manner in which monies and services were transferred to the poor, but, as one looked over the types of problems that seemed to have developed, a change in values. Money seemed to be the least of the problems facing the nation's poor. Their lives were in ruin because they had been stripped of, or had rejected, the very values and behaviors necessary for stable and successful lives. Any meaningful and effective change would have to provide not only the material resources to help but, more important, the moral and spiritual resources they needed. From the religious and cultural right, to the communitarian middle, to the reflective left, many stood aghast at the social and cultural catastrophe that seemed to be occurring before their eyes.

This growing feeling that the situation demanded a transformation of personal values led many to turn their attention to religion. Politicians and cultural analysts looked increasingly to religion and religious organizations as important actors in the welfare arena. This attention focused on two broad areas. One saw religious organizations as able to play a greater role in providing services of both a material and spiritual kind to the poor, weak, and suffering. The second saw religion as a source of the stability and values needed as people moved from dependency and irresponsibility to responsible community membership. For many, these presumptions overlapped. They felt that the delivery of services by and through religious organizations was the means by which the poor could be aided materially while simultaneously experiencing and observing the importance of certain values and ways of living.

There was no more powerful and influential articulator of this position than Marvin Olasky in his book *The Tragedy of American Compassion* (1992), especially given its influence on politicians such as Representative Newt Gingrich. Olasky articulated, or more precisely argued for, a particular way of viewing and understanding poverty and welfare. This argument altered dramatically and drastically the basis of the public conversation over welfare. The perspective on religion and the provision of services was stated most concisely not by Olasky himself but by Charles Murray in his preface to the book:

> We have learned in this century that the search for human happiness is not well served by egalitarian systems, let alone socialist ones. We have relearned in the last few decades the age-old lesson that narcissism and materialism are not satisfying bases for a fulfilling life. Marvin Olasky recognizes openly what most of us sense less articulately; the problems of America's social policy are not defined by economics or inequality, but by the needs of the human spirit. The error of contemporary policy is not that it spends too much or too little to help the poor, but that it is fundamentally out of touch with the meaning of those needs. By reminding us that it was not always so, this badly needed history points us toward a possible and better future [Murray, 1992, pp. xvi-xvii].

Although this view that people are more than just physical appetites and have other needs was articulated by one whom many regard as a spokesman for the political right, it resonates across the political spectrum. What else is the language of empowerment, dignity, and human rights than a statement that within human beings exist certain ways of being that are more important and higher than just their gross physicality?

The concern that people are more than physical beings explains why many turned their attention to religious organizations. Nearly all major religious traditions care about the whole person, about what a person is, not just about what she or he has. If a change from one way of being to another depends less on what one has than on who one is, then greater interest must be shown to that part of the person.

The recognition that the transformation of lives was necessary demanded that welfare provide not only goods but also the means by which people could be transformed. Pundits and politicians turned to religious organizations and the services provided by and through them for the intangibles that many believed were key to the success of welfare reform: the ability to move people from dependency to independence.

One result was the decision by many politicians to aid the work of religious organizations engaged in human service delivery and to develop greater government partnerships with them. Numerous local examples abound. In Indianapolis, the mayor established the Front Porch Initiative designed to bring all local organizations, including religious ones, to bear on the needs of their neighborhoods. The family court has encouraged the development of faith-based counseling programs for juvenile offenders and their families. In Chicago, home of the nation's first family court system, a Cambodian Buddhist temple provides a place of discipline and refuge for Cambodian youth who find themselves in trouble with the law. While such state and local initiatives could be multiplied, one of the most potentially important and influential initiatives has come from federal legislation as part of the 1996 welfare reform bill. One section of the law, known as the charitable choice provision, is directed explicitly at the use of religious and faith-based organizations for the delivery of services provided under certain federal block grants.

Using religious organizations to provide services paid for with governmental monies is not new; it is common in the international development field and significant domestically. Organizations such as Lutheran Social Services, Jewish Welfare and Family Services, and Catholic Charities receive nearly 50 percent of their operating budgets from public funds. The charitable choice provision for the first time explicitly addressed the ability of religious organizations to receive such funds on an equal basis with other nonprofits and to do so without having to alter their religious character substantially. It is worth quoting the section at some length:

Sec. 104 (b) Religious Organizations

The purpose of this section is to allow States to contract with religious organizations, or to allow religious organizations to accept certificates, vouchers, or other forms of disbursement under any program described in subsection (a)(2), on the same basis as any other nongovernmental provider without impairing the religious character of such organizations, and without diminishing the religious freedom of beneficiaries of assistance funded under such program.

(c) Nondiscrimination Against Religious Organizations

In the event a State exercises its authority under subsection (a), religious organizations are eligible, on the same basis as any other private organization, as contractors to provide assistance, or to accept certificates, vouchers, or other forms of disbursement, under any program described in subsection (a)(2) so long as the programs are implemented consistent with the Establishment Clause of the United States Constitution. Except as provided in subsection (k), neither the Federal Government nor a State receiving funds under such programs shall discriminate against an organization which is or applies to be a contractor to provide assistance, or which accepts certificates, vouchers, or other forms of disbursement, on the basis that the organization has a religious character.

(d) Religious Character and Freedom

(1) Religious Organizations.—A religious organization with a contract described in subsection (a)(1)(A), or which accepts certificates, vouchers, or other forms of disbursement under subsection (a)(1)(B), shall retain its independence from Federal, State, and local governments, including such organization's control over the definition, development, practice, and expression of its religious beliefs.
(2) Additional Safeguards.—Neither the Federal Government nor a State shall require a religious organization to—
    (A) alter its form of internal governance; or

       (B) remove religious art, icons, scripture, or other symbols;
           in order to be eligible to contract to provide assistance,
           or to accept certificates, vouchers, or other forms of dis-
           bursement funded [under this act]. . . .

(h)(2) Limited Audit

If [a religious] organization segregates Federal funds provided under such programs into separate accounts, then only the financial assistance provided with such funds shall be subject to audit.

Although the law states what freedoms a religious organization that accepts federal monies under this law has, there remain numerous constraints on both religious organizations and the states in the provision of these services. These include that no undertakings under this law are to be seen to breach the establishment clause. Monies are not to be used to support the religious work of the organization. They shall not be used, as subsection j states, for "sectarian worship, instruction, or proselytization." In addition, the law seeks to protect the religious rights of beneficiaries seeking services. Recipients objecting to the religious character of a provider have the right to receive services of an equal value from an accessible, alternative provider. The state is required to provide such an individual with assistance within a reasonable period of time of her or his objection (section e(1)). Religious providers contracting with the state are forbidden to discriminate against recipients "on the basis of religion, a religious belief, or refusal to actively participate in a religious practice" (section g).

Although this act provides a major opportunity for well-organized and well-managed faith-based organizations to increase their funding pool, it does not provide a source of infinite funds that all religious organizations should chase. Since the monies will be allocated on a competitive basis, those organizations with a successful track record will be at an advantage. They will be aided as well by their level of sophistication in the field—in writing proposals, knowledge of contracting opportunities, and, often, personal relationships with state decision makers.

Applying for and accepting these funds will bring religious organizations, especially those with an explicit faith-based component, into greater contact with governments at all levels. Although this legislation is intended to minimize the legal conflicts that might emerge from the practice of using religious organizations to deliver governmentally funded human and social services, the legislation does open the way for increased governmental oversight. Any organization attempting to garner these monies as well as any other previously untapped sources of funds must accept that potential funders may ask serious and probing questions about the program's success, costs, and management. Reporting demands will increase, and an ability to track funds will be demanded.

The capacities necessary to meet standards expected by funders may bring new and unfamiliar organizational demands. To some extent, these demands result from highly publicized scandals among both religious and secular nonprofits, but they also emerge from the donors' needs to guarantee that their monetary gifts are used wisely and efficiently.

Although organizations with a history of gaining funds from governments and foundations might be accustomed to such precision, reporting schedules and measures of success may strike other organizations, especially those that are smaller and more focused on direct or emergency service, as puzzling and even unreasonable. Organizations and their leaders accustomed to making the case that the homeless should be housed or the hungry fed will see the value of their work in the fact that beds are full, tables are crowded, and many others are turned away. Yet this growing pressure to show success and prove efficiency will be one of the most powerful forces in the future.

To some extent, this is as it should be. Both donors and those in need have a moral demand on managers and organizations—the donors that their monies will be used correctly and wisely, those with needs that as many of them as possible will be met. Inefficient and irresponsible use of funds fails to meet these moral demands. In many ways, however, success is not an easily identified product. Certainly one can count the numbers fed, immunizations given, and children tutored, but these measure only outputs. They tell us nothing about the impact of those services on people's lives. Similarly, low-output programs that strongly emphasize a close relationship to the recipient at a higher cost per person served might prove much more successful, perhaps even more efficient, in the long term.

The determination of quality will cause numerous difficulties. "Success" has become increasingly contested as many organizations are called on to define and meet certain "outcomes." Obviously faith-based service providers will (and should be) required to produce results of the same quality as secular providers, but who determines the results and the means by which they are produced? Invariably, it will be those who have a secular social science or social work background or vocabulary. The possibility of cultural clashes is high. If one of the assumptions behind "Charitable Choice" is that faith-based services provide a qualitatively superior service (and that was one of the assumptions), what happens when determinations about services are made by those whose training and education have formed them in a radically different way? When added to the administrative demands of government, issues revolving around procedures, bookkeeping, and rules, the possibility of radical differences in approach becomes quite obvious. This does not mean that religious organizations do not and cannot meet serious objective criteria. Many do. In fact, many religious services are as professional as most secular social services, and perhaps more so. If the purpose of the act, however, was to enable smaller, allegedly more responsive, and more humane organizations greater access to monies in order that they could do more of what they already were doing well, the very nature of the law may mitigate against it. Indeed the very act of accepting contracts may constrain the flexibility, responsiveness, and human contact that appear necessary to deal adequately with the needs of those suffering from poverty and its consequences.

Two problems exist, embedded in the assumptions of the drafters of the legislation and the categorical nature of governmental policies. The assumptions focus on flexibility, responsiveness, human contact, and the willingness to spend time with those in need. Simultaneously, the categorical nature of government assumes everything is the same, that procedures must be followed, outcomes must be measured, and all must be served. Those judging programs on the latter bases will be unable to see the former.

This does not deny the legitimate expectation of accountability, which lies behind an emphasis on procedure. News reports of waste, mismanagement, and inefficiencies have destroyed many good programs. While we may cheer in novels the soldier, the lawyer, or the social worker who bends the rules for a greater purpose, in real life too often we are resentful, suspicious, and condemning. The preacher whose work may save hundreds of children receives our applause, but when the money cannot be found, suspicions abound and rumors spread.

Fraud and corruption are real. Those charged with spending tax monies have an obligation and a duty to ensure that they are rooted out or prevented. Those allocating monies under the welfare reform bill must ensure that procedures are followed and will bring oversight into any project. Government will stand in judgment on programs.

Social Context: The Organization as Teacher

Faith-based service providers must become more aggressive in educating others about the nature of their work. There must be greater attention to real education rather than merely providing information, especially that which only demonstrates how benevolent the organization is. A process of education will enable the organization to articulate the reasonableness of its view of success, demonstrate its importance to those who use its service, and show concern for those who support it.

This education must take various forms and should be directed and led by someone within the organization. Certainly everyone in an organization should be capable and willing to make the case for it, but management and administrators, including board members and volunteer leaders, are obligated to take the lead. The main responsibility falls on the executive director and other senior staff. Larger organizations, especially those that undertake significant life-changing services—job training and placement, rehabilitation for substance abuse, and turning around at-risk youth—often find that those touched by the service are grateful and eloquent spokespersons. While one must guard against exploiting the population one serves, nothing prevents an organization's leaders from asking people to tell about what receiving a service meant to them, their families, and their futures. This point must be emphasized. Too often people focus on the benefit of their services to individuals and their lives (with good reason) and ignore the fact that changed lives have important social consequences. They produce marked community goods. A person freed from addiction or drunkenness can now hold a job, pay taxes, need not resort to theft and prostitution, and may be able to reconnect with estranged family members. The single mother with a job, adequate day care, and a support system undoubtedly will have markedly improved parenting skills. Her children will be better fed and treated and will fare better in school. The mentally ill who receive treatment and counseling may become functioning members of society. If an organization's work produces important goods in the lives of individuals, it also produces many goods for the wider society. They should not be ignored, and as part of the process of education, one must argue strongly for this significance, especially when convincing people of the importance of this work.

This highlights a peculiar anomaly in this arena. An increasing emphasis on the social value of human services has emerged at a time when individual donors give more readily when they know that their gifts touch concrete individuals. Research has shown that this is particularly true of women donors, who tend to become much more involved in the activities of the organizations to which they contribute than do men. Part of the function of public teachers is to help supporters see the real impact of their gifts in people's lives.

The statement of women's charitable donations also brings us to a new reality. Women of independent means—those who are successful in business and the professions—make large gifts. Organizations need to be aware of that fact and ensure that these donors are recognized as independent moral agents and their gifts acknowledged accordingly.

Just as independent and financially successful women constitute part of the emerging context of faith-based service agencies, so too does a marked shift in the overall way in which people approach their giving. There is a powerful and growing trend toward individual selection and accountability. To meet this challenge, organizations need to become clearer and more direct about their activities and successes. As many communal organizations have begun to discover, connections of ethnicity or faith no longer provide sufficient reason for receiving support. Those within a religious tradition may have internalized the obligation for giving, but that does not necessarily mean that such giving needs to be directed toward religious organizations. Certainly this is not new. My mother tells of a virulent argument between her aunt and a local Methodist minister in the 1940s over giving. My aunt set aside 10 percent of her salary, of which she gave half to the church and the remainder to other charitable enterprises. When the minister remonstrated with her, arguing that all of it should be given to the church, she quickly informed him that he was sorely deluded if he thought she was going to change her giving patterns.

This tendency has become more marked. The increasing number of organizations designed to receive charitable donations, the weakening of certain forms of traditional loyalties, and an increasing emphasis on ensuring that gifts are used wisely and effectively have acted to exacerbate this tendency. Donors want and deserve to know what an organization does with their money. They have a right to be convinced that their gifts are used wisely and for the purposes for which they gave them. Given that resources always are finite, the donors and volunteers want to know that they are putting their limited resources into an organization, program, or project doing something important, doing it wisely, and doing it well. Part of the obligation in meeting these expectations rests with one's function as a teacher and educator. Everyone in the organization must be able and willing to make the case for what it is doing to anyone who asks, to provide the appropriate information to those who have a legitimate need for it, and to help them to see why certain costs are the way they are.

The need to provide this information, to make sure that organization members can speak articulately and honestly about their work, demands finding ways to gather, assemble, understand, and interpret the necessary information at a level appropriate to the organization's size and activities. Gathering such information serves several important purposes. Most important, it helps the organization judge its successes and determine the areas where it needs to improve. The need to be a teacher about the organization's work requires that the organization itself becomes one that learns. Success in the future will not come to those organizations that regularly repeat the same old activities but only to those that struggle to learn first what they ought to be doing and then how to do it better. The bureaucratic mind-set that focuses on not erring and simply on fulfilling its duties will not be a successful one in the future.

Management Context:
The Organization as Learner

This process of learning first requires that organizations determine the context in which they are working; this is true both for existing and for planned programs. Is what they think they are accomplishing and what they are accomplishing the same thing? Organizations find this out by talking to staff, those whom they serve, and thoughtful outside observers. Where is the real value of their activities? Sometimes they will discover that it often is radically different from their perceptions and a small alteration in their programs may serve to distort terribly certain goods they are producing but about which they may be quite ignorant. Related to this is the fact that certain individuals working in the organization may be producing tremendously successful work, yet it might be invisible. The ability to see clearly what is going on and why the organization is being successful, if it is, depends on a willingness to understand the components of the organization's life.

This examination also will reveal what the organization is not doing well, where it is slipping, and where it is sacrificing too much to sacred cows. Really knowing what it is doing is both very important and very, very difficult. While often the discussion of organizational mission has led to pointless wordsmithing, the essence beneath it is unassailable. Organizations exist for reasons, for purposes: to accomplish some good (at least a perceived good), to meet some need, to attain some end. At its best, the language of mission reminds us that we need to attend carefully to these purposes, means, and ends. More important, it asks us to think carefully about what those ends ought to be.

The appropriate end of the organization depends on multiple factors: the expressed needs of those being served, the abilities of those who have created and sustained the organization, the supporters' vision of the good, and the distinctive calling or chrism that motivates the organization and those who support it. There is much in need of doing, and each organization has its distinctiveness. At the same time if the organization has a supply and no demand, it will be unable to accomplish anything unless it manages to create the demand. Coming to grips with its vision and supporters' abilities is the first step, and it requires careful thinking and discernment, just as does the next task: determining how an organization's abilities will enable it best to accomplish the ends for which it was created.

Becoming a learning organization means constantly comparing the activities undertaken with the mission and with the strengths and gifts of the organization. Another consideration is the interests and values of the various stakeholders within the organization. Insofar as it is humanly possible, these components should find themselves working together. Things should fit. If there is not a fit, then the organization must struggle to bring the various components back into a relatively cohesive whole. If it does not, the negative results will be large.

A lack of coherence will lead to a long-term dissipation of energies and a decrease in efficiency. When an organization's energies and resources are wasted, it cannot fulfill the purpose for which it exists. Perhaps one activity or two may be successful, but the overall success of work may be far less than it would be otherwise. This may seem like a relatively minor effect, but the populations being served by human and social service organizations are the weakest and most vulnerable, so any undertaking that "cheats" them in any way must, at the most basic level, be considered immoral, especially for a religiously based organization.

On a more powerful level, the failure to meet stakeholder expectations or to provide promised goods will result in a marked decrease in support, both financial and in terms of social goodwill. The loss of support will produce powerful and immediate effects on the organization's ability to continue its work, resulting in greater failures and a long-term downward spiral. It will begin to focus increasingly on institutional maintenance and less on providing the services it was created to provide. Such undertakings usually produce even greater dissipation as the organization struggles to generate revenues, identify and cultivate supporters, and manage in a crisis mode.

The implications of this way of working are both obvious and marked. Activities become diffuse, morale plummets, and work quality decreases as projects are undertaken for the revenue they generate and not for the good they accomplish. These weaknesses feed on each other as the organization spirals downward. Good employees move to more secure organizations, acrimony and conflict emerge between the executive director and the board, and any attempt at critical reflection and evaluation becomes a way to allocate blame rather than to adjust the organizational course and to right the ship.

This brings us to another significant change within the corporate environment. Organizations not only have to be thoughtful and reflective and encouraging of their staff, but they must learn how to evaluate and judge their activities in a way that produces greater learning and encourages responsible creativity. Too much concern in evaluation has focused on apportioning blame, on determining who made what error, rather than on asking what can be learned from activities that succeeded less than optimally. Little attention has even been given to the question of how organizations can learn from their successes. If we were unwilling to take the time to dissect our victories, what are we to do when we are faced with failures?

This is most definitely a place where we need to draw a lesson from professional sports, especially football, where the attention paid to every detail of the most recent project—the last game—is immense and is almost completely focused on improving the work for the next project and the overall quality of people's work. Organizations need to learn from both their failures and their successes, and they need to learn that often the best planned and most carefully organized project can fail. The failure of a project, or its incomplete success, does not necessarily reflect a failing or weakness of the people running that project. Often it is impossible to manage the external environment sufficiently. Events out of the control of an organization can have dramatic effects on the success or failure of some undertaking. One must be aware, therefore, of how to discriminate between failures that emerge from irresponsibility and incompetence and those due to simple mistakes, unanticipated events (especially those that no reasonable person could have anticipated), and sheer bad luck. One or two failures from incompetence can provide important learning experiences for staff, but they will not learn from them if their energies are directed toward covering up errors. In addition, an unreflective, judgmental corporate culture encourages bureaucratic numbness and time serving, not creativity, flexibility, and autonomy.

As we are called to do more and more, the need for flexibility and creativity will increase. Flexibility and autonomy ought to be the hallmark of faith-based services—the ability to deal with people where they are and with what they need. The genius of the faith traditions in so many ways is that they do not treat everyone similarly. The Jesus who could rebuke powerfully one of his closest followers also could speak comfortingly to the Syro-Phoenician woman, expressing his disapproval of her life, yet treating her as a child of God. Buddhism and Judaism are replete with stories about how teaching should be geared to the needs of the pupil and to her or his personality. Hinduism provides perhaps the most formalized set of this, articulating different duties to different ages of a human life, yet recognizing that there always will be those whose way is different.

Faith-based organizations need to focus carefully on the gifts of those in them. We must never forget our obligations to those people and their commitment to the organization. In our management and in our styles we must model the values we claim to hold. This does not mean that we are free to overlook and ignore incompetence and irresponsibility, but that in the way we handle all personnel matters, we must behave differently than many other organizations do.

We must do this particularly because as organizations driven by religious motivations, we look to higher standards than other organizations. We begin from a particularly exalted view of the individual: as a child of God, a fellow sentient being. The gifts and strengths of those around us should be honored and acknowledged. Staff are not simply instrumental to the ends of the organization; they are essential to it. An organization that respects them and honors their giftedness can attain successes previously unconsidered.

An organization's strength rests with its gifted people. The quality and creativity of staff and volunteers will make a major difference in the work accomplished and the successes achieved. In the future, the most productive and successful organizations will be those that find the best way to tap into the creative potentials of these individuals. The corporate and management culture of a organization must create an environment that gives people flexibility, rewards creativity, and values people for what they are and what they do.

This requires more than the superficial gesture and the awarding of meaningless recognitions. It demands that management attend seriously to the real value of those working in the organization and their contributions to its success. We have to learn how to give up power and the presumption that we have all the answers. Current management techniques such as teams are designed to do this, but as with many other management undertakings, they often are only shifts in form and not substance. As a result, evaluations of the process focus only on whether the model has succeeded, not whether it has accomplished the purpose for which it was designed. Simultaneously, rather than decreasing pointless meetings and busywork, they often increase it as greater emphasis is placed on making sure that the model "works."

Like much of the work on developing mission statements, this misses the point. Indeed restructuring may at best be a way to bring the goals to the fore, but it is not sufficient to accomplish them. Indeed it may not even be necessary. Probably one of the most successful organizations in encouraging flexibility and creativity is also one of the most hierarchical and tradition bound: the U.S. Marine Corps. The backbone of the marines is the smaller squad or group based around a noncommissioned officer and its ability to respond, within the wider purposes of the organization's mission, to situations as they emerge and develop. Within this context, incompetence, irresponsibility, and dereliction are punished severely while flexibility and initiative are rewarded. This fact should remind us that although certain management forms can facilitate the movement to a more flexible organization, they are no substitute for a work environment that gives both responsibility and authority to individuals and honors and rewards success.

Similarly, success comes only to organizations that value and undertake training and retention of individuals. Again the military provides a powerful example. It invests heavily in the training of new employees, recognizing the value of those employees and the expenses incurred; it also struggles to help them work through minor weaknesses and failings in order to improve their skills and to retain trained employees.

Training and retention are going to be keys to organizational success in the future. As the level of demand becomes greater, especially for more sophisticated services, the ability of staff—both paid and volunteer—to meet those demands will be crucial. Costs incurred by losing high-quality employees could spell the difference between success and failure for the organization. As margins become thinner, anything that provides an advantage should be grasped. In doing this, both what is good for the organization and what is right, morally and religiously, converge. Investing in staff, board, and supporters will help them to succeed marvelously, and an organization will be doing what is right in honoring and valuing them for what they are and what they do.

Personal Context: Respecting Individuals

This commitment to the value of the individual, especially framed in religious ways, must manifest itself increasingly in the organization's commitment to and struggle with worship. The emerging context for faith-based organizations is the reality of their distinctiveness. The key to this distinctiveness, the centrality of faith, will come into tension with the growing nature of pluralism and interfaith partnerships. While it may be appropriate, theologically and structurally, for some organizations to limit their staffs to those who share a particular faith commitment, for others this will be neither a desirable nor acceptable alternative. These organizations must find some way to maintain their distinctive religious character while simultaneously respecting and honoring the religious sensibilities of others.

Such an undertaking will not be easy, but it will be necessary and is not as difficult as many imagine. Numerous organizations have been successful at it, Habitat for Humanity and the Catholic Worker being among the most obvious examples. Those whom the organization serves, its staff, and its partners will all come from different religious faiths and none at all, yet the shared commitment to service and the shared nature of the need will bring everyone together.

To do this successfully, everyone in the organization must keep to the forefront that their commitment to service functions as an expression of faith. However, it should not necessarily be accompanied by any overt or explicit presumption on their part. To undertake to provide a service to those who are in need as a leading wedge to conversion is ultimately a violation of their personhood and fundamentally diminishes the morality of the undertaking. This differs, however, from a position that views the good produced by religious belief as paramount and therefore presents it in a straightforward way as a part of the service provided. At any time, however, to dangle food before a starving person as bait for a sermon is not and cannot be considered appropriate.

In the future, religious individuals and organizations engaged in delivering services to others must increasingly come to understand that the faith component of their service is more about them and less about those being served. Doing unto others must be viewed as part of a religious obligation, something from which one cannot escape and not simply as instrumental to other ends.

This respect for others also has to extend to those with whom those in the organization find themselves working as they struggle to meet the pressing needs of the community or the population served. The future will mean partnerships, working together. While many use the term, few know its true meaning and significance. Preeminently, just like the organization, the partnership has a purpose and an end. Partnerships are designed to help accomplish broader goals more readily, through building on differing strengths, reducing inefficiencies, and avoiding redundancy. Approaching any partnership with the view that the organization must get something out of it is wrong. There is nothing more likely to kill or destroy a partnership more quickly than such an attitude. For that reason, although there may be legitimate debates over governance and resources as partnerships are formed, these always must be viewed as secondary to the reasons for creating the partnership. Differences in faith and practice should be dealt with in similar ways. Partnerships always must be undertaken as though they are partnerships of equals. The organization has an obligation to treat partners in service as equals and to provide respect and support for their faith traditions. The requires respect, curiosity and honest questioning where necessary, and a constant focus on the wider context of the shared work together—not an attitude of indifference or denial.

Organizations in the future must be able to adjust to emerging realities and new needs. Only by planning for these, with a clear and well-articulated statement of the nature of the organization and its values, can the mission be fulfilled. It is a constant struggle to do this amid everything else and to do it in a way that does not become a drain on organizational life. Careful planning and implementation, however, will pay off markedly.

References

Murray, Charles. (1992). Preface to Marvin Olasky, *The Tragedy of American Compassion*. Washington, D.C.: Regnery.

Olasky, Marvin. (1992). *The Tragedy of American Compassion*. Washington, D.C.: Regnery.

Additional Readings

Bolman, Lee G., and Deal, Terrence E. (1991). *Reframing Organizations: Artistry, Choice, and Leadership*. San Francisco: Jossey-Bass.

Center for Public Justice. (1997). *A Guide to Charitable Choice: The Rules of Section 104 of the 1996 Federal Welfare Law Governing State Cooperation with Faith-Based Social-Service Providers*. Washington, D.C./Annandale, Va.: Center for Public Justice/Christian Legal Society's Center for Law and Religious Freedom.

Churchman, C. West. (1971). *The Design of Inquiring Systems*. New York: Basic Books.

De Geus, Arie. (1988). "Planning as Learning." *Harvard Business Review, 66*(2), 70–74.

Griffin, Emilie (ed.). (1993). *The Reflective Executive*. New York: Crossroad.

Harvard Business Review on Nonprofits. (1999). Boston: Harvard Business School Press.

Kearns, Kevin P. (1996). *Managing for Accountability: Preserving the Public Trust in Public and Nonprofit Organizations*. San Francisco: Jossey-Bass.

Mason, David H. (1994). "Scenario-Based Planning: Decision Model for the Learning Organization." *Planning Review,* Mar.–Apr.

Michael, Don. (1973). *On Learning to Plan and Planning to Learn*. San Francisco: Jossey-Bass.

Schwartz, Peter. (1991). *Art of the Long View*. New York: Doubleday Currency.

Senge, Peter. (1990). *The Fifth Discipline: The Art and Practice of the Learning Organization*. New York: Doubleday.

Wack, Pierre. (1984). *Scenario: The Gentle Art of Reperceiving*. Cambridge, Mass.: Harvard College.

Wack, Pierre. (1985). "Scenarios: Uncharted Waters Ahead." *Harvard Business Review, 63*(5), 72–79.

Wack, Pierre. (1985). "Scenarios: Shooting the Rapids." *Harvard Business Review, 63*(6), 139–150

Wilkinson, Lawrence. (1995). "How to Build Scenarios." *Wired* [Special Edition], Sept., pp. 74–81.

CHAPTER 2

Congregations and Social Ministry
Preparation and Development
Carl S. Dudley

From the time of Jesus' ministry of teaching, healing, and caring for the poor, the humanitarian concerns of Christians have been embedded in their religious response to people within and beyond the community of believers. In the pervasive religious foundations of the earliest American colonies, the integration of church and state provided for minimal care of the poor, while health care and education found private financing. In the nineteenth century, the responsibilities for health and care of the poor shifted toward voluntary societies and market forces, while education became increasingly supported by the state. In the twentieth century, the responsibility of caring for the poor shifted significantly toward national, state, and local governments, and health care, while remaining private, was subject to numerous government regulations. We are in a fascinating and precarious moment of history when the burdens of health, education, and welfare are not lodged clearly in any institution or agency. Mobilizing congregations for community social ministries must be seen in the context of this complex and confusing historical moment, as they try to sort out the way that faith has moved them to care for others (Jeavons, 1994).

Congregations as Caregivers

Throughout our national history, congregations have served as centers in immigrant communities for education and social welfare in the New World (Warner, 1994). Although the government increasingly assumed responsibility for funding and managing social welfare throughout the twentieth century, Presidents Reagan, Bush, and Clinton increasingly challenged churches, synagogues, mosques, and temples to initiate and sustain programs directed toward community social welfare. In the mid-1980s the Lilly Endowment responded with an initiative to encourage Christian churches to become more aggressive agents for social programs in their local communities. This chapter focuses on the findings of that work, emphasizing factors that were most significant for the success (and the failure) of congregationally based social services.

Between 1987 and 1991, funding from the Lilly Endowment allowed the Church and Community Project in Chicago to encourage the development of twenty-five church-based community ministries (Dudley, 1991, 1996). This assistance included training in the areas of community analysis, organizing, fundraising, and supporting volunteers. It also studied patterns of leadership, decision making, resource development, personal beliefs, and social location, along with other factors associated with developing congregation-based community ministries.

The variety of these services was great. They were, in order of frequency, education, from preschool through adult literacy programs; broad community efforts to expand human services and strengthen civic life; and programs of housing, elderly care, and advocacy for social change.

During this period, despite the collapse of several programs, most of these ministries matured and grew. Their movement from a combined annual budget of $550,000, composed of seed money provided in 1991, to a combined budget in excess of $7 million in 1998 offers a tribute to the value of their contributions to their communities. What was learned about religious support of community ministries can benefit many others.

Motives for Ministry

Different congregations explain themselves differently even when they engage in similar acts of compassionate outreach to help people in need and to transform unjust conditions. They may organize and support similar programs, but their explanations are distinctive to the congregation's own character and conditions. Some congregations respond to the needs of families and individuals in their community whom they know personally. Others act from fear, especially of changes in the local neighborhood. Some ministries grow from the efforts of a few committed members who do it alone for a while, and then recruit others to help. Some evolve from programs of evangelism that bring members into personal contact with the community, and the community in contact with their faith.

Caring ministries do not just happen (Dudley, 1996). Some congregations resist outreach because their energies are spent caring for their own members. Some believe that faith is so spiritual that physical and material help is not called for. The initiative for ministries of compassion and justice usually can be traced to someone who hurts for others. No personal pressure or organizational procedure can make someone love another enough to step forward and help. Unexpected crises of personal pain, hardship, loss, and sadness are often triggers for sensitive persons of faith. Sometimes this personal crisis expands to include others as well. Personal contact with an infant in poverty, an unemployed friend, a broken family, or an isolated elderly person, through the strange power of the divine spirit, often produces the necessary energy and endurance to organize a ministry in response.

To explain their motives and broaden their base, these individuals draw from the traditional language of their faith. Christians, we found in the Church and Community project, turn to their biblical foundations. When reaching out to the poor, they recall that Jesus began his ministry with these compassionate words from the prophet Isaiah: "The Spirit of the Lord is upon me, because he has anointed me to preach good news to the poor. He has sent me to proclaim release to the captives and recovery of sight to the blind, to let the oppressed go free, to proclaim the year of the Lord's favor" (Luke 4:18–19). More frequently organizers quote the great commandments: "You shall love the Lord your God with all your heart, and with all your soul, and with all your mind, and with all your strength . . . and you shall love your neighbor as yourself" (Mark 12:30–31). They want to enact the expectations of the Lord that they will feed the hungry, clothe the naked, welcome the stranger, and minister to the infirm and imprisoned, remembering that "just as you did it to one of the least of these who are members of my family, you did it to me" (Matthew 25:40). Beyond the biblical witness, many volunteers said that they experience a spiritual sense of "being with Jesus" in the act of caring.

Social ministry begins when one or two individuals care enough to act. They must gather others who share their hopes for touching individuals, changing systems, and empowering people. The group may be official or informal, homogeneous or diverse; it may focus on a specific ministry or share a wider concern for the welfare of the community. The members of this initial group, however, must be willing to make the development of this ministry a priority in their lives.

Taking the Pulse of the Community

Discovering that we care about our neighbors is the first and foundational step toward social ministry. The next is knowing those neighbors. Those who care about their communities must take a hard look at their community together, to try to see the world through the same eyes. Without disciplined study, familiarity binds us to the past and blinds us to new possibilities. Mapping the community—learning and identifying the people and places there—helps congregations connect to the real place. Congregations tend to float without contact to a specific location unless they look carefully and frequently at their specific context. In community study, myths are displaced and real people are discovered; trends are verified and fears are openly discussed. As congregations begin to imagine possible new ministries, they discover allies who share their concerns and resources, which can help make the work successful. (This point is made quite clearly in Chapter Three.)

Most guidelines for community study assume that during the process of mapping communities, congregations will recognize the conditions that need changing. We found, however, that they cannot see those needs until they have been empowered to mobilize resources and take appropriate action (see Heifetz, 1994). A process of empowering the concerned person of faith must accompany community study. When leaders believe God has called them to this work and the congregation supports them in it, they then begin to recognize and approach specific problems that must be addressed.

Further, in contrast with the scholars and policy analysts who focus on social issues, our study found that church leaders cared about people they could name in their communities—specific individuals who had problems and needed assistance (see also Claman and others, 1994). After making contacts in the community, they would name elderly families whose homes needed repairs and young people who were poorly educated yet needed a job. Knowing their neighbors in crisis forced congregations to break their complacency and become involved. A lay leader told us, "It hurts more when you call them by name," and another added, "And when they call you by name, that's family."

In listening to the community, we found that social networks were especially helpful in developing social ministry (Daloz, 1996). Although church members were often scattered and out of touch with the neighborhood, their social networks often provided connections to business, professional, educational, and other resources that became significant aids to the ministry. We also found networks of church neighbors who were not part of the congregation but, surprisingly, often had a higher esteem for the congregation than those who belonged. The community often viewed the local church building as a symbolic anchor for the community even though they had not joined it. Uniting these networks made ministry a program not *for* the community but *with* the community—indeed with new friends.

Invisible People and Intangible Forces

Leaders familiar with their community engage in a more revealing search for those oppressed segments of the population whom familiarity has rendered invisible. The early church gave special attention to "widows and orphans," the biblical symbol of invisible people in every society. Many congregations have been energized to launch a social ministry after discovering the marginal lives of neighbors, especially the poor and elderly—those whom we call the invisible people (a term that is, of course, a measure of our limitations, not theirs). One church member reported that "our invisible folk are the elderly who live in the apartments and homes of our neighborhood, but often they have neither the strength nor financial resources to maintain property. Some participate in community groups, but others are hidden behind drawn drapes and closed doors." Others talk about the homeless, unemployed youth, mental patients who have been mainstreamed, or long-time residents who have lost their jobs and self-respect. Frequently, by the grace of God, recognizing invisible people mobilizes a congregation to help them personally and challenge the schools, hospitals, and other institutions that have failed to help them.

In such personal relationships, church members see social ministry differently. They seek to empower the alienated people, not simply assist them. They ask new questions. "What are the needs of people in our community?" can be a condescending approach by those who hold positions of power. When we begin with the perspective of powerless, invisible people, we begin to ask, "What needs to be changed?" The question also takes on a more prophetic form. For the churches in our study, it began to embody the revolutionary words of the prayer, "Thy Kingdom come, Thy will be done, on earth . . ."

Those who discover the invisible people increasingly become more aware of the intangible forces that shape communities. Religious traditions, all of which have promoted the spiritual powers of prayer for centuries, should have a special feeling for the unseen social, economic, political, and religious forces operating in communities. These forces may be intangible, but they have real power over people's lives. One volunteer reported, "The lines at our soup kitchen are getting longer, because of a vicious cycle of unemployment, hunger, and people moving away looking for something better; as more moved, businesses closed in our town and houses are being boarded up."

Congregations that care but see no way to respond often become discouraged and despondent, feelings that give way to apathy and disinterest. Hope distinguishes congregations engaged in social ministries not because they believe they are winning, but because they offer members an opportunity to express their faith in action. When a ministry includes both personal contact with previously invisible people and time for reflection, it more readily discerns the intangible forces, including the power of God to form and transform us individually and together. Seeing invisible people and feeling intangible forces provide the emotional and spiritual nexus for ministry to begin.

The simple act of studying community produces profound changes in the members' perceptions of their own congregation (Rasmussen, 1993). During the process of community mapping, when we asked congregations to locate the anchor institutions and gathering places in their communities, they began to see themselves existing alongside other socially concerned institutions that compose their community. Prior to the community study, congregations were aware of how population changes in their community affected their membership, but they rarely saw themselves as one institution among others. Mapping enables members of the congregation to see themselves as existing alongside other anchor institutions, such as major employers, and among gathering places such as the parks, pubs, and settings central to community life and interaction. While assessing needs, they also discover resources, allies, and potential partners. In making these discoveries, most congregations also recognize old limits and new potentials. They find friends and allies for their work.

Leadership for Social Ministry

In order to break loose from business as usual, the launch of social ministries demands fresh energy from a new group with a clear mandate (Ammerman and others, 1998). To facilitate congregational ownership of community ministries, we adopted a policy designed to locate and empower lay leadership as the organizational leaders in ministry. We discovered that clergy blessing was essential, and clergy opposition was fatal. Neutrality on the part of clergy led to a long period of precariousness. Every new ministry needed both the pastor's blessing and energetic lay leaders.

Since most social ministries include a degree of risk and uncertainty, planning is essential. Effective ministries develop slowly but start quickly. It is important that participants do not get bogged down in the planning process, which deadens commitment and passion. Participants should be allowed to learn while doing (Senge, 1990). In the Church and Community program, church leaders called this experience "building an airplane while flying." Once they began the initial work, they could see more clearly what was needed. In the process, they learn to risk losing control and to expect events to happen for which they were unprepared. This managerial style requires a process of constant learning and adaptation.

It encourages continuity but accepts that the future is open and that crises will occur. An organization, however, must learn to distinguish between carelessness and poor planning, and those contingencies for which one could not plan. To a great extent, a good planning process includes a means by which the organization creates a structured and considered way to adapt to changes, new realities, and unanticipated crises.

As the ministries developed, we discovered that dominant leaders, clergy or lay, who overshadowed the ministry contributed to failure. In every discontinued project, we found a leader who could not let go. "Founder's pride" regularly proved fatal. In selecting project leadership, congregations often are attracted to strong, natural leaders who seem capable of doing it all. Ministries achieve lasting success, however, not by looking for superstars to save them, but by nurturing and forming committed, solid workers into confident and competent leaders (McKnight, 1995). These people often need encouragement to take on leadership responsibility as well as a supportive setting. They stand in particular need of models so they can see what others do and how they go about it. When they visit other ministries where ordinary citizens, average laypeople, are doing the job, they begin to believe in themselves and that they can do it too.

Pastoral leaders are essential to many dimensions of launching a ministry (Carroll, 1991; Schön, 1983). In the early stages, they must have a vision of the ministry and the ability to help lay leaders imagine doing what does not yet exist. Clergy who bless congregational social services give them the power of legitimacy, and clergy who support a project often are in the best position to mobilize an array of resources, from funding to volunteers. Clergy are appreciated most when they take the time to help volunteers understand the meaning of their activities and see the connections between their beliefs and the ministry. The clergyperson's most important role is as an interpreter of faith in action. This ability to place the social ministry in the context of the faith tradition transforms the lives of those who participate.

Using History Constructively

If we view history as the memory of the congregation that is used to interpret its present and imagine its future, then that past is a powerful tool for mobilizing to strengthen community ministry. Of the many ways to access history, church stories are the most available carriers of communal memory. Sometimes we hear these stories in formal situations, but more likely we share them in conversation, where humorous memories transmit community values and carry lessons that strengthen membership commitments. These stories also surface during decision-making crises, providing models for choices and the energy to seal the choice with action. The stories live through the social network, helping it to select what is authentic to its identity. Sometimes they guide us, like a rudder, through hard times. They confirm a sense of belonging for those who tell them and those who listen (Heilman, 1973).

Throughout the ministries studied, we found that new energy was rooted in memories associated with a heritage or value that members carried from the past. Housing ministries pointed to earlier efforts to repair homes in the community, elderly programs named families of former generations who had been sustained by the church, and youth activities harkened to earlier experiences that current leaders recalled with some humor from their own teen years. We could not predict what elements of the congregational history would be lifted up to energize the new ministry, but without exception we discovered power of precedent in creating new efforts. Although we worked with congregations that had no substantial social ministries, after they had launched their new ministry we discovered that they would say, "We've always done this." That is the power of selective memory to institutionalize and sustain their ministry.

Expanding Resources

Clergy voiced a common reservation about undertaking new ministries. They were almost unanimous in feeling that the congregation's financial and human resources already were stretched to the maximum. They feared that a new program would push them over the limit. However, as we worked with congregations in developing new social ministries, all—without exception—found far greater resources than they expected within and around them, especially when their programs clearly strengthened individuals and added value to communities. Even small congregations located in poverty-stricken areas found ways to expand their income and tap additional funding, find new workers and redeploy existing volunteers, develop multiple uses for existing space, and locate unused buildings in the community. In the process of observing this, we became convinced that every congregation has the potential physical, financial, human, and spiritual resources to begin community ministries that will succeed when the leadership has the energy and imagination to risk the effort.

Along with the pastors, we worried that new ministries might compete with existing church programs and reduce their financial support. Rather than draining these resources, we found that community ministries were able to expand their income faster than the churches that initiated them. The income for these ministries increased tenfold in five years, without any negative effect on the funding for other congregational programs. These social ministries generated their own independent sources of money that were much more broadly based in the various sectors of the community than was the funding for the local churches, which remained limited to the membership base.

Participation in social ministries does not change the profiles of an individual's beliefs. In standard measures of belief, conservatives did not become more liberal or liberals more conservative. There was, however, a significant increase in measures of commitment to the church and to programs of community ministry (Dudley, 1996, chaps. 1, 10). Although individuals did not change *what* they believed, they changed significantly in *how much* those beliefs meant to them and the intensity of their support. They gave more of everything: more time, money, and energy. Participation, in short, impassioned their giving.

Theologically, we found no difference in levels of participation between congregations that were predominantly liberal and those that were more conservative. Congregational participation cut across popular theological differences. They quoted the same scripture and, after looking together at their communities, shared the same social concerns. They named the same neighbors, and together built ministries in response. To highlight this emphasis on common practice rather than theological differences, Dean Hoge (Hoge and others, 1994) has used the term *lay liberals* and Nancy Ammerman *Golden Rule Christians* (Ammerman, 1997). Although both terms reflect the margin of a common faith, neither fully expresses the depth of commitment by these Christians to enact their faith by their work in social ministries.

In a similar way, the congregations' work transformed local institutions not by confrontation but by providing viable alternatives (Hinsdale and others, 1995). In one city, the government's housing rehabilitation program incorporated the programs and staff of two church-based ministries. In another, the courts designated the church-based mediation ministry as an alternative to mandated sentencing, and in a third the church-based literacy program was adopted by United Way as their flagship ministry for community support. Without confrontation, these ministries transformed the existing but inadequate institutions simply by practicing their beliefs, not by challenging the alternative.

Partners as Problems and Potential

Congregations often have surprising difficulties working comfortably with other congregations and with community agencies. Although these relationships are important to expanding the physical, financial, personnel, and spiritual resources of new ministries, they also require a kind of letting go—of sharing the vision, the work, and the public recognition with others. Some resistance comes from inexperience among partners, some from institutional myopia, and some can be traced to ugly memories of past efforts.

Partners can be negotiated in a variety of ways (Kretzmann and McKnight, 1993). Many congregations have a positive history of working with one or more partners, and they can build on that experience to initiate a ministry together. In these situations, they usually share a common perception of their community and need only agree on the focus and scope of their shared ministry. More often, partnerships begin when, after studying their community, the leaders of one congregation agree on a ministry that they recognize is too big to be undertaken alone. In this case, as each new partner is added, it must re-vision the ministry in a way that makes it their own.

In virtually every case, existing leaders must adjust the old vision to accommodate the views of new partners. This re-visioning is costly in psychic energy, particularly when the initiating members feel that new participants dilute their commitment. Furthermore, the need for new partners to negotiate their roles within the ministry, whether very limited (such as donating materials for a housing program) or highly specialized (like fundraising or management consulting), created periods of ambiguity and tension. Energy was restored to most projects, however, as the ministry matured and relationships became more comfortable. Especially when recognized in the public press and television, all the participants seemed to take extra pride in "our baby."

No particular organizational form was more successful than others, but ministries seemed to shape the mixture of structural, relational, political, and symbolic organizations to fit their polity, faith, and community culture (Bolman and Deal, 1991). Most troubling, although understandable, was the fact that the largest number of failures occurred across cultural boundaries, especially in racial-ethnic and low-income settings. Some of this was attributable to the lack of viable leadership, from either inexperience or stress. More often the problem was a disconnect between the organizational requirements for program ministry and the relational, interpersonal style that characterized racial-ethnic and rural congregations. In these churches we discovered the importance of a "translator," or bridge person, who could traverse both worlds and explain why evaluation might be helpful or demonstrate how to keep financial records. In all the failed racial-ethnic ministries, the loss of this bridge person was determinative. Although the bridge people were not the chairpersons, the projects could not survive without their gift of bicultural translation.

Although bridge people are a dramatic example of the fact, personal relationships are essential to the survival of every partnership. Common interests create temporary coalitions, but personal trust relationships sustain partnerships over the long and difficult struggle necessary to maintain community ministries. While pastors are often the most visible bridges between partners, friendships among lay leaders should be intentionally encouraged as equally significant links and those often more readily more extended.

Great Expectations

In a strange combination of political forces that allowed President Clinton to fulfill his campaign promise "to change welfare as we know it," Congress passed the Personal Responsibility and Work Opportunity Act of 1996. In addition to restructuring the entitlement funding for millions of Americans, the bill includes language that denies states the right to refuse to fund explicitly religious programs that include faith as a major factor in helping move people from welfare to work.

Journalist Joe Klein (1997) has described the ambivalence of President Clinton, Governor John Edgar of Michigan, and other political leaders who had wrestled with ways to maintain First Amendment patterns of nonsectarian government programs, yet at the same time harness the unique power of religious beliefs that transformed clients in church-sponsored poverty programs. He reported that participants find the strength in their faith to move from dependency to economic self-sufficiency, but when government funding strips these programs of their religious teachings, the procedures become ineffective. The strange combination of political pragmatism, conservative theology, and economic relief comes together in the charitable choice section of this new law (Carlson-Thies and Skillen, 1996). It invites creative partnerships between congregations and state agencies in attacking the most tenacious problem of the ages: "The poor you have with you always."

No consideration of initiating new ministries should ignore this shift in resources and potential alliances. Faith-based partnerships with government agencies offer new possibilities for community ministries. While congregations should not assume the burden that rightly belongs to government, neither should they shirk their calling to challenge the massive problems of disproportionate distribution of wealth and power that offends God and contributes to human misery.

Amy Sherman (1997) speaks of the remarkable effectiveness of "restorers of hope": those individuals in faith-based programs who effectively challenge captivity to the culture of poverty with the power of transforming faith. Such programs are slow, labor intensive, and highly personal. They also are problematic for deeply concerned Christians committed to structural change rather than personal salvation. Still, one must hear the testimony of a storefront pastor: "We pray with jobless people and the Lord blesses them with new opportunity." As Klein reminds us, religious groups have something unique to offer; in faith, people are transformed.

As a social service rooted in a religious tradition or traditions, this fact cannot and ought not be forgotten.

Steps for Beginning

- Find believers who care enough to act in faith.
- Help your congregation rediscover its neighborhood, community, and region.
- Finding the "invisible people" and "intangible forces" renews vision and commitment.
- Organize your ministry your way, that is, any way that works for you.
- Remember past ministries as the seedbeds from which new ministries grow.
- Expect resources and partners when your ministry touches the lives of real people.
- Let risk (faith) and effort take you beyond proved skill and past performance.

References

Ammerman, Nancy Tatom. (1997). "Golden Rule Christians; Lived Religion in American Mainstream," In David Hall (ed.), *Lived Religion in America*. Princeton, N.J.: Princeton University Press.

Ammerman, Nancy, and others. (1998). "Congregational Leadership." In *Studying Congregations*. Nashville, Tenn.: Abingdon.

Bolman, Lee G., and Deal, Terrence E. (1991). *Reframing Organizations: Artistry, Choice, and Leadership*. San Francisco: Jossey-Bass.

Carlson-Thies, Stanley W., and Skillen, James W. (eds.). (1996). *Welfare in America*. Grand Rapids, Mich.: Eerdmans.

Carroll, Jackson W. (1991). *As One with Authority*. Westminster/John Knox.

Claman, Victor, and others. (1994). *Acting on Your Faith: Congregations Making a Difference, A Guide to Success in Service and Social Action*. Boston: Insights.

Daloz, Laurent A. (1996). *Common Fire: Lives of Commitment in a Complex World*. Boston: Deacon Press.

Dudley, Carl. (1991). *Basic Steps Toward Community Ministry*. Washington, D.C.: Alban Institute.

Dudley, Carl. (1996). *Next Steps in Community Ministry*. Washington, D.C.: Alban Institute.

Heifetz, Ronald A. (1994). *Leadership Without Easy Answers*. Cambridge, Mass.: Harvard University Press.

Heilman, Samuel C. (1973). *Synagogue Life.* Chicago: University of Chicago Press.

Hinsdale, Mary Ann, and others. (1995). *It Comes from the People: Community Development and Local Theology.* Philadelphia: Temple University Press.

Hoge, Dean R., and others. (1994). *Vanishing Boundaries.* Westminster/John Knox.

Jeavons, Thomas. (1994). *When the Bottom Line Is Faithfulness.* Bloomington: Indiana University Press.

Klein, Joe. (1997). "In God They Trust." *New Yorker,* June 16, 1997.

Kretzmann, John P., and McKnight, John L. (1993). *Building Communities from the Inside Out.* Evanston, Ill.: Center for Urban Affairs, Northwestern University.

McKnight, John. (1995). *The Careless Society.* New York: Basic Books.

Rasmussen, Larry L. (1993). *Moral Fragments and Moral Community.* Minneapolis: Augsburg Press.

Schön, Donald A. (1983). *The Reflective Practitioner.* New York: Basic Books.

Senge, Peter. (1990). *The Fifth Discipline.* New York: Doubleday.

Sherman, Amy L. (1997). *Restorers of Hope.* N.p.: Crossways Books.

Warner, Steven. (1994). "The Place of the Congregation in American Religious Configuration." In James Wind and James Lewis (eds.), *American Congregations: New Perspectives in the Study of Congregations.* Chicago: University of Chicago Press.

CHAPTER 3

Congregations and Communities Working Together

John P. Kretzmann

For many congregations and other local religious groups, building connections with their surrounding community involves either evangelism or service—or often a combination of the two. The goal of the evangelists is to enlarge the faith community, while services aim to help or to "fix" individuals who are hurting. Both are important strategies, yet neither addresses an increasingly critical concern for mission-driven congregations: how to become effective community builders. In fact, many church-based community builders have come to recognize that service delivery alone not only fails to strengthen local capacities but may even contribute to their diminution. John McKnight (1995) argues persuasively in *The Careless Society* that human service systems tend to disable communities in three ways: they divert resources from lower-income to professional, credentialed helpers; they teach people to focus on their needs and deficiencies rather than their resources and potentialities; and they displace community-based citizens' organizations and their power to solve problems.

Recognizing the limitations of a strategy centered on service provision, many congregations surrounded by communities in distress have accepted the challenge to help rebuild those communities by exploring alternative approaches. Chief among these approaches have been congregation-based community organizing and community economic development. Currently, these two strategies engage the energies of several thousand local congregations across the United States. More recently, these two approaches have been modified by a set of perspectives sometimes called "asset-based community development." (Chapter Eleven illustrates the merger of these elements.)

Congregation-based community organizing has developed and expanded significantly since the mid-1970s. Often affiliated with one of four major organizing networks providing training and valuable professional support (the Industrial Areas Foundation, the Gamaliel Foundation, the Pacific Institute for Community Organizing, and the Direct Action Research and Training Institute), these congregations provide leaders, supporters, meeting and office space, dollars, and other resources for efforts to build more powerful communities. The concrete results of these efforts are apparent in hundreds of communities across the country. Affordable housing units (both new and rehabilitated), increased investment in enterprises and infrastructure, and public officials more responsive to demands for higher-quality schools, parks, libraries, and police are evident because of this work in neighborhoods from the South Bronx to East Los Angeles, from Minneapolis to the Rio Grande Valley.

In many instances, congregational investment in community organizing has led to or been joined with efforts to rebuild local economies. Beginning in the mid-1960s with New York's Bedford-Stuyvesant neighborhood, communities began to act on the recognition that economic revitalization lay at the core of the challenge to rebuild areas devastated by the exodus or elimination of employers, particularly those in traditional industries. The community development corporation (CDC) has proved to be as significant as the power-building community organization in providing local citizens with strategies for rebuilding localities.

Over the past fifteen years, the involvement of religious congregations in community economic development has expanded significantly. The major network of church-based community development efforts, the Christian Community Development Association, constitutes a significant subsection of the more than two thousand community development corporations across the United

States. Particularly for churches in the African American and Hispanic communities, the CDC's emphasis on the development of affordable housing has been critical. As with their involvement
in community organizing, congregations whose members support
community economic development see immediate benefits to
themselves and to their neighborhoods.

These two strategies—community organizing and community
economic development—have engaged increasing numbers of
congregations over the past two decades. In many cases they have
been powerful tools for reinvigorating both communities and the
congregations within them. Not only have they produced concrete
results in the forms of jobs and affordable housing, they also have
functioned as vital incubators for community talent. Hundreds of
clergy and lay leaders have discovered leadership capacities and
developed skills necessary to operate effectively in the public
realm.

But effective and necessary as community organizing and community economic development are for congregations committed
to a community-building mission, they nonetheless represent only
partial strategies. In fact, as many congregational leaders are recognizing, they beg to be stretched in two different directions. First,
community organizing and community economic development approaches exist in a much larger context, one that involves regional,
state, national, and even international policy decisions. For community action to bear fruit over time, these larger arenas must be
entered creatively and effectively. Building public policy from the
grassroots up is a daunting challenge, but one that must be met if
communities are to survive and thrive.

The second stretch is one that congregations are beginning to address with remarkable faith and creativity. It is the mandate to reach back, to make sure that everyone in the congregation
and everyone in the community becomes an integral part of the
community-building action. If the first stretch reaches to the macro
world of policymaking, this second challenge focuses on the micro
world of the very local, the critically personal and interpersonal.

For many congregational leaders, this shift to the immediate and
local has been accompanied by a simple realization. Despite their
power and effectiveness, community organizing and community

economic development represent strategies built on the view that all the important challenges that struggling communities face are caused by external forces and that all solutions are held in the hands of outside players.

For community organizers, designating (and personalizing) an outside "target" or "enemy" is the centerpiece of a successful campaign against city hall or a land-hungry developer. Among the core assumptions underlying the community organizing strategy is the effort to build a community voice powerful enough to speak effectively to outside interests that are both invested in the community and able to respond to the community's organized pressure. But what happens when the "enemy" is no longer either local or capable? What happens when the ownership of the departing corporation is headquartered in Europe or Asia, or when the mayor lacks funds for job expansion or affordable housing?

Community economic developers face a similar challenge. For twenty-five years, these specialists have targeted resources outside the community as the necessary core ingredients for rebuilding disinvested economies. They have attracted millions of dollars from both public and private sources. But some now wonder whether we have been ignoring the resources within our congregations and communities. Should not community economic development use both necessary external and extant internal resources?

These questions have led many congregational leaders to explore the emerging field of approaches and tools—those referred to as asset-based community development. These strategies begin with the assumption that successful community building involves rediscovering and mobilizing the resources already in the local community. These internal resources fall into three major categories: the skills and resources of local residents, the power of voluntary citizens' associations, and the full range of assets held by local public, private, and nonprofit institutions.

In many communities, congregations have begun to develop tools and methods for rediscovering these local assets and for mobilizing their power. Following are some examples of effective congregation-based community building that began not with a focus on the neighborhood's needs, problems, and deficiencies but on its resources and strengths.

The Gifts of Individuals: Building Blocks for Congregations and Communities

Vital congregations have long recognized that every person has capacities, abilities, and gifts and that the quality of an individual life depends in part on the extent to which these capacities are used, abilities expressed, and gifts given. Just as individual lives are enhanced by the opportunity to contribute, communities and congregations are strengthened when more members and residents direct their skills and capacities toward the well-being of the whole.

In practice, the process of uncovering individuals' gifts and abilities often focuses first on the members of the congregation and later on the residents of the surrounding community. These two different foci prove useful in different ways. When accompanied by a commitment to use the skills discovered, a thorough "gift inventory" process can reveal vital new leaders and help reenergize a congregation. But experienced clergy and lay leaders warn that without a plan to follow up the inventory with invitations and opportunities to put members' abilities to meaningful use, the congregation will have wasted its effort. Disillusionment spreads when congregants report, "They asked me about my skills and about what I'd be willing to contribute. I told them, but they never called me." On the other hand, when the congregation constantly creates new opportunity structures for the giving of members' gifts—when the skills of cooks, drivers, gardeners, basketball players, computer whizzes, plumbers, and readers are consistently mobilized—then the sense of community and interdependence within the congregation is continuously renewed.

While many congregations have understood their obligations to be faithful stewards of their resources to include the wise use of their members' capacities and skills, fewer have applied the same understanding and approach to their surrounding communities. For many, in fact, the community is useful partly because it provides an endless supply of needs, problems, and deficiencies that can be "treated" and "served" by the resources of the congregation. This classic religious service or charity orientation only perpetuates a debilitating sense of powerlessness and dependence. It cannot build a stronger community. Recognizing this, a few congregations have begun to apply tools such as the capacity inventory, or gift survey, to the residents of the community around them. Some cases point to the potential for community-building outcomes that emerge with this shift in perspective.

In one particularly daring effort, a group of ministers and lay leaders in inner-city Cincinnati decided to reexamine their relationships with the people they were "serving" in their soup kitchen. "We were feeding folks, but we weren't getting to *know* them," explained one kitchen volunteer. "We knew nothing about their experiences, and especially about their skills and their talents."

The congregation designed a "gift interview" (see Exhibit 3.1), and after refining the questions among themselves, they began one-on-one interviews with the people coming into the soup kitchen. What they found astonished them: here were carpenters, plumbers, artists, musicians, teachers, and caregivers—gifted and talented people with dreams who had not been asked recently about who they really were and how they would like to contribute to their community.

As the interviews proceeded, the congregation volunteers began to notice that one skill in particular was being reported more than any other. In fact, more than 50 percent of the people interviewed cited cooking as one of their talents. Gradually the church leaders began to understand what this message was meant to convey. As one pastor put it, "Folks were telling us, 'We don't want to stay over here on the receiving end of the table. We're not just recipients. We want to cross over to *your* side of the table. We want to cook and to serve too. We want to belong by contributing.'"

And so the journey continued. More and more, recipients served and servers received. The power the server held over the served began to disappear, and real, reciprocal relationships blossomed. The Soup Kitchen's "Wall of Fame," a large display highlighting the gifts, skills, and dreams of the folks coming to the kitchen, became one way of celebrating this reunification of people in expanded community.

In another setting, a group of congregations in Minneapolis expanded their traditional involvement in community organizing to include a process of finding and mobilizing the skills of congregation members and community residents. As the leaders of Interfaith Action began to focus particularly on economic development

Exhibit 3.1. Gift Interview.

Survey Guidelines:

INTRODUCTION

My name is _____

What is your name?

Thank you for coming over. Did someone talk to you about what the "Gift Exchange" is all about? What do you understand it to be?

Basically, we believe that everyone has God-given talents and gifts that can be used to benefit the community. I'd like to spend a few minutes talking to you about your gifts and skills.

Before we get started, let me give you a small gift.

GIFTS

Gifts are abilities that we are born with. We may develop them, but no one has to teach them to us.

1. What positive qualities do people say you have?
2. Who are the people in your life that you give to? How do you give to them?
3. When was the last time you shared with someone else? What was it?
4. What do you give that makes you feel good?

SKILLS

Sometimes we have talents that we've acquired in everyday life such as cooking and fixing things.

1. What do you enjoy doing?
2. If you could start a business, what would it be?
3. What do you like to do that people would pay you to do?
4. Have you ever made anything? Have you ever fixed anything?

DREAMS

Before you go, I want to take a minute and hear about your dreams—those goals you hope to accomplish.

1. What are your dreams?
2. If you could snap your fingers and be doing anything, what would it be?

CLOSING

First, I'd like to thank you. We're talking to as many people as we can and what we'd like to do is begin a Wall of Fame here in the Soup Kitchen highlighting the gifts, skills, and dreams of as many people as possible. The ultimate goal is to find a way to use those gifts in rebuilding the community.

Before you go, can I get your full name? Address? Age?

challenges for members of the Hispanic community, they decided to explore what skills and abilities that community possessed. Their community talent inventory (Exhibit 3.2) centered on economic skills and sought to uncover business experience and entrepreneurial dreams. In their first two hundred interviews, they discovered a huge array of talent, with significant numbers of people experienced in food and catering, sales, theater, arts and crafts, and music. These congregations now focus on using these skills and talents to enhance what Interfaith Action calls "whole community economic development." Among the other concrete outcomes are these:

- Both the skills possessed and the interests expressed have led to the development of a computer literacy center.
- Having found more than sixty members and residents with serious business development ideas and interests, Interfaith Action is developing a small business incubator, which it is planning to expand into the first Hispanic *mercado* (market) in the upper Midwest.
- New bilingual technical assistance and training opportunities have been developed, as has a new development association linking businesses and residents.

Interfaith Action's organizers and leaders continue to explore ways in which the rich array of talents and skills in Minneapolis's Hispanic community can be transformed into community wealth.

One final example illustrates the ways in which refocusing on gifts and talents can reconnect people to the life of the community, particularly those who have been pushed to the margins by being labeled primarily as deficient. A small congregation in a struggling South Bend, Indiana, neighborhood decided to redirect its youth ministry toward finding, using, and celebrating the skills and energies of the community's young people. To kick off the effort, they hired three neighborhood youth as "animators of the human spirit." The animators' assignment was simply to discover and use the gifts of as many of their young friends as they could. The positive results became evident almost immediately. Older youth became tutors and mentors for their juniors. Young

Exhibit 3.2. Community Talent Inventory.

ADDRESS: ZIP:

PHONE: INSTITUTION:

LIST BELOW THE ANSWERS YOU GET TO THE FOLLOWING
QUESTIONS:

1. What do you do well? For example, cooking, "I'm a good listener,"
   cross-stitching, public speaking, plumbing, etc.
   (We want to know practical skills and social skills.)

   Have you ever been paid for any of these skills?
   No   Yes   Which ones?

2. When you think about all of these skills, which would you say are
   the ones you are best at or enjoy doing most?

   Would you be interested in making money doing them or
   teaching someone else to learn them (i.e., a gardener selling
   produce, someone who makes quilts selling them at a craft
   fair, teaching someone carpentry skills).

   Which skill would you like to use to:
   Make money?
   Teach others?

   Have you tried to make money on a skill and been successful?
   No   Yes
   What skills?
   What happened?

3. Have you ever thought of starting a business at home or in the
   neighborhood?
   No   Yes

   What kind of business would you start?

   Why haven't you started it?

   What would lead you to try?

4. What are some of the groups you belong to? Do you have a role in
   these groups (for example, chair, fundraiser, treasurer, troop
   leader)?

5. Can we list these skills in a published inventory for the community?
   Volunteer   Yes   No
   Paid   Yes   No

   This inventory was completed by:

writers produced and bikers delivered a neighborhood newsletter. Musicians and dancers began to perform for church and community groups, and in one major community project, a large group of young people produced a huge public mural portraying this troubled neighborhood as a place with a peaceful and hopeful future. Today a new group of animators of the human spirit are hard at work organizing their peers to be teachers, business owners, and spiritual leaders.

Clearly we too seldom regard young people as gifted. Congregational and community leaders may value them as the "leaders of tomorrow," missing the obvious fact that they can also be the contributors of today. And young people are not the only group pushed to the margins of our congregations and communities. Other "strangers" among us often include our elders; the poor; those of a different color, culture, or language; or people with disabilities. A commitment to building vital communities must also be a commitment to inclusion, to providing the opportunities for every person's gifts to be recognized and given. Faithful community builders take seriously the pledge, "There are no strangers here."

As more congregations begin to work with their own versions of a capacity inventory process, they identify critical lessons about what works and what does not. The most important lesson concerns the mandate to act on the information and find ways to put people's skills and talents to good use continuously. The act of collecting the information can never be an end in itself. The information cannot be thought of merely as data; in fact, the frequent appearance of the term *data* in discussions about a capacity inventory strategy might be one sign that community members are being left behind. What we mean by data frequently is aggregated and generalized information. The more we have, the more accurate and informative the data are.

But community-building information about the capacities of individuals is important for the opposite reason. The more concrete and disaggregated it is, the more useful it can become. Community builders are less interested in finding out how many of something there are in a four-block area than in discovering that Mary is a wonderfully skilled gardener and is willing to teach what she knows to young people after school on Tuesday, or that she would be excited to meet with other gardeners to brainstorm about a community garden. The specific skills and talents of particular individuals are the human capital that can be invested in denser relationships and a stronger community.

Again, one key to retaining the community-building focus (as opposed, for example, to data gathering) is to revisit continuously the purposes of the project and the results that the participants hoped for. Following are a few examples of tangible results reported by congregations and community groups that have conducted capacity inventories among local residents:

Economic Development

- Linking existing businesses with new markets
- Making employers aware of the skills of potential employees in the community
- Sponsorship of the start-up of new businesses
- Producing a community income statement and balance sheet
- Establishing an advisory group for a primary business corridor
- Showcasing the talents of local start-up businesses at a fundraiser
- Mobilizing community creative talent to produce a community celebration and arts fair
- Raising funds for community projects
- Establishing new public transportation routes to enable isolated consumers to patronize local businesses
- Increasing availability of critical resources such as child or respite care
- Identifying retirees in the community who can assist local groups with professional expertise
- Identifying opportunities for local employment so that local residents can work within the neighborhood economy

Organizing People to Address Issues

- Identifying new participants for community organizations and local issue campaigns
- Organizing resident management groups
- Establishing a senior center
- Starting a food bank that incorporates homebound disabled people and seniors in its management structure

- Establishing a network of local people to supervise visitations among family members separated by child and family service agencies
- Organizing a neighborhood skills center where participants decide what will be taught

Building Trust and Social Capital Through Connections and Linkages

- Creating intergenerational linkages between elders and children
- Connecting two troubled teenagers in different parts of the country who now share a supportive pen-pal relationship over the Internet
- Identification of a homebound man with computer expertise who can tutor young students
- Connecting families of children with mental illnesses so they can jointly advocate for their children
- Linking a man who lost everything in a fire to an advocate who could assist him in the process of rebuilding his life
- Creating supportive links among families with problems
- Providing opportunities for people to volunteer to share with others

Civic Involvement

- Registering voters and providing transportation to polling places
- Creating volunteer advocacy networks to assist families in their interactions with institutions and agencies
- Involving more adults in youth activities such as sports teams or clubs
- Monitoring an urban greenspace project
- Identifying neighborhood people who can act as spokes-persons on issues of concern to community members
- Opening opportunities for volunteer action for the benefit of the community

These examples indicate the impressive range of tangible community-building results that congregations can obtain by focusing on the gifts and capacities of their members and neighbors. Intangible results are sometimes harder to identify, but they are no less important. Parishioners and residents involved in the process of discovering and mobilizing local capacities frequently report that community pride and spirit are enhanced, and individuals feel themselves more capable and authoritative. Community members previously identified only by their problems (too old, too young, too poor) are now viewed as contributing members of the community. People are more willing to reach out to their neighbors and to build trusting relationships, and residents develop a renewed sense of hope about their community's future and their own ability to steer toward that future.

Additional Community-Building Blocks: The Power of Citizens' Associations, the Resources of Local Institutions

Most congregations begin to explore the asset-based approach to community building by focusing on the gifts and talents of individual members and community residents. But some are expanding their strategies beyond individuals to the sectors of their communities that are already organized. They are reconnecting first to the voluntary sector—the small, face-to-face citizens' groups that Alexis de Tocqueville called associations—and then to the more formally organized public, private, and nonprofit institutions in their community.

The groups that Tocqueville saw as the inventive engines of a new kind of democracy have much in common with healthy congregations. They are characterized by their reliance not on paid staff (pastors, rabbis, priests) for carrying out the duties of ministry, but on the lay or voluntary members. Tocqueville described his astonishment at discovering the audacious agendas these self-selected groups adopted: to decide together what a problem was, take up the task of figuring out a solution to that problem, and finally listen to their own advice to act together to solve the problem.

What was true some 165 years ago remains relevant today. Small, voluntary associations are the most powerful amplifiers of individual gifts and capacities. They invite people to come out of their homes to connect with their neighbors, sometimes for civic or community improvement purposes, but often simply to join with others to help one another or to sing or play together.

In the late twentieth century, many observers have been worried about the weakened state of associational life in North America. Recognizing the importance of this sector as a seedbed for both a healthy economy and a vibrant democracy, observers such as Robert Putnam have lamented the decline of older forms of social capital such as the Lions, Kiwanis, Elks, and PTA. But some local congregations have recently joined with other community builders to examine once again the associational sector of their communities.

The first reports about the kinds and numbers of small, voluntary groups that exist in even the most challenged urban communities are quite astonishing. Exhibit 3.3 is the initial summary of the associations uncovered in one of the most devastated city neighborhoods in the United States, a community called Grand Boulevard, on the South Side of Chicago, with slightly over twenty-five thousand residents.

Clearly the seventy-one churches and thirty-one other religious organizations (these include many groups related to congregations, such as choirs, mission groups, and Bible study circles) form a critical part of this neighborhood's associational sector. These and the scores of other voluntary associations were uncovered by residents using very simple methods. They consulted all the written records they could locate; canvassed local institutions such as schools, parks, and libraries; and asked friends to list all of the clubs, groups, and organizations in which they and their family members participated.

With this information in hand for Grand Boulevard and other neighborhoods, some of these congregations and religious organizations have sought ways in which they could help nurture and invigorate this array of community resources. After conducting a thorough inventory, or "map," of their community's associations, these congregations have asked how these associations might be involved more effectively in the community-building process.

The information collected about Grand Boulevard's local associations—which included their addresses, telephone numbers, and names of leaders—allowed community leaders to build relationships with the local associations and to explore ways in which

Exhibit 3.3. Associational Map of Grand Boulevard.

Type	Types of Groups Included (Number)	Number
Religious congregations		71
Age/gender defined	Youth (24), seniors (12), women (5), men (4), parents (4)	49
Public institution connected	Schools (15), public housing (14), parks (8), police (7)	44
Social/recreational/ cultural	Special interest (12), athletic (9), local chapters of national groups (4), cultural (6), social (2)	33
Nonpublic housing residents	Tenants (8), block clubs (25)	33
Religious (not congregations)		31
Neighborhood improvement/advocacy	Improvement (16), advocacy (12)	28
Physical health	Self-help (9), health and disability (6)	15
Economic	Business (6), employment (1)	7
Political	Party (1), district (2)	3
Racial/ethnic	History (2), political (3)	5
Total		319

they might contribute to building the community. In building on the progress made in establishing relationships with local associations, they then moved to an inquiry that involved designing, testing, and administering a survey aimed at discovering what functions these neighborhood associations currently fulfill, which associational activities have already affected the wider community, and what kinds of community economic development and more broadly defined community-building activities these associations would be willing to undertake.

Follow-up interviews with the local associations probed their experience, current activities, and potential future activities in three major areas: how they provided mutual care through work on neighborhood projects, how they addressed issues in the community, and how they contributed to the neighborhood economy and economic development.

What the interviewers discovered in Grand Boulevard, and in other neighborhoods where similar surveys have been conducted, can be summarized very simply. The associational life of Grand Boulevard is rich and varied, consisting of at least 319 groups. The associations are already engaged in significant community-building activity, especially that which provides mutual care. Large numbers of the associations of Grand Boulevard expressed their willingness to become even more thoroughly engaged in contributing to the social and economic health of their community by participating more fully in providing mutual care, working on community issues, and supporting community economic development.

Congregational and other community leaders are recognizing that local associations in low-income communities represent an extraordinary and diverse array of energy, creativity, and mutual support. Grand Boulevard's community leaders have explored ways in which they could be encouraged to contribute even more than they already do to the economic and human development of their neighborhoods. Following are some of their ideas:

- Community leaders could contact voluntary associations to discover which groups were willing to pursue particular economic and community development strategies.
- Interested associational leaders could then, as a group, develop such specific economic development strategies as "buy local" campaigns, form local purchasing councils with institutional partners, and assist local employers to hire local residents through job networks, skill banks, and hiring pacts.
- In the same way, interested associations could convene around their common interest in the mutual care of neighborhood residents.
- The mutual care groups could be organized around specific interests, such as young people or senior citizens. They could explore ideas for maximizing mutual care, first focusing on the capacities of associations and then exploring ways that

associations' own agendas can be supported by local human service agencies.

- To facilitate these ideas, a group of local leaders may invest in a neighborhood association organizer whose task would be to convene community associations to enhance their contribution to community development.
- A useful organizational outcome might be a congress of associations, designed as a forum for maximizing the associations' mutual care, issue-focused activity, and economic development involvement. Such a congress could also emerge as the principal community planning and development group in its neighborhood.

In addition to the significant community-building potential of local citizens' associations, every neighborhood contains an array of public, private, and nonprofit institutions. Too frequently these institutions are not engaged in the community development process. Thus, one further challenge for congregation-based community building is to capture these institutions and their resources for the development agenda. If every local school, park, library, hospital, human service agency, and business were mobilized to contribute to a commonly developed neighborhood plan or vision, that plan would be advanced quickly. Congregationally based leaders often are well positioned to convene and activate their institutional neighbors and to lead them to greater recognition of their mutual interest in a healthy community.

Asset-based community development, then, is simply an orientation toward community building defined by three interrelated characteristics. It begins with resources—the capacities of congregation members and local residents, the associations and institutions in the area—*not* with what is absent, problematic, or needed. It understands that both needs and capacities are real, that the proverbial glass is both half-empty and half-full, but also that the full part of the glass contains many of the resources necessary to address the emptiness effectively.

The second characteristic is that this development strategy begins with an emphasis on the *local*. It is focused internally, not driven initially by the impulse to react to outside forces or attract outside resources. This intense internal focus is not intended to minimize the role that external forces have played in devastating some communities or to deny the need for external investments. It simply stresses the primacy of local definition, investment, control, creativity, and hope.

Finally, an asset-based, locally focused process always will be driven by the mandate to strengthen relationships, especially those that involve residents, local associations, and local institutions.

For many congregations, the process of engaging with the community in an asset-based, internally focused, and relationship-driven development effort is a regenerating experience. New leaders emerge, unused energies are discovered and unleashed, and hope replaces cynicism as community ties are strengthened. Mission in and with *this* place renews not only the community, but the congregation and its spirit as well.

Reference

McKnight, John L. (1995). *The Careless Society.* New York: Basic Books.

Additional Readings

Kretzmann, John P., and McKnight, John. (1993). *Building Communities from the Inside Out: A Path Toward Finding and Mobilizing a Community's Assets.* Evanston, Ill.: Center for Urban Affairs, Northwestern University.

Kretzmann, John P., and McKnight, John. (1996). *A Guide to Mapping Consumer Expenditures and Mobilizing Consumer Expenditure Capacities.* Evanston, Ill.: Asset-Based Community Development Institute.

Kretzmann, John P., and McKnight, John. (1996). *A Guide to Mapping Local Business Assets and Mobilizing Local Business Capacities.* Evanston, Ill.: Asset-Based Community Development Institute.

Kretzmann, John P., and McKnight, John. (1996). *A Guide to Mapping and Mobilizing the Economic Capacities of Local Residents.* Evanston, Ill.: Asset-Based Community Development Institute.

Kretzmann, John P., and McKnight, John. (1997). *A Guide to Capacity Inventories: Mobilizing the Community Skills of Local Residents.* Evanston, Ill.: Asset-Based Community Development Institute.

PART 2

Capacity Building

CHAPTER 4

Holding the Mission in Trust
Effective Board Leadership
James B. Lemler

Religious human and social service organizations, like other organizations in our society, find themselves facing rapid, significant, and challenging change. There are new expectations, new constituencies, new problems, and new opportunities. Congregations and religious organizations are confronted simultaneously by financial constraints and rising demand for services.

This reality has been identified and studied by researchers, both religious and secular. Peter Vaill, one of the best, has described this fast and ferocious change as resulting in a "whitewater society": a society in which people and organizations feel as if they are rafting on difficult, fast-moving, and treacherous whitewater rapids. Things move fast, and immediate responses are required. Often, Vaill notes, traditional responses do not work. A new repertoire is required.

Stories of congregations in such whitewater change and circumstances abound. One congregation struggles to welcome the newcomers that their rapidly growing suburban area offers up to them. A congregation in the heart of urban America has faced decline in its community and membership and works to provide needed programs of outreach and compassion. One congregation faces a serious shortage of financial resources, while another wonders how to use new endowment resources wisely and in keeping with its faith.

These challenges are not limited to congregations alone. They are found throughout all religious organizations. Seminaries face declining enrollments because of the changing profile of individuals seeking ordination. Social and human service ministries and programs face increasing demand as government programs are cut. National and denominational bodies search for new vitality and identity because they can no longer assume traditional and familial loyalties from their members.

Amid this change, congregations, religious organizations, and secular organizations need competent and caring leaders. In fact, the quality of leadership remains the most significant ingredient for organizational success and effectiveness. Strong leaders and leadership accomplish the following work:

- Define a mission that is authentic and vital.
- Are stewards of its human and financial resources.
- Know the organizational context.
- Listen to constituencies and stakeholders.
- Build connections and collaborations for mission.
- Envision its future and develop strategies and responses to that future.

The scriptural stories of Judaism and Christianity are full of images and reflections on leadership. In the Hebrew Scriptures, leaders such as Moses and Aaron lead people through immense difficulties, anxieties, and insecurities in their wilderness sojourn to enter a land of hope and promise. The prophets of God provide leadership by speaking truth to power, calling for justice, and proclaiming God's Word. Great women of faith lead, often at the boundaries of society, as they demonstrate faithfulness and integrity. In the New Testament, Jesus of Nazareth models and calls for a leadership rooted in servanthood, not domination; in compassion, not competition. His followers emulate that leadership in their practices of invitation, love, and service.

In the Qur'an, the stories of the Buddha, and the Hindu texts of law, stories of leaders and leadership abound. There exists a compelling and powerful dimension in them all. Leadership is a gift given by God to people. Leaders receive gifts from God to lead—gifts of spirit, perseverance, compassion, insight, discernment, and vision. These gifts equip leaders to guide communities of faith, and these gifts have remained operative among the leaders of communities of faith through the centuries. They abound in the leaders of communities of faith today.

Organizations need leaders, but individual leaders alone are insufficient. They need a strong community of leaders and leadership as well. This community of leadership often is met informally as individuals move into positions of responsibility as need demands. Projects and programs emerge for which an individual or group is particularly well suited or about which they are particularly passionate. Such constant and continuous movement not only is healthy for an organization, it is wise stewardship of the different gifts that individuals bring.

This chapter addresses the element of formal leadership, particularly the institution that has been given legal or functional responsibility for the organization: boards of directors or trustees and their functional equivalents. Virtually every religious organization (and most secular ones) have boards to provide leadership. These boards are essential and can offer powerful leadership to the religious organizations that they lead. Often, however, they are underused, caught up in day-to-day, operational, and managerial issues instead of being equipped and freed to provide the deeper and more powerful leadership for mission and vision that they are called to do.

Ronald Heifetz (1994) makes an important distinction between the technical and the adaptive. Technical problems and issues can be met with responses of technique and mechanics. Leaders can call on tried, true, and often traditional methods to meet an issue or problem that is readily defined or contained. If the roof needs to be fixed, leaders know the technical issues and responses necessary to do it. Adaptive problems and issues are much more difficult and challenging. They are complex and often involve deep philosophical issues that reflect the core purpose and meaning of an organization. They allow no easy answers. Leaders cannot call on the tried and true. These problems cannot be solved with technical expertise. Instead, leaders need to do adaptive work. They need to probe deeply into the meaning, values, and purposes of an organization and address questions of deep social change and shifts of understanding. Often leaders attempt to solve serious, adaptive issues with technical responses, thereby avoiding the deep, substantive, and often painful questions that are the real issues at hand.

The boards of congregations and other religious organizations are called to lead in both technical and adaptive ways. They have responsibility for setting policies and developing plans that reflect good governance. Board service requires commitment, perseverance, and discernment and corporately board members have responsibility for substantive areas of organizational life.

Development of Human Resources

Human beings are the greatest single resource in all organizations. This is particularly true in faith-based organizations. People lead, people serve, people care. Religious organizations depend on people to accomplish their mission. Because they are religious, they have a particular calling to the value of these individuals. Faith-based service organizations, especially those run by congregations, often are volunteer intensive even when there is professional staff.

Boards have responsibility for the development of human resources. This responsibility includes establishing clear personnel policies, guidelines, and evaluation procedures. Job descriptions for professionals and key volunteers are of great importance. Defining work relationships and organizational structure belongs to the board as well. Although sometimes overlooked, boards are responsible for nurturing and sustaining the human beings who serve. Whether the religious organization is large or small, the board must have specific and intentional ways of nurturing people who serve the organization's mission.

The same is true for the board itself. Many boards now have governance committees that have expanded on the tasks of traditional nominating committees. Although still responsible for raising up and nominating good leaders to shape and implement mission, a governance committee also has the duty to identify and create opportunities and methods for the development of the board itself. For example, a governance committee can assist the entire board in developing ways to evaluate its effectiveness; chart ways for the board to engage in its adaptive work by providing occasions (such as board retreats) to go deeper into mission reflection and planning than general meetings allow; and provide input into meeting agendas to balance time spent on reports and decision making with time for prayer and reflection.

A fundamental theological stance should undergird the board's development of human resources: that God has given people gifts for ministry and for mission, and people bring these gifts to the community of faith in which they serve. The board of a religious organization ignores these gifts to the peril of its call and mission. The board has the duty to set the tone and create the structures for equipping people to use their gifts and for ensuring that these gifts are used wisely and with integrity.

Support of Clergy, Senior Executives, and Staff

Boards need to relate to clergy, senior executives, and staff in intentional and supportive ways. This means, among other things, having a clear awareness that the professional staff (and often senior volunteers) have the responsibility for the organization's daily ministry and operation. This is a realm usually separate from the board's responsibility for setting policy and providing general oversight. When these boundaries and responsibilities are ignored, much misunderstanding, anxiety, and even anger emerge. Stories abound of board members' intruding inappropriately into the daily life of an organization. Such actions often undermine the work and authority of clergy, senior executives, and other staff and lead to internal dissension.

The truth is that it is difficult to be a religious professional today. A preeminent danger for ministers and staff is being overwhelmed by fatigue and anxiety. At its worse, the stresses and challenges of leadership for ministers and staff can be toxic. One of the primary responsibilities of the board is to support clergy, senior executives, and staff. The marks of this support are awareness of the challenges of clerical leadership, open communication with ministers and staff, and clear policies of support and accountability. Boards should ensure that personnel policies ensure just and adequate compensation, continuing education, and professional growth. The stewardship responsibility of boards extends to individuals who work professionally in religious organizations, and boards should attend to that responsibility carefully.

Development of Financial Resources

Boards have primary responsibility for the development of financial resources to support the organization's mission. Experienced board members know what a challenging responsibility this is. The threshold for financial viability has become increasingly higher in many religious organizations, particularly congregations. Individual giving has not increased proportionately with increased responsibilities or with the increased income of members and supporters. When faced with financial tensions, leaders feel stretched and confused.

As a result, they attempt to approach the challenge through technical solutions. They search for techniques to address the financial pressures—a new stewardship plan, different fundraisers, or new visitation methods. Although good methods for financial development are important (see Chapter Five), the overall financial health of an organization is at its heart an adaptive challenge and needs to be addressed as such by boards. The board needs to focus on the development and articulation of a compelling mission that attracts financial support. Only out of that mission can the board work to create financial resources that support it. Implicit in much of the emphasis on "the ask" explored in Chapter Five is the sense that many people feel uncomfortable with asking because they are not sufficiently convinced of the importance or power of the organization's mission. Boards have an obligation to create that compelling mission and to ensure that the work being done is equally compelling. Such adaptive work is the key to financial viability.

Although annual giving is part of the whole picture, boards need to expand their horizons of financial giving. They need to look for ways to generate planned gifts and endowment resources, as well as seeking funding from new sources and in new ways. Most important, board members need to examine their own giving to the organization. If the organization's mission does not compel them—the individuals who are most intimately connected to its work—to give, then how can they expect significant support from others?

Boards also are called on to be stewards of financial resources. Legally this is the most important function the board has. Policies for clear accountability are the responsibility of the board. Regular financial reports and audits, intentional financial plans, and open disclosure are required. All of these technical activities are essential for building institutional integrity (as Chapter Seven emphasizes).

Clear and consistent accountability measures serve to build confidence within the organization and within the wider community. They aid greatly in seeking funds. Most important, however, they express the organization's values of integrity, honesty, and respect. Ensuring commitment to such values is the responsibility of the board, as is requiring the implementation of procedures that reflect that commitment.

Relationship to the Wider Community of Faith

No faith-based organization exists apart from the wider community of faith. One of the important responsibilities of boards is to overcome isolation within organizations and connect them to the other levels of religious organization and with other entities. Although there is considerable variety in the structure of connection, depending on the various polities of American religion, the board still must keep its eye on wider relationships and collaborations.

Some of the most effective collaborations are to be found in the local community. Other faith-based services, congregations, and interfaith and ecumenical organizations can be powerful local partners. Resources can be maximized and presence intensified as local churches, synagogues, mosques, temples, and missions work collaboratively for a common goal. Boards have the important responsibility of seeking these collaborations on a local level through their communication linkages and vision for service.

Boards also are the points of connection with regional and national partners. They are stewards of collaboration with these wider bodies, and in congregations they often shape the flow of human and financial resources to them. There is no question that the primary lens for viewing religious life at the beginning of the twenty-first century is through local organizations, especially congregations. Since the local is where most people function on a daily level, these organizations determine much of the nature of religious life. This tension has created much hostility and suspicion. Local faith-based organizations have questioned the effectiveness and stewardship of middle judicatory and national religious bodies, which in turn have accused the former of parochialism and isolationism. What is called for is not recrimination and accusation, but the forging of a new spirit and style of collaboration between these levels. Local organizations need to discover new ways to forge partnerships with middle-level judicatory and national religious bodies, and these bodies must realize that their vitality and support depend on the effectiveness of their support for local religious life. In addition, depending on the polity of a faith community, a faith-based service organization's board may actually have no ultimate governance or legal function. When this is the case, the board of the local organization and the responsible judicatory board must develop clear lines of responsibility.

Defining and Supporting Programs

The special relationship that boards have to program definition, implementation, and evaluation begins with the board's success in defining mission clearly and succinctly so that it provides the foundation for the organization's programmatic activities.

The sheer proliferation of programs presents a danger to American religious life. Often leaders of religious organizations feel that the number of programs they initiate expresses the vitality and effectiveness of their work. That is not the case. Numbers of programs simply as numbers can drain the organization of effectiveness, energy, and resources. A clear understanding of organizational mission is the way to shape coherent and connected programs.

Board members must understand and support the organization's programs. When they are not sufficiently informed about the programmatic life of the organization, they are unable to monitor and evaluate effectiveness. Boards need to develop clear lines of communication regarding programs. These should include regular presentations by the program units and board participation in program activities for the purpose of learning.

As stewards of the organization's mission and resources, board members have to understand how each program serves that mission and whether it does so effectively. Good programs that are misunderstood by the board often may fail to receive the support they deserve. They also may be terminated during periods of financial retrenchment or administrative reorganization, to the organization's detriment.

In the absence of good information, lethargy may allow outmoded, ineffective, or inappropriate programs to continue unnecessarily, draining organizational resources and energy. Occasionally such programs may even be an embarrassment to the organization.

Only with complete information, presented in a coherent and understandable manner, can boards make good decisions regarding programs. The gathering and analyzing of this information must be a collaborative undertaking by the board, senior executives, and appropriate staff and volunteers.

Board members not only review programs for their appropriateness to mission and their effectiveness, but also are called on to be advocates for those programs, interpreting them to the public and supporting them aggressively. They can do this only if they understand those programs well.

Legal and Fiduciary Responsibilities

Boards today have increasing legal and fiduciary responsibilities. Unfortunately, many boards choose to remain oblivious to these obligations. Ignorance, whether willful or inadvertent, will protect neither the board nor the organization. Governmental and legal responsibilities relating to finances, personnel, property, and reporting cannot be avoided. Every board must meet these responsibilities, using outside expertise and counsel as necessary.

A good source for assistance is the insurance company that provides coverage for the organization. Insurance companies are good partners, because they desire to limit their liability and exposure. Many do property and liability audits for clients as a part of their services.

Boards are also responsible for financial review (and many times for audits) to ensure that they are sound and faithful fiduciaries. The board's careful attention to financial control mechanisms can eliminate the potential for massive difficulties. Even where no one has done anything illegal or unethical, the public airing of financial incompetence cannot help the organization.

Board members must be aware that the expectations for fulfillment of legal and fiduciary obligations become greater all the time. Today's world requires a certain level of sophistication of every board. Boards can increase their capacities in this area by calling on outside resources to assist them in policy definition and decision making. (Chapter Seven provides a detailed discussion of how to improve financial accountability.)

Theological and Ethical Foundations

There are significant theological and ethical foundations for the boards of faith-based organizations. Unfortunately, awareness of the theological and ethical imperatives often escapes leaders. A recent study of congregations in one Christian denomination with large endowment resources discovered that leaders seldom undertook explicit theological reflection or used it to guide their decision making. In a similar vein, the sociologist Robert Wuthnow (1988) concluded that many of the financial crises and challenges in mainline Christianity are directly connected to the pervasive spiritual malaise in the same religious traditions.

Board members in faith-based organizations are called to be aware of the theological foundations that enable and empower their service and their leadership. Rich resources of prayer, spirituality, Scripture, and tradition undergird their work. The board itself ought to be a community of prayer and theological reflection, and a certain amount of its time together should be spent in these activities and practices. If faith-based service organizations are distinctive from secular ones, it must be that the spirit of God enriches their work and their deliberations. The tradition of so many faiths in viewing decision making as a spiritual and prayerful process needs to be reinvigorated and revived.

The board also has important ethical responsibilities. (Chapter Seven demonstrates the connection between ethics and practice.) The moral capacities of the board assist it in its ongoing work. While all boards are called to sound ethical and moral practice, this is particularly true of boards called together out of religious purposes. It is even more important for those who serve the weakest and most vulnerable populations. Board members have numerous ethical responsibilities or duties:

- A duty to serve the common good
- A duty to treat all publics and other stakeholders as children of God
- A duty to act honestly and fairly
- A duty to ensure that all applicable laws are followed in letter and spirit
- A duty to refrain from self-dealing and directly using board membership for private gain
- A duty to oversee the management of the organization actively and impartially
- A duty to donors to ensure their funds are used for the designated purposes and in a wise and prudent manner
- A duty to those served that guarantees quality service, a safe environment, and respectful treatment
- A duty to volunteers that recognizes and respects their effort, diligence, and passion
- A duty to staff to ensure fair, equitable, and respectful treatment for all, to guarantee a wage appropriate to their abilities and the organization's financial state, and to provide those benefits necessary for a safe and healthy life
- A duty to self to follow the dictates of one's conscience

The ability to realize these rules in practice often is hindered by the fact that the realization of one may prevent or hinder the realization of another. Although this list does not attempt a ranking of these duties, except for the duty to the common good, clarity about the duties and about what is unacceptable increases the likelihood of making the right decisions in difficult times.

The theological and moral framework of the organization demands serious and ongoing attention and response by board members, and indeed by everyone else affiliated with it. These religious and moral demands, however, should not be perceived as burdens. They reflect the great traditions and strong foundations that undergird the work of boards in faith-based organizations. Theological virtues and moral perspectives are given to the leaders of religious organizations for their practice of leadership. Not only do these religious and moral imperatives strengthen the faith and commitment both within the board and the organization as a whole, they provide powerful models for the wider society. They are a gift of good leadership.

Certainly the responsibilities of leadership are significant and profound, as well as demanding. The stewardship of human and financial resources, building and maintaining connections with the wider community of faith, defining programs and seeking support, legal and fiduciary responsibilities, and maintaining the theological and moral foundation all mean that board service is not casual or occasional. Board membership is a commitment, a challenge, and a great opportunity for service.

Adaptive Work

For a board to do adaptive work, moving from the technical to the substantial and entering deeply into the life and mission of the organization, it must expand its horizons of understanding and reflection. Board members need to consider a wide and deep framework for their service.

At the heart of this consideration is the meaning of trusteeship itself. Board members are trustees of the religious organization they serve. They hold the organization, and its mission and vision, in trust. The work of Trustee Leadership Development, a national organization that works with varieties of boards and their leaders, has yielded a wealth of reflection about trusteeship as trust holding. Its work has yielded these insights:

- Leaders enter a deeper level of their service and work by realizing that they hold powerful and rich things in trust.
- Trusteeship as trust holding is a vital perspective for understanding the work of board service.
- Boards that spend time to consider that which they ought to hold in trust have the potential for greater mission faithfulness and effectiveness.

The power of the dynamic of trust should not surprise leaders of religious organizations. Trust is the foundational component for communities of faith and service. It joins human beings in relationship to God as creator, sustainer, and redeemer, and it builds a sense of connectedness and union within a community of faith. Trust is at the very heart of leadership.

Leaders can lead because of the trust given to them by the organization they serve. In turn, they constantly weave a fabric of trust within that organization that empowers people to serve, to be committed, and to give of themselves.

Leadership is trust holding, and board leaders are trust holders. They bring, or ought to bring, qualities and characteristics of trust holding to bear on their leadership: commitment, vision, perseverance, truth telling, nurturance, love, and faithfulness. Leaders hold important and vital things in trust: the institutional mission, the people who are served, institutional resources (including staff and volunteers), the tradition of faith, and a vision of the future. A board's capacity for leadership is strengthened when its members seriously reflect on their trusteeship obligations—on what it means to hold powerful and important things in trust—and the responsibilities that come with this position of trustee.

Trusteeship is a call to servanthood, to servant leadership. Thanks to the work of Robert Greenleaf, as a society we are much more aware of the nature and pattern of leadership as servanthood. Greenleaf (1977) is direct: "The servant-leader is a servant first. It begins with the natural feeling that one wants to serve, to *serve first.* Then conscious choice brings one to aspire to lead." Greenleaf called for a trusteeship revolution rooted in leaders' awareness of the call to serve as their primary motivation and foundation.

This is particularly true for the leaders of religious organizations. An entire pattern and structure of servanthood undergirds this special and particular form of leadership. The biblical and theological tradition underscores the call to servanthood for this leadership. At their very heart religious organizations are servant institutions. They exist to serve—to serve God and to serve human beings. Boards of religious organizations need to be particularly alert to this call and meaning. Unfortunately, other issues often cloud this call. Day-to-day operations, competing demands of stakeholders, and the sheer volume and pressure of work all draw the attention of leaders away from their primary vocation of servanthood. Boards that take the time to reflect on the meaning of their servanthood have a better chance of realizing their authentic mission.

Trust holding and servanthood are deep and powerful dynamics for leadership. They help a board and its members to see their work much more clearly than they otherwise would be able to do and give a board greater capacities for discernment and mission than they would otherwise possess. Boards that are congruent and committed to their leadership have natural instincts and inclinations toward these dynamics, but every board needs shaping and education to realize these more fully.

A different form of education is required for boards that aspire to lead in this way, approaching their adaptive responsibilities and serving as effectively as possible. In the descriptive words of Robert Lynn, former senior vice president of the Lilly Endowment, this form and type of education would best be described as depth education, that is, education that allows leaders to go deeply into the elements of an organization's life that truly reflect its purpose, service, and vision (personal communication). Depth education requires a board to move from the technical and managerial to analyze the deeper issues of why the organization exists, whom it serves, and what it hopes to accomplish in its service.

Depth education requires a board to step out of its usual patterns of work and deliberation, to delve into organizational purpose and meaning. To be truly successful, this form of education cannot to be momentary and occasional. Its goal is to affect the ongoing life and nature of the board and of the organization itself. A board must consider four essential elements as it pursues its education in depth: history, mission, publics, and future. These elements are interconnected and of ongoing importance to leaders and to effective leadership by a board. They are particularly essential for boards of religious organizations to attend to.

History

A board needs to make a deep and careful review of the history of the organization it serves. This is more than a cursory look at a few key events or people. The board should examine the entire stretch of organizational history, reflect on the developing patterns of mission, and hear the stories of organizational life. James Hopewell's classic *Congregation: Stories and Structures* (1987) describes in rich detail how the history and stories of congregational life over time shape the realities of congregational life in the present. (This insight is emphasized in Chapter Two.)

Deep and careful consideration of the organization helps board members see how current issues are rooted in past patterns and decisions. It frees them to plan for the future from a sense of awareness of how the organization reached its present form.

Mission

Mission—which encompasses purpose, identity, foundational beliefs, and the reason for existence of an organization—is at the heart of an organization's life and work. Board members are responsible for the mission and its definition. A depth education approach requires leaders to examine organizational mission carefully and intensely. It seeks to assist leaders in reflecting on the organization's core beliefs and activities to ensure congruence among them. Many boards fail to do this important work. They assume that a mission exists or quickly write a mission statement or description. Depth education asks them to take the time to enter deeply into mission consideration so they understand and can communicate the essence, identity, and purpose of the organization they serve.

Publics

Religious human and social service organizations serve people. This harkens back to the basic vocation of religious organizations to service and servanthood. Boards of religious organizations have the responsibility of knowing who is served and how. In addition, they have the obligation to be aware of those who are affected by their work and those whose actions affect their work—those individuals identified as stakeholders in Chapter Six.

Time and again boards fail to focus on the people who are served, and they rarely possess the mechanisms necessary for identifying those individuals, let alone for conversations with and learning from those who are served. Depth education invites board members to a new level of knowledge and relationship with people who are served or affected by their organization's activities. It asks leaders to identify these individuals and groups, establish communication with them, and learn their hopes and needs. This undertaking enables boards to make better-informed decisions about program and the use of resources.

Future

"Without a vision, the people perish," proclaims the Book of Proverbs. The ancient wisdom writer's words remain true today.

Vision is essential for the continuation of the life and service of any organization. One of the most significant opportunities and responsibilities of the board of a religious organization is that of envisioning the future. The leaders of the board dream the dreams for the future of the organization they serve, dreams grounded in the understanding of history, mission, and the people who are served and that stretch the vision and possibilities of the organization. In the work of depth education, boards are encouraged to envision the future of the organization, and then to develop goals and plans for that vision to become reality.

The depth work of a board is full and invigorating. It allows the board to enter the organizational life fully and to make plans and decisions out of that fullness. Boards that engage in depth education are more competent and prepared to approach the adaptive challenges and issues that confront them. The deep knowledge that they have gained through their own assessment, reflection, and work enables them to lead more effectively. To date Trustee Leadership Development has worked with over six hundred boards (more than twelve thousand board leaders) to assist them in their work of leadership. It has discovered the potential and vitality of board trust holders and leaders who do this work and make it a continuous part of board life and leadership.

Board service is an important ministry, call, and opportunity for people. People give their time and talents (and often their treasure) to this service because they care deeply for the religious organization and the human beings that it serves. They experience a congregation or another religious organization as a community in which people are changed and transformed in trust and faith. These leaders serve on the board because they have known and experienced this transformative power and want to ensure its vitality for others.

It is the responsibility of all the leaders to develop their capacities for leadership within the board. Leadership is sustained as these capacities are strengthened through depth education, as well as improvements in technical skills and abilities. They are strengthened through the practices of prayer and discernment that belong to a board. The board can be a locus for spiritual growth and renewal, especially if the board leadership shapes occasions and structures for that dynamic.

Leaders bring commitment to board service. It is the responsibility of the board as a whole to nurture and encourage that commitment. Some of this nurture and encouragement occurs through the common work of the board. Much of it happens as individual leaders seek ways to discern their own personal gifts and strengths for leadership and to identify ways to put them to service for the organization.

Certainly there are forces that resist good leadership within all boards. The danger of intrusion into daily operations has been identified, and there are also other forces of resistance. The inability of the board to recognize or address conflicts openly hinders board effectiveness. Board work can also be resisted by passive, antagonistic, and pessimistic members. It can be adversely affected by the lack of commitment by members to do the work that they are called to do. This lack of commitment often combines with a lack of faith and hope, thereby retarding the strength and future of the board and the organization's success. Sometimes individuals are recruited or elected to the board without having been given a clear picture of what will be expected of them or of the degree of commitment required. This too common occurrence hinders the board's effectiveness.

This is a critical time for attending to the development of boards of religious service organizations. Resources that offer frameworks, learning, and support for the building and sustaining of leadership exist to assist boards in their work of leadership. At the same time, there is a growing awareness of the challenges and opportunities that face religious organizations. People who serve on boards want to make a difference as they meet these challenges and opportunities. They want to lead their organization, to be good servants, to be faithful trust holders.

Every board of religious organizations needs to examine its own life and it effectiveness. Individual members need to examine their commitment, their focus, and their gifts. Leaders cannot be casual or timid in this. They must understand their own capacities and potential and seek the structures and resources that will enable them to make a difference in the mission to which their organization is called. They need to lead. It is a time of unique and special possibility for the boards of religious organizations. Gifts for leadership exist within the membership of these boards, and gifts are given by God for the exercise of leadership. What is necessary is this: each and every board must be called to move from a stance of management to a stance of leadership. They must be called to approach the adaptive issues and challenges and to go deeply into their purpose and future. Boards that do these things will not be disappointed. They will find rich and abundant new possibilities for leadership, faithfulness, and effectiveness in their service.

References
Greenleaf, Robert K. (1977). *Servant Leadership: A Journey into the Nature of Legitimate Power and Greatness.* New York: Paulist Press.
Heifetz, Ronald A. (1994). *Leadership Without Easy Answers.* Cambridge, Mass.: Belknap Press.
Hopewell, James F. (1987). *Congregation: Stories and Structures.* Philadelphia: Fortress.

Additional Readings
Andrings, Robert C. (1997). *Nonprofit Answer Book: Practical Guidelines for Board Members and Chief Executives.* Washington, D.C.: National Center for Nonprofit Boards.
Bell, Peter D. (1993). *Fulfilling the Public Trust: Ten Ways to Help Nonprofit Boards Maintain Accountability.* Washington, D.C.: National Center for Nonprofit Boards.
Bryson, John M. (1996). *Creating and Implementing Your Strategic Plan: A Workbook for Public and Nonprofit Organizations.* San Francisco: Jossey-Bass.
Carver, John. (1997). *Boards That Make a Difference: A New Design for Leadership in Nonprofit and Public Organizations.* San Francisco: Jossey-Bass.
Eadie, Douglass C. (1997). *Changing by Design: A Practical Approach to Leading Innovation in Nonprofit Organizations.* San Francisco: Jossey-Bass.
Greenleaf, Robert K. (1996). *Seeker and Servant: Reflections on Religious Leadership.* San Francisco: Jossey-Bass.
Greenleaf, Robert K. (1998). *The Power of Servant Leadership: Essays by Robert K. Greenleaf.* San Francisco: Berrett-Koehler.
Houle, Cyril Orvin. (1997). *Governing Boards: Their Nature and Nurture.* San Francisco: Jossey-Bass.
Howe, Fisher. (1995). *Welcome to the Board: Your Guide to Effective Participation.* San Francisco: Jossey-Bass.
Howe, Fisher. (1997). *The Board Member's Guide to Strategic Planning: A Practical Approach to Strengthening Nonprofit Organizations.* San Francisco: Jossey-Bass.

INDEPENDENT SECTOR. (1991). *Ethics and the Nation's Voluntary and Philanthropic Community: Obedience to the Unenforceable.* Washington, D.C.: INDEPENDENT SECTOR.

Jeavons, Thomas. (1994). *When the Bottom Line Is Faithfulness: Management of Christian Service Organizations.* Bloomington: Indiana University Press.

Jinkins, Michael, and Jinkins, Deborah Bradshaw. (1998). *The Character of Leadership: Political Realism and Public Virtue in Nonprofit Organizations.* San Francisco: Jossey-Bass.

Lang, Andrew S. (1993). *The Financial Responsibilities of Nonprofit Boards: An Overview of Financial Management for Board Members.* Washington, D.C.: National Center for Nonprofit Boards.

Mason, David E. (1996). *Leading and Managing the Expressive Dimension: Harnessing the Hidden Power Source of the Nonprofit Sector.* San Francisco: Jossey-Bass.

National Center for Nonprofit Boards. Available at: http.www.ncnb.org.

Nelson, Judith Grummon. (1995). *Six Keys to Recruiting, Orienting, and Involving Nonprofit Board Members: A Guide to Building Your Board.* Washington, D.C.: National Center for Nonprofit Boards.

Powell, James Lawrence. (1995). *Pathways to Leadership: How to Achieve and Sustain Success.* San Francisco: Jossey-Bass.

Scribner, Susan M. (1991). *Boards from Hell.* New York: Scribner.

Senge, Peter. (1990). *The Fifth Discipline: The Art and Practice of the Learning Organization.* New York: Doubleday.

Smith, David H. (1995). *Entrusted: The Moral Responsibilities of Trusteeship.* Bloomington: University of Indiana Press.

Wilbur, Robert H., and others (eds.). (1994). *The Complete Guide to Nonprofit Management.* New York: Wiley.

Zander, Alvin Frederick. (1993). *Making Boards Effective: The Dynamics of Nonprofit Governing Boards.* San Francisco: Jossey-Bass.

CHAPTER 5

Funding the Dream

Sara Robertson

"God called me to help women in crisis, not to do fundraising." The speaker was irate. She found my suggestion of how she might deal with diminished government funding absolutely unacceptable. Her resistance was rather shortsighted. She dreamed of an exciting vision, growing out of her desire to carry out biblical social justice, but without funding no one would be helped. Ministry takes money.

To ask for money is biblical. God expects people to give to those in need. The apostle Paul put it plainly: "Thieves must give up stealing; rather let them labor and work honestly with their own hands, so as to have something to share with the needy" (Ephesians 4:28). Nearly half of Christ's recorded parables concern the subjects of poverty and wealth. The Bible contains over 2,350 references to stewardship—not only of money but of life as well. In Isaiah 58:6–7 giving to others is raised to the level of worship, replacing fasting: "Is not this the fast that I choose; to loose the bonds of injustice. . . . Is it not to share your bread with the hungry, and bring the homeless poor into your house; when you see the naked to cover them."

The apostle Paul did not hesitate to invite people to give. He used direct mail to call for generous giving, enlisted volunteers, and stressed the benefits of participation. He was accountable for how he handled funds (II Corinthians 8–9).

These are principles for twenty-first-century ministry opportunities as well. Giving people the opportunity to exercise personal stewardship is a privilege. We cannot make the decisions for them, but we can offer them a partnership in serving. Whether people volunteer their time, expertise, or resources, we need them to help advance our causes. Just as important, they need our causes to help satisfy their need to give.

In fundraising, the goal is not to manipulate people into parting with their money. Integrity demands caring for the donors as well as the cause we represent. Those of us in faith-based service organizations do not dare treat donors as mere money machines, whom we are out to exploit. Donors give gladly when they believe in the organization and share its values. Our job is to establish a clear, honest, and compelling message of our organizations and their work, then to take that message to those who might be interested.

Once we have our philosophy of stewardship in place and exercise that philosophy through our own giving, we can ask others to join us. That is the key to fundraising: *You have to ask.*

Getting the Cause Concept Straight

If you believe that something vital to the well-being of the world would be lost if you went out of business tomorrow, you are ready to consider fundraising. Until you can articulate why you need money, you are not ready to ask.

The case for support is a foundational document, though not necessarily a document shared with others. Once you have thought it through and written it out, you might communicate the contents orally, in a brochure, or even solely as an internal organizational guide to shape this work. The case for support lays out the organization's special mission and uniqueness, while providing direction for all who work for it.

Primarily the case answers basic questions that donors want addressed:

- Who are you?
- Why do you exist?
- What do you intend to accomplish? (Notice that this is not worded as, What do you hope to accomplish?)
- How will you go about accomplishing your goals?

The case for support should answer other questions, too:

- What problem are you addressing?
- Are there other groups dealing with this problem? If so, what is this organization's unique opportunity or distinctive approach?
- What is the proposed solution? In other words, what opportunities lie ahead? Remember that the goal is not to raise money for this organization but for those who will benefit. Moreover, the organization does not even *need* to raise money, but people have a *need* to give and to help. The goal is to match people with the opportunities to make a difference.
- Exactly what will the funds be used for? This is a question often asked by baby boomers and generation Xers (sometimes known as Generation *Why*). They want to know there is a sense of urgency requiring their commitment and involvement, and they want to see results.

Perhaps this sense of urgency will be conveyed by emphasizing the consequences of inaction. You want to intervene to prevent a tragedy, and you are providing an opportunity for others equally concerned with preventing that tragedy to partner with you. You are helping them to accomplish some goal they want to see accomplished yet cannot do on their own.

This is not begging, as some would characterize it. The organization is looking for money not out of desperation but out of hope. Gifts flow more readily to organizations with exciting visions and solutions, not to those with financial problems. You are working to create a better future, and donors can be part of that future. Since astute donors want to know whether you are actually doing what you have set out to accomplish, once the case is set out in writing, you have to live by it. Be sure, therefore, that not only is it stated compellingly but accurately as well.

A Marketing Plan

Once the case is mapped out, the next step is to determine a marketing strategy. To whom will you go to with the case? What methods will you use to communicate to those who share your concerns? Where will you find people with an emotional connection to your cause, who share your passion? If they are to be successful, the marketing methods must match the target audience.

People must be connected to the organization before they will contribute. Although a comprehensive marketing plan considers the giving potential of foundations, businesses, government sources (especially local, county, and state connections), and churches, individuals are the priority. Fundraisers must look for people who care, or who can be challenged to care, about what the organization does, has done, or might do in the future.

Perhaps these people are already involved in the organization or are being served by it. Do not miss potential donors right in your back yard. Equally, if not more important, never fail to respond promptly and courteously to those who approach the organization with requests for information. My interest in contributing to a Reye's Syndrome organization was occasioned by my nephew's death from the illness. Although my gifts would not have been large, the organization lost out entirely when no one responded to my request for information.

Begin by developing a cadre of volunteer supporters from within the congregation. Those who give their time are in the best position to see the need and are therefore more likely to share financially. Indeed, all volunteers should be current donors, and you are remiss if you do not start by asking them for pledges. To paraphrase Luke 12:34, "Where your heart is, there your treasure will be also."

This corps of donors can multiply your effectiveness and build a list of prospects from their families, friends, colleagues, and other acquaintances. Enthusiasm is contagious, and their excitement over the shared mission is bound to draw in other supporters.

What about those whom you have served in the past or who have served with you? Recently I was asked to consult with a nonprofit agency that realized it had to be more active in fundraising. As I was touring the agency office, I recognized the wealthy head of a family foundation in a picture of former board members. I was amazed to learn they had never asked him for a grant. This was the first place I suggested they start. In response to this suggestion, a board member who knew the gentleman went to see him and was assured of a gift. All they had to do was ask.

Assume that anyone you meet is a prospect and can be cultivated to become a donor. What you are really doing is building relationships, which is the entire process of fundraising. It is constant and ongoing. You must not let relationships die through inattention, regardless of whether those contacts are with a corporation, a foundation, a church, or an individual. Are they disgruntled? Talk to them. Are they feeling neglected? Do something to connect again. Are they happy and pleased with what is being accomplished? Help them know how much more could be done with greater resources.

Occasionally individuals do their giving through a private family foundation. A donor list may disclose such possibilities in addition to other foundations that are receptive to particular mission opportunities. Nevertheless, foundations are not the best places to expend solicitation energies. Only rarely does as much as 10 percent of the budget come from foundations. Logically it follows that you will not want to spend more than 10 percent of your time seeking this kind of funding.

This does not mean that you will never find a foundation willing to partner with you. Indeed foundation support should be part of your overall fundraising program, and as Chapter Ten shows, relationship building and responsiveness are as important to those funders as to individuals.

Consider the benefits received by those food banks, food pantries, and soup kitchens that profited from businessman Alan Shawn Feinstein's passion to do something about hunger. In 1998 he began an annual campaign in which he pledged to match, dollar for dollar, all donations of twenty-five dollars or more that hunger-related causes raised in two weeks in February, up to a total of $1 million. Those organizations willing to put forth the effort to mobilize their constituency were the ones that profited. One group said that the value had not been just in money. After all, there were at least thirty-five hundred groups across the country participating, so each group's individual share of the money would not be huge, although surely it was quite welcome. However, the group still feels the impact in the increased awareness of the local community, which responded so generously to the need. This group expected the challenge to help it raise $50,000 with the matching funds. In fact, it sent copies of checks totaling $145,221.39 to the Feinstein Foundation. Because this phenomenon happened all over the country, their matching funds were just $300, but hunger resources were greatly multiplied through this campaign. The value over the long run extended way beyond one matching gift.

As an individual, Feinstein raised the consciousness of millions regarding the needs of the hungry in the United States. Yet the responsibility for connecting with these funds lies at the local level. We should commend the unnamed social worker who invited him to visit Elmwood Community Center in inner-city Providence, Rhode Island. "Until then, Mr. Feinstein had made some charitable donations and had volunteered but was not a significant philanthropist. He agreed to go. . . . 'When I saw it I was encouraged to help'" (Gray, 1998, p. 10).

This social worker had done her homework. She knew Feinstein had the capacity to give and that he had already volunteered, so there was some connection to the charity. The next step was up to her, and this is significant: she had to have the courage to pick up the telephone. The thousands who have benefited since owe their good fortune to that woman's initiative.

Another concept to note is the leveraging of gifts through matching funds. An outside philanthropist is not necessary to do this. Perhaps the organization's board would take on a challenge gift related to a specific project. In addition to encouraging the board's generous giving, a challenge can also inspire other donors to new levels of support.

Some ministries may begin with the concern of just one or two people, but if they can enlarge their vision to inspire an entire congregation, much can be accomplished. Drawing in the congregation also is a matter of building and nurturing relationships through informing people about the opportunities for service or ministry, being creative in any communication, and using every possible means to let people know what is happening and how they can be part of it. Before you know it, you may have waiting lists of people wanting to be involved. Some of those people may be senior citizens; some may be in junior high school. You never know the possibilities until you ask.

Even if the organization is not congregationally based, the congregation may offer a base of support. Proceeding cautiously is advised here. Some evidence suggests that members' giving to congregations is decreasing and that congregations are more likely to spend their money on their own needs rather than on outside missions (Billetteri, 1998). Nevertheless, many congregations are very service minded and, as Chapter Two shows, resources for social ministries flow from different directions than that for congregational work. The task is to discover these congregations and then ask. There is that important word, *ask,* again. Search for ways to share your case with the decision makers: perhaps the official board or benevolence committee or perhaps small groups within the congregation that would be glad to partner with you. This partnership may take shape in ways other than financial support. Often fellowship groups, youth groups, and educational classes are looking for service projects. Such small groups can be an important source for committed volunteers and donors.

Consider the difference one suburban church makes with its inner-city tutoring programs, job counseling, transitional housing for ex-prisoners and people without resources, senior support services, and food and shelter for the homeless, to name just a few of their direct involvements. Almost 50 percent of the annual budget of this church goes to fund local and international missions. But this church also has a policy of not funding any program in which members of the church are not directly involved, so no one can ask to be on the budget unless they can demonstrate their own commitment of time and effort.

Cultivating the relationship is vital to keeping the funding. This begins with keeping the congregation informed of both the organization's successes and its needs and ministry opportunities. Be sure the right person gets the information and that she or he communicates it appropriately to others. Write articles for the newsletter. Speak in person as often as possible to any group willing to listen. This might range from a religious school class to a fellowship group. You might even be able to participate in the worship service. Your organization must not be a secret partner, heard from only at the annual budget time.

Partnerships can offer many different kinds of creative funding opportunities. An article in the newsletter *Partners Make It Possible* featured a two-year partnership that a crisis pregnancy center had entered into with a computer consulting firm. As the president put it, "Our appreciation for their work ethic and the impact they are making has grown. We like to think that to the extent the computer systems help the staff do their work more effectively, we have advanced the goals of the ministry" (Molsen, 1998).

In another partnership, a group of restaurants offered an evening's income to an AIDS hospice group. One restaurant contributes a brunch to playgoers at a nonprofit theater working with children with special needs. Some grocery store chains offer a contribution to certain groups on certain days as a proportion of shoppers' expenditures. A food pantry set up a coalition with a Rotary group and a church. It receives six hundred buckets of cleaning supplies annually to be distributed to its clients, a much-needed commodity that cannot be purchased with food stamps. And Oscar Mayer has dedicated the Wienermobile to help fight hunger (McNamara, 1999). It is the first time the corporation has partnered with anyone.

Think creatively to come up with possible partnerships for activities. Brainstorm and then ask.

Methods of Communication

The most effective method of fundraising is through face-to-face contact. According to an INDEPENDENT SECTOR survey, the most frequently cited reason that individuals give a first-time gift to a new organization is "being asked to give by someone you know well" (Hodgkinson, Weitzman, Noga, and Gorski, 1992). This linkage is important for ongoing support as well. Results will be greater by asking in person and maintaining contact with donors. Of course, a relationship cannot be developed with every name on the list of supporters because of time and resource availability. This is where careful planning and ordering come in. An ongoing program of cultivation should be established to target people who can make major gifts. The goal is to lift people to higher amounts than the organization would get without personal intervention. Direct mail does not work here. No one ever got milk by sending a letter to a cow.

In everything undertaken, careful record keeping is crucial. The search for major donors starts with the organization's own list, by identifying those who have already demonstrated a high level of loyalty. Those who examine the list should check people's giving patterns to determine when their last gift was made, how often they have given, what programs or appeals they have given to, and how much they have given. Ultimately the goal is to find donors who have the potential to give from their assets, not from their cash flow. These are people to consider for a planned giving program. Although their annual giving might not be great, even fifty dollars a year adds up to five hundred dollars over a faithful ten-year span of support.

There is a need for a means of accessing this information, which means a computerized system. A state-of-the-art system is not necessary. Perhaps a request will yield the perfect in-kind gift (with the caution not to take someone's worn-out, obsolete system). One organization had a donor who helped get brand-name equipment and then work out a program that allows that group to track every bit of information it needs about its donors. It is also helping the group keep accurate financial records. In addition, this group's web page brings in about fifty new members a week. Clearly this group is making good use of the technology, which is helping it to develop a donor base.

Let us assume that your computer has enabled you to identify people who deserve a face-to-face contact. How many people an organization can reasonably be expected to visit in a year clearly depends on how many other responsibilities there are, but such visits should be a priority. At the very least, the top ten to twenty-five donors ought to have the personal attention of the organization's senior person. The ultimate goal of that attention ought to be a significant gift. If these donors are local, seek numerous opportunities for cultivating their interest. Let them get to know you and your work as you get to know them and their particular interests. Give them opportunities for personal observation. Develop their enthusiasm and commitment to the cause. That way you can tailor your request to match their concerns.

You may realize that you are reaching only a tenth of the people who ought to have personal visits. With that recognition comes a wonderful opportunity for you to train and use volunteers who share your passion for your cause. People give to people. For some donors, the right person is the executive director. For others, it might be the chair of the board—or their sister-in-law or next-door neighbor. And that donor might be the next person to send on a face-to-face call.

Volunteers need to be trained. This is not their full-time job, not even their part-time job. They cannot be expected to make ten calls in two weeks. But if time frames and expectations are reasonable and careful and there is follow-up, good results will flow.

Ideally, many of the volunteers willing to do fundraising are on the board of directors. Although the primary responsibility of the board is to set policy and maintain fiduciary responsibility for the organization, they must also realize that they are key fundraisers. Henry Rosso (1991), founder of The Fund Raising School, emphasized that "willing involvement by board members in fundraising has been the hallmark of successful programs." Maurice Gurin (1981) also pointed out, "Boards should recognize that they are central to the success of all fundraising, and that their strength in this effort determines the organization's fundraising effectiveness."

This expectation should be spelled out clearly when individuals are asked to join the board. In fact, except in rare instances, no one should be asked to serve as a board member who is not already a donor. John Pearson (1995), executive director of the Christian Management Association, asks all individuals whom he is cultivating for board membership, "Could you envision that you could make (XYZ Organization) your highest giving and time priority beyond your church for the next three years?" Giving is something all board members can do, indeed, must do, hopefully at a major gift level.

Not all board members feel qualified or comfortable asking for money, so the fundraising effort should start with those who are willing to try. The others can participate in other ways, by helping with mailings or a telephone campaign or by helping to develop a mailing list.

Those willing to make personal visits will have the most fun. If they know that their role is simply to make the request and that they bear no responsibility for a donor's decision, they may feel more confident about the process. A person who declines to give is not rejecting the caller personally. We have no control over the many factors that influence giving decisions. Perhaps the timing is not right. In many cases no is not final; it may just mean "not now." In those instances, continued cultivation and relationship building are crucial to future success.

If board members understand the fundraising expectation and have been trained appropriately, they will be less reluctant to try. Board members themselves can model helpful examples that can encourage others. According to G. Douglass Alexander (1994), "The behavior of the members who accept this responsibility works on the reluctant ones, so that in time the practice becomes accepted."

The second most effective method of communication is by telephone. Telephones provide an opportunity for ongoing contact with key supporters. It should be a regular practice to pick up the telephone and express appreciation for their latest gift or simply to give an update on the status of the program it supports. They can share the excitement about the good things that are happening or sorrow about areas in which you need encouragement. Listen to their ideas for turning around a negative situation. As special friends, they may be the ones to provide special resources. Working in at least one telephone call a day should be standard.

A complete fundraising campaign can be conducted by telephone, a wonderful way to maintain contact with all donors. It provides an opportunity for dialogue as well as for expressing gratitude for their support. The results will make this a very cost-effective way of raising funds, especially with volunteers, including board members, as callers. Volunteers need to be trained. They can be given a call guide for talking points, but should not read a script. Expect at least a 20 percent affirmative response rate. If the people who are being called already share the vision, the campaign will do much better than that.

The least effective method of communication is direct mail. Nevertheless, you cannot do without it. If the donor list is small, mailings may not be cost-effective. Mail anyway, and let all information pieces include a reminder of gifting opportunities. Written pieces enable communicating the accomplishments of the organization. They provide an opportunity to tell your story. The power of a story cannot be overlooked in helping people remember your organization when it is time to make their charitable contributions. Some people stack appeal letters on their desks until they get around to writing checks. What happens to you if your request is not in the pile?

Direct mail can also be used for donor acquisition by renting a list and mailing a letter. But even with a carefully targeted mailing to people you are reasonably sure share your concerns, you will be lucky to break even. Carefully follow up those who do respond with subsequent appeals. You are likely to get further gifts, so the initial mailing investment may not be a loss.

Cost-Effectiveness

Direct mail is costly, but it can pay by following some basic principles:

- Control the cost. For example, use corporate stationery to take advantage of quantity purchases.
- Think of the one person to whom you are writing. Be conversational, but do not waste words.
- Make an emotional impact by telling the story powerfully while conveying facts.
- Be specific about your request for funds.
- Convey a sense of urgency about the appeal. Remember that this letter is one among many. If there is no deadline and no specific need, the donor will probably send her funds to someone else, for whom her gift will make a difference.
- Begin by writing the response device—that portion of the letter the donor will return. Often that is all the donor keeps after reading the letter.
- Be sure the reason for giving and the amount requested are clear. By the time the check is written, this may have been forgotten.
- Include your name and address in case the reply card gets separated from the envelope.

As nonprofit mailing rates continue to change, mail gets more and more costly. You cannot afford to waste this communication. Recently, I received a plain white envelope with a handwritten address. It was delivered in spite of the misspelling of the street name. There was no return address, but there was a first-class stamp, so I opened the envelope. Enclosed was a "Dear Friend" appeal from a camp I had been remotely connected with. They were sure I would want to know that the Lord wanted "to lay the need for a computer on my heart. . . . Please mail your gift to our treasurer." Nothing told me who the treasurer was, where she lived, and when they needed this money. The letter ended with "Thank you from the board."

Although donors who support the cause may be forgiving about the methodology, they also may be suspicious about an organization (or an executive director) that is so irresponsible and lax. Do you dare take such a chance with your mailings?

Whatever method of communication you choose is bound to be influenced by budget. This is where careful record keeping will help you make good decisions. You must be able to calculate the return on your investment. Whatever you hope to accomplish requires funding. That funding can come as readily from what you save by not spending foolishly as from what you raise by spending wisely. Know how much you raise for each dollar spent. If you adjust your fundraising activity according to the level of each donor's giving, analyze your results. Try some testing too. Even with a small list, you can examine such variables as color, the amount of the request, the teaser copy on the envelope, and first-class versus bulk postage. Just be sure to vary only one aspect each time.

Clean the mailing list on a regular schedule, but do not delete a donor without warning. It is more cost-effective to renew a lapsed donor who is on the list than to pay to find new supporters.

You will have to spend money to make money, so I am not making a case for no spending at all. Rather, no one should spend money that does not bring results. Know whether face-to-face contacts and telephone activity bring in more money than they cost. Learn to seek the expertise of printers by understanding the options of paper and printing costs. If you want a four-color brochure, perhaps the best way to do this is to use blank brochures that come preprinted with a four-color picture. Use the computer to modify the message to fit the available space, and print as needed.

For the results achieved, the telephone can be a highly cost-effective tool. One small organization has had no trouble raising three dollars for every one dollar spent in acquiring new donors by telephone. The organization's renewal record for these donors is very good also. Not only do these telephone donors give again, but they have also increased their average gifts.

Seeing people face to face can also be extremely cost-effective. Even if you have to travel long distances to maintain contact with major donors, the results are usually worth it. A thousand dollar trip may seem exorbitant, but if it results in a $100,000 gift, it is money well spent.

In-Kind Gifts

In-kind gifts can provide cost-effective fundraising. Businesses often are open to helping causes they believe in, especially when they consider the potential benefits. Giving away stagnant inventory can free valuable warehouse space and reduce administrative expenses. (Like all other gifts and donations, however, do not take anything that distorts your mission or hinders your work.) Depending on the type of business and the type of incorporation, businesses can deduct up to twice the cost of the donated inventory according to section 170(e)(3) of the Internal Revenue Code. The fact that a product has outlived its identified life may not matter to the benefiting organization at all. Many foods are still edible past the shelf life, and many medicines are still effective. An older packaging design does not harm the contents.

The only way to learn of such gifts is to ask. Let the request lead to a productive partnership. The successes can be immense. One homeless shelter serves a bountiful breakfast to its overnight clients because the director contacted a local bakery. Each night at the 9:00 P.M. closing time, a volunteer picks up bags of unsold bagels, bread, and other baked goods. The bakery gets a tax write-off, and the hungry are fed. None of this would have happened, however, without the director's initiative. He had to ask.

Another source of in-kind gifts is expertise from people whose knowledge can serve your organization. Be alert for lawyers, fundraisers, business people, special event organizers, and others who can make important contributions as board members.

Special Events

An organization that has a history of special events will have difficulty discontinuing them, even if research shows them to be neither time- nor cost-effective. But if creative, energetic volunteers are available who like to run special events, the organization has nothing to lose. Some service organizations take care of the entire enterprise. You have nothing to do but accept the check. A silent auction or a noisy one, a walkathon, a dinner, a craft fair, a golf marathon, a concert, a book sale, or sales of magazines, candy,

or ornaments offer potential funding. They hold potential pitfalls, too.

Before plunging into the special event swamp, ask some
questions:

- What is the purpose in holding such an event: to find support
  or to find supporters?
- Will all the effort bring long-term results? The goal is to build
  a base of donors who ultimately will renew and upgrade their
  gifts, perhaps even eventually endowing the organization.
  Rarely are these lofty goals attained through concert goers or
  product buyers.
- Are there enough volunteers to hold a successful special
  event? While special events can be a wonderful way to use volunteer support, they can also quickly lead to volunteer
  burnout.
- Can you afford a special event?
- Do you have the time and the lead time necessary to ensure
  success? One group learned to its dismay not to rely on bulk
  mail for publicity. Mailing announcements three weeks in advance meant that nearly everyone got the notice after the
  event was over. Fortunately there had been other kinds of publicity, so it was not a total loss, but they were highly embar-
  rassed not to have a better crowd for a speaker they had flown
  in from a distant city. They were even more disappointed in
  the financial results. A net gain had turned into a net loss
  through inadequate planning.

Funding the Future

By far the most cost-effective fundraising is planned giving. Many
of the most faithful donors would like to be able to give more, but
believe that they lack the resources. Yet even small organizations
can show their donors how they can make major gifts that do not
affect current cash flow.

The simplest program to undertake is a wills emphasis. Studies have shown that even when people have wills, they do not think
of including charitable bequests unless the idea is suggested to

them. Awareness can be created by placing a notice in the organization's newsletter: "Have you remembered us in your will?"

Seize conversational opportunities as well. When you thank someone for annual support, ask if he or she would be open to endowing that support in perpetuity.

In fact, many people do not have a will or their will is out of date, so the first task is to motivate them to do something about their wills. Preprinted materials can be personalized, and you can use them to set up regular mail contact. The hope is that this program will lead to a bequest for the organization, but this might not be the case. Your role is to serve the donor. If you are fortunate, you will also be served.

Be sure the board is behind this effort. The members need to understand that for a while, there will be expenses that do not bring an immediate return. This concern will be quickly assuaged the first time a lawyer calls with news of a bequest. The board members too need to be asked about whether they have named the organization in their wills

No planned giving program should be launched without carefully thinking through the organizational policies for such a move:

- What will you do with bequests? Will you immediately sell gifts of stock? While donors can benefit from giving appreciated assets, most organizations do not play the stock market.
- Will you set up an organizational endowment plan for the future? If so, what investment policies will you follow to minimize risk and maximize return? To whom will you turn for investment expertise? Is there a local community foundation or a bank or trust company that could handle this work with fees the group can afford?
- Plan for pitfalls. What procedures will you follow the day a donor calls and says, "I'd like to give you a house"? Be particularly cautious about accepting gifts of real estate. You do not want someone else's problems.

Other planned giving options can be through life-income gifts, such as a charitable remainder trust or a charitable gift annuity. The organization may not be in a position to manage such gifts, but it should understand them. Know how to work with donors so they can take advantage of these win-win gifting opportunities. Often their own financial advisers may be unaware of options that minimize tax consequences. You do not want to be in the position of giving legal advice, but you do want to help donors ask the right questions of their advisers. Donors will be grateful to learn of ways to make large gifts to the causes they care about while setting up a stream of income they cannot outlive.

Another future gifting option is through insurance, although this option should be handled carefully. Do not turn into an insurance salesperson, marketing guaranteed issue insurance where your organization would own the policy in the donor's name and use a portion of the donor's contribution to pay the premium. If such a program is presented to you, scrutinize it carefully, and challenge any assumptions that promise huge sums. Exactly what rate of return will you be getting? Under what circumstances will you receive no money at all?

This does not mean that you should never accept a gift of life insurance. Donors can take the initiative to give such a gift. They can easily assign a policy that no longer serves the purpose for which they purchased it. Another way to give insurance is for a donor to purchase a new policy, making the organization the beneficiary. Each year their payment of premiums is tax deductible.

The Receipting System

No matter how a gift comes, whether immediate or deferred, and no matter how large or small that gift is, the donor should be thanked immediately. A simple receipting system can help build the relationships that are so vital. It does not take much effort to add a short handwritten thank-you note when the receipts are mailed. Some groups thank immediately with telephone calls. Any giver of $100, either cumulative or in one payment, gets a timely thank-you call from the director of development. When the amount is $250 or more, the president calls. Such appreciation contributes to continued giving. Donors continually express gratitude for this personal contact.

You also need to express gratitude for all volunteers. Be creative, but be sure they know they are appreciated. The food pantry that puts a billboard on a busy road saying, "Thank you, volunteers, for giving the time of your lives," probably will see those volunteers come back time and again.

Be sure receipts go out promptly (within three working days), and be sure they include some kind of request for a return gift. This reminder can increase the frequency of contributions. There is no reason that an annual gift cannot be turned into a semiannual one, or even a quarterly or monthly payment. The secret is to *ask*.

Careful records must be kept. If contributions are ever questioned, the organization needs to know exactly when it received a gift and what the amount was, and it must be able to substantiate the claims. All computerized systems must have a current backup that is not kept in the organization's office.

Accounting practices must adhere to federal standards. If the organization does not know the current requirements, it should work with an accountant who does. The annual report to constituents, as well as to the government, needs to make very clear the sources of income, the costs of raising that income, and what is being done with that income.

The board of directors carries fiduciary responsibility for the organization. This reaches to the very heart of the organizational mission, as Chapter Seven aptly reminds us. Are you spending the money for the purposes for which it was raised? Are appeals truthful? Do you touch the emotions without being sensational? Are your records in good order? It will neither enhance your reputation nor further your mission to be the target of the next newspaper investigation. But if you are operating with the highest integrity and disclosing all necessary information, you need not worry. Instead, you can enjoy being the kind of fundraiser described by Jerold Panas (1994): "These are exciting times to be in the business of potential. What will be required are professionals who think smarter, work harder, plan bolder, and commit themselves with greater fervor and missionary zeal to the needs of their institution."

Checklist for Fundraisers

Do you have:

- Staff, board members, and volunteers who have an understanding of stewardship?

- Access to successful fundraisers whom you can call for advice?
- A positive public image?
- A mission statement that can be summarized by the board, staff, and volunteers?
- A persuasive, well-written case statement?
- A comprehensive marketing plan?
- A systematic plan for soliciting every donor annually?
- An up-to-date computer database that allows you to track donors by gift history, personal history, gift size, and appeal response?
- An accurate record of all fundraising activities and results for the past three to five years?
- Several board members who are active in fundraising? Board members who have included your organization in their estate plans?
- A system to acknowledge all gifts within three working days?
- A process for continuously identifying new donor prospects?
- A planned giving program, complete with written policies for gift acceptance and investment?

References

Alexander, G. Douglass. (1994). "10 Things I Wish I Had Known 24 Years Ago." *Fund Raising Management,* May, p. 50.

Billetteri, Thomas J. (1998). "Protestants Found to Donate a Reduced Share of Their Incomes to Social Services." *Chronicle of Philanthropy,* Jan. 15, p. 14.

Gray, Susan. (1998). "Rhode Island's Accidental Philanthropist." *Chronicle of Philanthropy,* Apr. 8, pp. 9–10.

Gurin, Maurice. (1981). *What Volunteers Should Know for Successful Fundraising.* New York: Stein and Day.

Hodgkinson, V. A., Weitzman, M. S., Noga, S. M., and Gorski, H. A. (1992). *Giving and Volunteering in the United States: Findings from a National Survey.* Washington, D.C.: INDEPENDENT SECTOR, 1992.

McNamara, Don. (1999). "My Fundraiser Has a First Name ... It's O-S-C-A-R." *NonProfit Times,* May, p. 5.

Molsen, Mike. (1998). "Partners Make It Possible." *Life Matters,* Fall, p. 7.

Panas, Jerold. (1994). "The Future Isn't What It Used to Be." *Fund Raising Management,* Apr., p. 29.

Pearson, John. (1995). "Enhancing the Board's Ministry in Development." Unpublished paper presented at the Christian Stewardship Association, Schaumburg, Ill., Sept. 26, 1995.

Rosso, H. A., and Associates. (1991). *Achieving Excellence in Fund Raising: A Comprehensive Guide to Principles, Strategies, and Methods.* San Francisco: Jossey-Bass.

Additional Readings

Hartsook, Robert F. (1998). *Closing that Gift: How to be Successful 99 percent of the Time.* Wichita, Kans.: ASR Philanthropic Publishers.

Nichols, Judith E. (1995). *Growing from Good to Great: Positioning Your Fundraising Efforts for Big Gains.* Chicago: Bonus Books.

Sturtevant, William T. (1997). *The Artful Journey: Cultivating and Soliciting the Major Gift.* Chicago: Bonus Books.

CHAPTER 6

Identifying the Organization's Key Stakeholders

Mary Tschirhart
Eric Knueve

Father Bill sighed. The volunteer music director just announced that without more resources, she is unwilling to coordinate the Christmas concert. The budget is tight, and the music director's request competes with requests from the director of religious education for new educational materials. A group of parishioners formally asked for materials that reflect more ethnic and gender diversity. But one of the oldest church members (and its most generous donor) just called to complain that he does not like the "newfangled" music being played in church and thinks the music director is rude. All this comes at a time when the church is adding a food pantry for impoverished families to its programs and is experiencing increased demand on its homeless shelter. And Father Bill is running late for a meeting with nonprofit and government representatives hoping to better coordinate social services for the community.

Father Bill faces a variety of stakeholder challenges. Faith-based nonprofit organizations have an obligation to a transcendent element and a particular set of religious values and structures. Their ultimate responsibility is to a divine mandate, an ultimate authority, and the demands of religious precepts rather than to a particular interest group. However, a variety of individuals and groups have stakes in faith-based organizations. How those organizations respond to the interests and claims of these individuals and groups can affect their effectiveness, their funding, and even their very survival. When stakeholder demands are competing or incompatible rather than complementary, organizational leaders may need to make tough choices. Statements of organizational mission and values rarely offer sufficient guidance for decision making in the face of competing stakeholder needs and pressures. Few organizations have the luxury of interacting only with stakeholders with compatible goals and similar value systems. Even a shared faith commitment among the stakeholders is not enough to ensure the absence of conflict between them.

This chapter presents stakeholder analysis as a decision-making and planning tool for faith-based organizations. A stakeholder is any individual, organization, or institution that influences or is influenced by an organization. Although the word itself may be unfamiliar, the concept should not be. Whether you call them stakeholders, constituents, publics, or interested parties, the idea is the same. These are the people and organizations that can affect the functioning of the organization or are affected by that functioning. The term *stakeholder* is useful because in a stakeholder analysis, it is essential to focus on the stakes of the entities with which the organization is interacting.

After completing a stakeholder analysis, leaders of organizations are better able to answer the following questions:

- Who are our stakeholders, and what are their stakes?
- Who are our most important stakeholders?
- How important are we to each of our stakeholders, and how do they judge us?
- What responsibilities and obligations do we have to our stakeholders?
- What challenges do our stakeholders present?
- How can we more effectively manage relationships with our stakeholders?

The answers to these questions can clarify the organization's vision, help articulate organizational values, increase awareness of core and discretionary programs, identify current issues and potential problems, provide direction to staff, increase effective responses to demands, and develop coherent and defensible decision making. Stakeholder analysis can be a key component of a strategic planning process, mission statement review, and establishment of a core values program.

The Stakeholder Framework

The stakeholder framework assumes that every organization has stakeholders. The stakeholders may be external or internal to the organization, and their activities may help or hurt the organization. The list of a faith-based organization's stakeholders may be long, encompassing staff, volunteers, consumers, funders, project partners, congregation members, competitors, suppliers, advisers, banks, regulators, accreditors, general public, umbrella organizations, terrorist groups, media, and future generations, to name a few. All of these, and many more unnamed, are individuals, groups, and entities that affect or are affected by the purposes, actions, decisions, policies, and practices of the organization. Indeed, many might be explicit in naming God as a stakeholder—the supreme stakeholder, as John Zietlow intimates in his chapter.

Leaders of organizations spend time and resources anticipating and responding to stakeholders' needs and pressures. Stakeholders often make competing or incompatible demands on an organization. Far too often the stakeholder demands commanding the greatest attention depend on the power, influence, and communication abilities of the stakeholder rather than the importance of the demands to the organization's mission, values, and strategic orientation. Stakeholders may use varying and multiple methods to exert pressure on an organization, and they may work with or through other stakeholders in their attempts to influence the organization. Often organizational leaders find themselves continually putting out fires set by stakeholders rather than strategically choosing which fires to address and which to ignore. The leaders may themselves be divided into competing interest groups. Given a potentially contentious and dynamic environment, organizations usually benefit from developing forms, policies, and practices for analyzing stakeholder claims, responding to stakeholders' demands, and encouraging stakeholder support of the organization. Ultimately organizational effectiveness is improved by analyzing and controlling, insofar as it is possible, an organization's relationships with its stakeholders.

Stakeholder Analysis Process

The stakeholder analysis process is accomplished by answering the questions listed at the beginning of the chapter. These questions promote a thorough review of the organization's stakeholder environment and, based on the review, the development of guidelines for managing relations with stakeholders.

Some attention needs to be given to planning for the analysis process. No single person in an organization is likely to be able to carry out the analysis and planning independently. An effective way to take advantage of multiple areas of expertise and knowledge is to assemble a group of individuals to work on the analysis. Finding representatives from a variety of internal stakeholder groups may be useful. Staff and volunteers operating on the edge of an organization in liaison roles may be best at representing the perspectives and nature of the external stakeholders with which they interact. Staff and volunteers operating at the core of the organization may be able to make sure that there is thorough coverage of all areas of the organization and appropriate ordering of organizational needs. Having representatives from key stakeholder groups participate in the analysis process can help create a more accurate view of the stakeholder environment.

The stakeholder analysis process is inherently messy. A variety of dimensions of stakeholder relationships need to be examined. Matrices and maps can be useful tools for organizing information but are unlikely to capture the richness of discussions of the questions. Stakeholder relationships are dynamic, and a stakeholder analysis quickly becomes outdated in a turbulent environment. Major changes in an organization's purposes, activities, values, norms, or outcomes should serve as prompts for new analysis. The process may question assumed mandates and require improved articulations of mission, values, and strategies. By formally working through a stakeholder analysis, organizational leaders can better understand the likely consequences of organizational actions and improve decision making.

Who Are Your Stakeholders, and What Are Their Stakes?

To understand who is a stakeholder, it is useful to understand the concept of a stake. According to Carroll (1996), a stake is an interest in a decision, share in an undertaking, claim on an asset or property, or a legal or moral right to be treated a certain way. A stakeholder is an individual, group, or other entity with a stake in what the organization does and plans to do. For example, congregation members may have an interest in maintaining convenient services. A project partner may have a share in work to improve the welfare of the community. Business suppliers have a legal right to payment of bills. Volunteers may have a moral claim to be treated fairly and with respect.

It is sometimes difficult to judge how specific one should be in constructing a stakeholder list. For example, under a broad stakeholder label such as "volunteers," one could create more specific stakeholder labels, such as food pantry workers, choir members, and others. A general rule is to add more specificity when the stakeholders under one label vary significantly in their interests and claims. An adequate stakeholder list will have enough stakeholders noted to represent all the existing stakes in the organization. A more richly developed list will have sublists for those who share the same stakes but differ on other dimensions useful to consider in preparing a plan for stakeholder relations—for example, the types of contributions the stakeholder makes to the organization, type of power, influence level and mechanisms, criteria used to evaluate the organization, and satisfaction level. Exhibit 6.1 presents a worksheet addressing these dimensions that can be filled out as part of the stakeholder analysis process.

Stakeholder identification can be complex because stakeholders do not always act independently. They may form coalitions or rival factions, and they also share communication mechanisms. For example, parochial school teachers and students' parents may team up to present a proposal for a special program. Different religious denominations may join together in an advocacy effort. Employees may form pressure groups based on their preferences for budget allocations. A sophisticated understanding of who an organization's stakeholders are requires an understanding of which stakeholders are most likely to work in concert or opposition.

Exhibit 6.1. Stakeholder Identification and Analysis Worksheet.

Stakeholders	Stake	Responsibility Obligation to Stakeholder	Importance to Organization	Importance of Organization	Performance Criteria	Satisfaction Level	Influence Means	Power Bases	Challenge & Response
Core:									
Secondary:									
Tertiary:									

Who Are Our Most Important Stakeholders?

Not all stakeholders are key or core stakeholders. It is useful to imagine a series of concentric circles around an organization. The stakeholders who play an essential or vital role in fulfilling the organization's mission are in the innermost ring. Stakeholders who affect or are affected by the organization in a more minimal or indirect manner are in rings farther from the core. Bryson and Alston (1996) suggest placing stakeholders into one of three categories or rings: core, secondary, and tertiary. This placement does not mean that the organization should ignore or does not have obligations or responsibilities toward stakeholders who are not in the core. It merely shows the relative degree to which the stakeholders influence or are influenced by the organization. The placement on a "stakeholder map" is also dynamic. For example, individuals who attend religious services only on holidays might be in the secondary ring, but they might move into the primary ring if they become more active and involved members.

Drawing a stakeholder map is relatively easy once stakeholders are identified and analyzed. The first step is to complete the stakeholder worksheet in Exhibit 6.1. Then the map is created by placing each stakeholder in one ring of a set of concentric circles. Group the stakeholders who are in coalitions together in the same area of the map. Dotted lines can be drawn around them to show their relationship.

Figure 6.1 shows the beginnings of a stakeholder map created for a Catholic parish. The map (only partially constructed) shows the concentric circles, stakeholder coalitions, and stakeholder sublists.

Faith-based organizations with complex operations may find it useful to develop a separate stakeholder map for each of their programs. A stakeholder map for a self-sustaining parenting support group, for example, may be relatively simple compared to the map for an international emergency relief effort. The stakeholder environment would look quite different for the two programs. Stakeholders vital to the success of one program may be irrelevant for others. Stakeholders may be placed in different rings when the program rather than the organization is the focus of the analysis. A program-level analysis can be helpful in developing guidance for

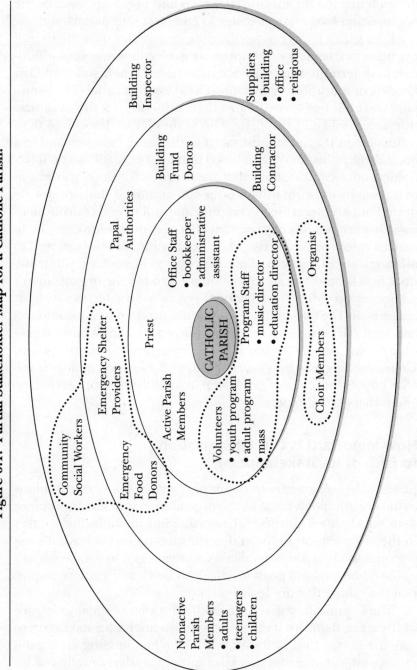

Figure 6.1. Partial Stakeholder Map for a Catholic Parish.

decision making for specific programs and may help to make the organization-level analysis easier to complete and understand.

Even with a focus on specific programs rather than the overall organization, leaders of nonprofit organizations may find it difficult to determine the relative importance of their stakeholders. Leaders of for-profit organizations have it much easier. They compare stakeholders according to their influence on the organization's survival and prosperity. This is simpler to determine than influence on the accomplishment of the more complex and less quantifiable missions of faith-based organizations. Still, some stakeholders offer contributions that are required for the organization to pursue its mission; others offer contributions that are not required but are nevertheless helpful, and still others contribute in ways that are not directly relevant. These contributions may be financial resources, expertise, skills, reputation, or effort, as well as other resources necessary for the provision of services. Contributions may be as disparate as a willingness to use the organization's services or providing the freedom to carry out the services without harassment. The establishment and maintenance of social, economic, and legal infrastructures that make the organization's mission possible or easier to realize must also be recognized as contributions. Understanding existing contributions to the mission and their relative importance is a necessary step in identifying core, secondary, and tertiary stakeholders.

How Important Is Our Organization to Each of Its Stakeholders?

Just as stakeholders vary in the importance of their contributions to the organization's mission, the organization varies in importance to its stakeholders' purposes. Understanding an individual's stakes in the organization helps in determining the organization's importance to the stakeholder. Stakes more integral to a stakeholder's welfare, identity, and goals are likely to be viewed as more important than those that are less central.

The organization may have a different view of the importance of the stake than the stakeholders do. In analyzing stakes, try to take the perspective of the stakeholder when judging an organization's importance to them. For example, leaders of religious organizations may place a higher value on the religious education of congregants than do the latter. Chapter Two provides several examples of differences in perspective by stakeholders. Knowledge of these differences can mean the difference between success and failure.

Not all stakeholders use the same criteria in judging an organization. There is no one measure of effectiveness for an organization. Government may judge an organization based on its obedience to laws and compliance with regulations. Employees' evaluation of the organization may be based on the quality of their work life or supervisors, pay, benefits, or ability to help a cause. Community leaders may focus most on how well the organization contributes to the well-being of the community. A clear understanding of how their organization is judged can help leaders anticipate stakeholder concerns and feedback.

An organization's success in satisfying a stakeholder may influence the level of importance the stakeholder places on the organization. A satisfied stakeholder may rely more on the organization, placing great importance on its continued provision of desired outcomes. An inability to satisfy a stakeholder's interests or claims may lead to escalating pressure. The stakeholder may make changing the organization a top priority, seek new influence mechanisms, or try to punish the organization. Or an unsatisfied stakeholder may decide to ignore the organization, sacrificing any particular stakes connected to it. In this scenario, the stakeholder no longer views the organization as important.

What Responsibilities and Obligations Do We Have to Our Stakeholders?

An organization's responsibilities and obligations to its stakeholders may be social, legal, and ethical. In general, nonprofit organizations are expected to provide goods and services that have public benefit and to act as trustworthy organizations, honoring social and legal commitments.

Among the many authors who have outlined the ethical responsibilities of nonprofit organizations, Jeavons (1993) has identified the expected ethical attributes of nonprofit organizations as integrity, openness, accountability, service, and charity. INDEPENDENT

SECTOR—a leading nonprofit advocacy organization—devised an ethical code for nonprofits that informs the development of standards for relationships with stakeholders. The code states that the behaviors of nonprofit organizations should express commitment beyond self; obedience of laws; commitment beyond the law; commitment to the public good; respect for the worth and dignity of individuals; tolerance, diversity, and social justice; accountability to the public; openness and honesty; and prudent application of resources (O'Connell, 1986).

Beyond these broad prescriptions, individual organizations may have distinct responsibilities and obligations to particular types of stakeholders. For example, some faith-based organizations such as Gospel Missions and the Salvation Army focus on meeting immediate human needs and transforming the lives of individual persons. Others focus on forms of work designed to change what they view as the social and political conditions that create those needs. Jeavons (1994) argues that faith-based organizations have special obligations to their staff to provide a working environment that allows for spiritual development. Other types of nonprofits would probably not see this as a responsibility.

A systematic discussion of general and specific responsibilities and obligations to stakeholders may develop new understandings of appropriate behaviors for an organization. Examination of responsibilities and obligations using a stakeholder context can highlight the trade-offs that organizations must make. It is impossible to please everybody all of the time. Knowing which stakeholders' interests and claims should receive the highest priority can ensure that decisions about trade-offs are made for the right reasons rather than for expediency or merely to silence a squeaky wheel. Understanding and accepting responsibilities and obligations will help in determining how to relate to a stakeholder even when the stakeholder has no expectations of the organization and is not exerting pressure on it.

What Challenges Do Our Stakeholders Present?

Stakeholders' values, norms, expectations, purposes, activities, and outcomes may not be congruent with those of an organization. This lack of congruence can create challenges. There are three general types of incongruence issues involving stakeholders: organizational legitimacy concerns, stakeholder legitimacy concerns, and technical clashes. Understanding the types of incongruence an organization may have with various stakeholders can help the organization develop strategies to improve its stakeholder environment.

Organizational Legitimacy Concerns

When an organization fails to satisfy a stakeholder's interests or claims, the stakeholder may question the organization's legitimacy. An organizational legitimacy concern arises if a stakeholder's values, norms, or expectations are incongruent with the organization's purposes, activities, or outcomes. For example, when the leader of the PTL ministry was found to be using donations inappropriately, the organization suffered a legitimacy crisis. Right-to-life advocacy organizations that support the bombing of abortion clinics are considered illegitimate by those who believe that no organization should break the law, no matter what the cause.

When an organization has legitimacy with stakeholders, it is more likely to attract resources, engender commitment, avoid opposition, and reduce demands for accountability and change. Organizations lacking legitimacy with a stakeholder face the challenges of losing the stakeholder's support, finding substitute sources of support, or changing the stakeholder's perception of the organization in order to regain legitimacy.

Stakeholder Legitimacy Concerns

A stakeholder legitimacy concern exists when the stakeholder is acting inappropriately based on the organization's values and norms. For example, someone who receives a service from a program that depends on or demands some commitment in sweat equity yet who refuses to participate is acting inconsistently with the programs values and norms.

Another stakeholder legitimacy concern occurs when satisfying a stakeholder's interests or claims would force the organization to violate its own values, norms, or expectations. For example, a board member may expect to receive a lucrative purchase contract from a program because of her or his work on its behalf. A large donor may demand a reduction in services to a particular class of people. Such demands present challenges to an organization. When stakeholders lack legitimacy, organizational leaders may take the opportunity to encourage the stakeholder to change or to diminish the stakeholder's importance to their organization.

Technical Clashes

A technical clash results if a stakeholder's or the organization's purposes, activities, or outcomes are not positive for the other party but do not violate values, norms, or expectations. The concern is not social or moral in nature, but nevertheless results in difficulties in achieving the organization's mission or the stakeholders' goals. For example, nonprofit organizations may compete for the same donations or grants. None violates the others' values or norms in pursuing such funds. If one organization receives them, the others face the challenge of finding other sources of support.

Once technical clashes are identified, it may be productive to consider ways to change them into win-win situations in which the stakeholder and organization help each other. Some technical clashes may be prevented through cooperation, coordination, and collaboration. For example, previously competing organizations may develop joint proposals for funding. For the technical clashes that cannot be transformed into win-win situations, the consequences often can be minimized. For example, an organization that has an on-street parking space shortage may choose to build its own parking facility so that its clients do not have to compete with others for parking spaces.

Additional Challenges and Concerns

Legitimacy concerns and technical clashes are not the only challenges and opportunities for organizations. Organizations may find that their stakeholders' relative importance to the organization is not consistent with the stakeholders' relative power over the organization. This may create accountability problems when the stakeholders' claims are competing or incompatible. The challenge is to make sure that the most important but less powerful stakeholders are satisfied while minimizing the negative impact of actions by more powerful but less important stakeholders. In some cases, an organization may be able to reduce the power of the more important stakeholders or increase the power of the less important ones. If one must accept existing power balances, leaders need to find ways both to resist this power and find opportunities to channel that power into productive directions.

How Can We More Effectively Manage Relationships with Our Stakeholders?

To develop policies and practices that can improve an organization's stakeholder environment, organizational leaders need to understand the characteristics of their environment. Answers to the previous question will reveal major challenges and perhaps present opportunities. Once these challenges and opportunities are identified, strategies can be developed to respond to them.

When the organization-stakeholder relationship is troubled, organizational leaders may choose to adapt to the desires of the stakeholder or change the stakeholder's interests or claims. Other strategies are to change the importance of the stakeholder to the organization or the importance of the organization to the stakeholder, and increase or decrease the stakeholder's power over the organization. The choice of strategy should be informed by knowledge of the responsibilities and obligations the organization has to the stakeholder.

Maintaining a good relationship with a particular stakeholder often depends on being tuned in to the performance criteria that the stakeholder uses to judge the organization and communicating to the stakeholder the criteria that the organization uses to judge the stakeholder. Instituting ways of detecting or surfacing stakeholders' views of the organization and clarifying stakeholder performance can aid in identifying concerns and addressing them before they create greater problems.

Conclusion

Organizational leaders who conduct stakeholder analysis can gain greater awareness of their organization's environment and develop carefully thought-out strategies and policies. The investment of time and effort offers the promise of benefits that can transform an organization that tends to respond best to the immediate demands of its loudest and most powerful stakeholders to one that more fully acknowledges its responsibilities and obligations to all stakeholders.

References

Bryson, J. M., and Alston, F. K. (1996). *Creating and Implementing Your Strategic Plan: A Workbook for Public and Nonprofit Organizations.* San Francisco: Jossey-Bass.

Carroll, A. B. (1996). *Business and Society: Ethics and Stakeholder Management.* (3rd ed.). Cincinnati: South-Western.

Jeavons, T. H. (1993). "Ethics in Nonprofit Management: Creating a Culture of Integrity." In R. D. Herman and others (eds.). *The Jossey-Bass Handbook of Nonprofit Leadership and Management.* San Francisco: Jossey-Bass.

Jeavons, T. H. (1994). *When the Bottom Line Is Faithfulness.* Bloomington: Indiana University Press.

O'Connell, Brian. (1986). *Obedience to the Unenforceable.* Washington, D.C.: INDEPENDENT SECTOR.

Additional Readings

Bacharach, S. B., and Lawler, E. J. (1980). *Power and Politics in Organizations.* San Francisco: Jossey-Bass.

Brynjolfsson, E., and Renshaw, A. A. (1997). "The Matrix of Change." *Sloan Management Review, 38*(2), 37–55.

Donaldson, T., and Preston, L. E. (1995). "The Stakeholder Theory of the Corporation: Concepts, Evidence, and Implications." *Academy of Management Review, 20*(2), 65–91.

Freeman, R. E. (1984). *Strategic Management: A Stakeholder Approach.* Boston: Pitman.

Mitchell, R. K., Agle, B. A., and Wood, D. J. (1997). "Toward a Theory of Stakeholder Identification and Salience: Defining the Principle of Who and What Really Counts." *Academy of Management Journal, 22*(4), 853–886.

Nielsen, R. P., and Bartunek, J. M. (1996). "Opening Narrow, Routinized Schemata to Ethical Stakeholder Consciousness and Action." *Business and Society, 35*(4), 483–520.

Reidenbach, R. E., and McClung, G. W. (1999). "Managing Stakeholder Loyalty." *Marketing Health Services, 19*(1), 20–30.

Savage, G. T., and others. (1991). "Strategies for Assessing and Managing Organizational Stakeholders." *Academy of Management Executive, 5*(2), 61–75.

Wallace, G. W. (1995). "Balancing Stakeholder Requirements." *Journal for Quality and Participation, 18*(2), 85–90.

CHAPTER 7

Developing Financial Accountability and Controls

John Zietlow

Recent news headlines have brought striking lessons about the negative consequences of having a weak financial accountability and control system. New Era Philanthropy reminded us that investment and fundraising returns that sound too good to be true no doubt are. Fraud and embezzlement at the treasury department of the denominational headquarters of the Episcopal Church and diversion of funds at the Jewish Education Center in San Francisco highlight the need for internal financial controls. Board members and managers have had their attention heightened by public scandals at PTL Ministries, the National Baptist Convention, USA, several Catholic dioceses, and local charities and congregations too numerous to mention. One thing is clear: faith-based organizations are not immune to fraud and other forms of malfeasance. Nonprofit decision makers must respond to the growing demand for greater accountability. Governmental and foundation funding have brought new requirements for reporting and for demonstrating effectiveness, and donors and other stakeholders increasingly are asking tough questions regarding ethics, efficiency, and effectiveness.

This chapter ties the concepts of accountability, control, and stewardship together. Throughout I use the following definitions for accountability, control, and stewardship. *Accountability* is defined as "liable to being called to account; answerable." A *control,* in a financial context, is defined as "a restraining device, measure, or limit; a curb." *Stewardship* denotes "managing another's property, finances, or other affairs." Except where addressing governmental or grantor information needs, I oversimplify in two ways. First, an organization may use the same mechanisms to be accountable to its mission (and therefore the divine mandate or founding parties behind that mission); its beneficiaries, clients, members, board, donors, employees, volunteers, business partners, and community; and society. Second, when conflicts exist between the interests of two stakeholders, these can be resolved in a way that maintains the credibility of your organization in both parties' eyes.

What Are We Accountable For?

Canada's Panel on Accountability and Governance in the Voluntary Sector (PAGVS) answered the question as follows:

> Voluntary organizations are self-governing agencies which hold a public trust related to a particular mission and they generally use donated funds to accomplish this mission. As a result, these organizations are responsible for what they chose to do and how well they do it. This means they are, at minimum, accountable for:
> - Establishing an appropriate mission and/or policy priorities and ensuring their relevance;
> - Setting goals to measure how well they do in meeting their policy objectives;
> - Sound management of funds received from donors and governments;
> - Effective organizational governance (including management and planning practices); and the outcomes, quality and range of their programs and services [at http://www.pagvs.com/helping.html].

Notice that overall accountability extends beyond financial accountability and control. The management implication is that an organization that follows all of the directives in this chapter and becomes financially accountable is not necessarily accountable in the broader sense.

Scriptural Bases

Accountability and control flow naturally from an organization's first principles. For a large majority of the faith-based organizations in the United States, biblical precepts lie at the heart of the Judeo-Christian ethic, and these will be the focus of examples in the chapter. Nevertheless, all of the world's religious traditions embody certain measures of accountability within their normative texts and precepts.

Stewardship

The key passage in the Bible relating to stewards, who are portrayed as household managers, is found in the New Testament (I Corinthians 4:2): "Moreover it is required in stewards, that a man be found faithful" (King James Version). In other words, a manager should be trustworthy, sure, and true. A stewardship litmus test for a human or social services agency is to answer this question: Would an objective outside observer agree that a particular organization is trustworthy, sure, and true in all of its dealings? Summarizing the findings from a group of funded religious grants at a Lilly Endowment grantees conference in late 1997, Avner Ben-Ner noted that trust in leadership is an important determinant of giving. The implication is that good stewardship begets more resources. The Greek word used for steward speaks of a "household manager." The concept extends beyond mere trustworthiness to include carrying out all that is implied in the role. Managers are to be efficient and effective.

Accountability

The accountability dilemma for most nonprofit organizations is that their service provision is mostly unobservable to interested stakeholders other than employees and clients or members. Donors, governmental agencies, foundations, and even board members rarely have the opportunity to observe their daily operations. The Bible speaks authoritatively to these situations. Specifically, it is expected that each person in a management role will give account to vindicate efficiency of resource use. In Luke 16:1–2 we read, "Jesus told his disciples: There was a rich man whose manager was accused of wasting his possessions. So he called him in and asked him, 'What is this I hear about you? Give an account of your management, because you cannot be manager any longer.'" (The same is said of unbelievers, in I Peter 4:5: "But they will have to give account to him who is ready to judge the living and the dead.") (Quotations are from the New International Version unless noted.) It is not the (possibly unobservable) output of services at issue here but the observed resource waste. Where service provision is observable, accountability may not be quite as important, as noted in II Kings 22:7: "But they need not account for the money entrusted to them, because they are acting faithfully." Even in such cases, there is accountability to God for one's actions: "Why does the wicked man revile God? Why does he say to himself, 'He won't call me to account'?" (Psalm 10:13). The fascinating extra dimension of accountability for faith-based organizations is their duty to answer to God.

Speaking to believers, whose roles may or may not include involvement with churches or other human and social services agencies, the apostle Paul says in Romans 14:12, "So then, each of us will give an account of himself to God." Perfect appraisal can be expected because God sees everything we do. "Nothing in all creation is hidden from God's sight. Everything is uncovered and laid bare before the eyes of him to whom we must give account" (Hebrews 4:13). Although the focus here is on financial accountability and control, human resource management also has its spiritual component: "Obey your leaders and submit to their authority. They keep watch over you as men who must give an account. Obey them so that their work will be a joy, not a burden, for that would be of no advantage to you" (Hebrews 13:17).

Control and Risk Management

Proverbs 22:3 tells us that "a prudent man sees danger and takes refuge, but the simple keep going and suffer for it." Financial controls exist to protect against dangers, attempting to prevent as many as possible. There is an element of rightness perceptible to people as well as God: "For we are taking pains to do what is right, not only in the eyes of the Lord but also in the eyes of men" (II Corinthians 8: 21). In modern organizations, a financial control system protects against risks that threaten the organization's financial well-being. A well-run organization envelops the financial control system in a broader risk management structure. We often think of embezzlement and altered financial records as breakdowns in control, and it seems that at best a control system has only a negative role. However, a control system works positively by providing relevant and accurate information to appropriate parties on a timely basis. For example, a church was fined $100,000 because it was late remitting its federal withholding tax; an adequate control system would prevent such events. The financial control system, as part of the broader risk management structure, is simply the proactive behavior of a prudent manager or board. It improves the organization's survival prospects, enhances its mission achievement opportunities, and builds the organization's reputation.

A Framework for Making Organizations Accountable

An organization may fully agree with being accountable, being a good steward, and managing controls and risks carefully. The issue of implementation may be hindering its ability to put them into action.

Accountability Pyramid

The accountability pyramid shown in Figure 7.1 fits with two public standards for financial accountability and control: the Evangelical Council for Financial Accountability (ECFA) standards and Statement of Auditing Standard (SAS) No. 78, which external auditors apply when evaluating an organization's financial controls and risk management structure. Both standards are sound benchmarks against which to judge any organization's policies.

Level 1: Integrity Level

Integrity is the foundation of any organization's accountability and stewardship. Integrity means: (1) steadfast adherence to a strict moral or ethical code; (2) the state of being unimpaired; soundness; (3) the quality or condition of being whole or undivided, completeness. Donors and other stakeholders hold faith-based organizations to a higher standard because such organizations are inherently values expressive and must practice what they preach. Honesty and trustworthiness are the attributes that must guide all actions and communications. Organizations that possess integrity

Figure 7.1. Accountability Pyramid.

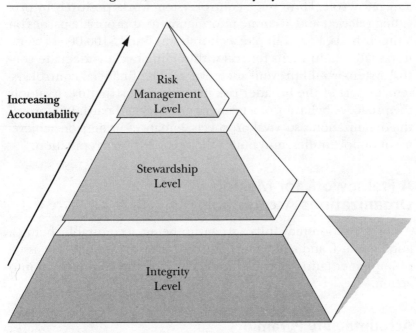

Increasing
Accountability

Risk
Management
Level

Stewardship
Level

Integrity
Level

are managed in a sound manner, including fair and honorable treatment of donors, clients, and employees. Finally, there must be a whole or undivided pursuit of the mission of the organization, with employee self-interest kept secondary. Agency problems, in which employee interests are placed at or above those of clients, are to be guarded against. Basic financial policies fit here.

Level 2: Stewardship Level

Organizations with strong integrity have some elements of stewardship, but more is required to be classified as good stewards. Evidencing efficiency and effectiveness and having working controls and control processes in place are the chief attributes of organizations that reach the stewardship level of the accountability pyramid. Although some accountability mechanisms are part of the integrity level, additional accountability processes and controls are in place for organizations in the second level. More activities and greater attention are paid to accountability, such as internal financial reviews and budget variance reports, outcomes assessment, performance reporting, and board involvement. Cost control, and not spending more than is reasonable for administration or fundraising, demonstrate stewardship. A strong, well-functioning financial management system is at the heart of such organizations. More detailed financial policies, addressing more issues than one would expect for basic integrity, fit here as well.

Level 3: Risk Management Level

The best-in-class organizations operate at an even higher level of accountability. At the risk management level, all potential threats to the organization's financial viability are monitored and managed. Managers who carry out the no margin, no mission directive by actively managing the net surplus—present and future—are at this level. Organizations susceptible to lawsuits, negative publicity, or negative word of mouth from either clients and members or funders reveal that they have not progressed to this level.

Threats to the organization's future cash position come not only from traditional financial risk factors—interest rate risk, foreign exchange rate risk, and commodity price risk—but insurance coverage, personnel decisions, and integrity. So risk management encompasses integrity and stewardship, along with other factors. Very few charities have reached this level in the accountability pyramid. For that matter, few businesses have either. Do not assume that having businesspersons on the board will provide all the necessary impetus and direction for advancing to this level of accountability.

ECFA Standards

All of the ECFA Seven Standards of Responsible Stewardship (see Exhibit 7.1) are in the category of integrity (except standard four, which refers to resource use). Having audited financial statements (and an audit review committee), providing requestors with a copy of current audited financial statements, avoiding conflicts of interests, maintaining the faith moorings of the organization, being governed by a board comprising a majority who are not employed by the organization, and maintaining truthfulness and careful reporting of fundraising activities are all part of basic integrity for the faith-based organization.

Exhibit 7.1. ECFA's Seven Standards
of Responsible Stewardship.

Standard #1—Doctrinal Statement:

Every member organization shall subscribe to a written statement of faith clearly affirming its commitment to the evangelical Christian faith and shall conduct its financial and other operations in a manner which reflects those generally accepted Biblical truths and practices.

Standard #2—Board of Directors and Audit Review Committee:

Every member organization shall be governed by a responsible board of not less than five individuals, a majority of whom shall be other than employees/staff, and/or those related by blood or marriage, which shall meet at least semi-annually to establish policy and review its accomplishments. The board shall appoint a functioning audit review committee, a majority of whom shall be other than employees/staff and/or those related by blood or marriage, for the purpose of reviewing the annual audit and reporting its findings to the board.

Standard #3—Audited Financial Statements:

Every member organization shall obtain an annual audit performed by an independent certified public accounting firm in accordance with generally accepted auditing standards (GAAS) with financial statements prepared in accordance with generally accepted accounting principles (GAAP).

Standard #4—Use of Resources:

Every member organization shall exercise management and financial controls necessary to provide reasonable assurance that all resources are used (nationally and internationally) to accomplish the exempt purposes for which they are intended.

Standard #5—Financial Disclosure:

Every member organization shall provide a copy of its current audited financial statements upon written request.

Standard #6—Conflicts of Interest:

Every member organization shall avoid conflicts of interest. Transactions with related parties may be undertaken only if all of the following are observed: 1) a material transaction is fully disclosed in the audited financial statements of the organization; 2) the related party is excluded from the discussion and approval of such transaction; 3) a competitive bid or comparable valuation exists; and 4) the organization's board has acted upon and demonstrated that the transaction is in the best interest of the member organization.

Standard #7—Fund Raising:

Every member organization shall comply with each of the ECFA Standards for Fund Raising:

7.1 Truthfulness in Communication: All representations of fact, description of financial condition of the organization, or narrative about events must be current, complete and accurate. References to past activities or events must be appropriately dated. There must be no material omissions or exaggerations of fact or use of misleading photographs or any other communication which would tend to create a false impression or misunderstanding.

7.2 Communication and Donor Expectations: Fund raising appeals must not create unrealistic donor expectations of what a donor's gift will actually accomplish within the limits of the organization's ministry.

7.3 Communication and Donor Intent: All statements made by the

Exhibit 7.1. ECFA's Seven Standards of Responsible Stewardship, Cont'd.

organization in its fund raising appeals about the use of the gift must be honored by the organization. The donor's intent is related to both what was communicated in the appeal and to any donor instructions accompanying the gift. The organization should be aware that communications made in fund raising appeals may create a legally binding restriction.

7.4 Projects Unrelated to a Ministry's Primary Purpose: An organization raising or receiving funds for programs that are not part of its present or prospective ministry, but are proper in accordance with its exempt purpose, must either treat them as restricted funds and channel them through an organization that can carry out the donor's intent, or return the funds to the donor.

7.5 Incentives and Premiums: Organizations making fund raising appeals which, in exchange for a contribution, offer premiums or incentives (the value of which is not insubstantial, but which is significant in relation to the amount of the donation) must advise the donor of the fair market value of the premium or incentive and that the value is not deductible for tax purposes.

7.6 Reporting: On request, an organization must provide a report, including financial information, on the project for which it is soliciting gifts.

7.7 Percentage Compensation for Fund Raisers: Compensation of outside fund raising consultants based directly or indirectly on a percentage of what is raised, or on any other contingency agreement, may create potential conflicts and opportunities for abuse. Full disclosure of such arrangements is required, at least annually, in the organization's audited financial statements, in which the disclosure must match income and related expenses. Compensation to the organization's own employees on a percentage basis or contingency basis is not allowed.

7.8 Tax Deductible Gifts for a Named Recipient's Personal Benefit: Tax deductible gifts may not be used to pass money or benefits to any named individual for personal use.

7.9 Conflict of Interest on Royalties: An officer, director, or other principal of the organization must not receive royalties for any product that is used for fund raising or promotional purposes by his/her own organization.

7.10 Acknowledgment of Gifts in Kind: Property or gifts in kind received by an organization should be acknowledged describing the property or gift accurately without a statement of the gift's market value. It is the responsibility of the donor to determine the fair market value of the property for tax purposes. The organization should inform the donor of IRS reporting requirements for all gifts in excess of $5,000.

7.11 Acting in the Interest of the Donor: An organization must make every effort to avoid accepting a gift from or entering into a contract with a prospective donor which would knowingly place a hardship on the donor, or place the donor's future well-being in jeopardy.

7.12 Financial Advice: The representative of the organization, when dealing with persons regarding commitments on major estate assets, must seek to guide and advise donors so they have adequately considered the broad interests of the family and the various ministries they are currently supporting before they make a final decision. Donors should be encouraged to use the services of their attorneys, accountants, or other professional advisors.

Auditing Standards

The internal control standards embodied in today's auditing standards (SAS No. 78) are modeled on the Internal Control—Integrated Framework, published by the Committee of Sponsoring Organizations of the Treadway Commission (COSO or the COSO Report). They have much to offer faith-based organizations, even if an organization chooses not to have its financial reports audited, a rarity if the organization contracts with governmental or grant agencies to provide human or social services. Five components of internal control are incorporated in SAS No. 78:

Control environment

Risk assessment

Control activities

Information and communication

Monitoring

These components map into the accountability framework as follows:

Integrity level: Control environment; information and communication

Stewardship level: Control activities; monitoring

Risk management level: Risk assessment

One thing immediately becomes clear. An external auditor will impose a higher degree of financial accountability and control than that laid out by the ECFA. While this will cost money and time, it should motivate the organization's management and board to progress up the accountability pyramid. Understand that these audit standards are set up only to ensure reasonably that objectives will be achieved in the areas of reliability of financial reporting, efficiency and effectiveness of operations, and compliance with applicable laws and regulations. The organization's leadership is still responsible to see that these three areas are carefully managed and monitored.

Action Steps Toward Financial Accountability and Control

An organization can "abstain from all appearance of evil" (I Thessalonians 5:22) principally by a commitment to integrity, reports and other communications, and a carefully designed and implemented and fully operational internal control structure.

Committing to Integrity

The nonprofit organization initiates its commitment to honesty and trustworthiness by realizing its importance. The biblical basis for this commitment has been examined. Further, managers recognize that charities, churches, and other faith-based organizations are (and should be) held to a higher standard of integrity than most other institutions in society. Third, consider the implicit contract in the donor exchange—one that other parties, particularly state regulators, the Internal Revenue Service, and the general public, expect to be honored. When money or goods are donated, the nonprofit is expected to use the funds in an efficient and effective way, and if they are designated (restricted gifts), then used for the purpose or within the time frame specified.

Once the commitment to integrity is agreed to in principle, it must be subscribed to by top management, the board, and all employees and volunteers. Lip-service assent is insufficient. Actions matter more than words in this arena. After making the organizational committal to integrity, it must be communicated throughout the organization to clarify and reinforce the initial commitment. Annual or more frequent communications are essential, as the temptation for moral lapses is unremitting. Episodes of high-level sacrifices to maintain integrity are especially valuable for inculcating the necessary culture throughout the organization. Including the organization's commitment to integrity in the mission or vision statement should be considered. Finally, membership in an organization such as ECFA or National Religious Broadcasters (NRB) can serve as an impartial, external certification of the commitment to ethics and accountability. (Exhibits 7.2 through 7.4 contain the NRB's code of ethics, standards of conduct, and financial accountability standards, respectively.)

Exhibit 7.2. NRB Code of Ethics.

Recognizing the vital and increasingly important role played by radio and television broadcasting as an agency of mass communication, and the desire of the National Religious Broadcasters to foster and encourage excellence in religious broadcasting by establishing and maintaining high standards with respect to content, method of presentation, speakers qualifications and ethical practices . . . , the Association also recognizes that the general public looks to us to bring conformity to ethical behavior into our broadcasting, programming, business, management, financial, and relational responsibilities. Recognizing the Bible as the standard by which we must evaluate all beliefs, instruction, policies and practice, the Association has adopted and each of its members has subscribed to the following Code of Ethics:

1. I will conduct my personal life and corporate business in a way that will not bring shame or reproach to the name of the Lord. [I Peter 1:14–16]

2. I will speak the truth in love without being unnecessarily offensive. [Proverbs 3:3]

3. I will recognize and respect what the Lord is doing through other individuals and organizations while refraining from unnecessary criticism of them or conformity to them. [I Peter 3:8–9]

4. I will honor my obligations to my vendors, neighbors, community, and government. [Romans 13:7–8].

5. In matters of dispute with other Christians I will attempt to submit my grievances to Christian arbitration rather than to the courts of the land to try and resolve issues. [I Corinthians 6:1–8]

These steps should not be regarded as burdens. After One U.S.-based ministry to the poor in Poland was called into question by a major network investigative report, the NRB conducted an independent audit that exonerated the ministry. These and similar agencies can protect an organization's reputation while providing accountability to donors and the public. Certainly mere membership does not guarantee that an organization is accountable, but it does evidence a striving for accountability.

Exhibit 7.3. NRB Standards of Conduct.

1. Sponsorship—Sponsorship of all programs broadcast by or in the name of the Association or any of its members shall be solely by a nonprofit organization whose aim and purpose is the propagation of the Gospel.

2. Character—The message disseminated in such programs shall be positive, concise and constructive.

3. Production—The content, production, and presentation of such programs, including both music and continuity, shall be consistent with the program standards of the station or network over which they are broadcast and with the legal requirements and of all regulations of the Federal Communications Commission.

4. Cooperation—Persons engaging in the broadcasting of such programs shall cooperate with the station or network management by prompt appearance, courtesy, and scrupulous conformity with the limitations imposed by the physical, technical, and economic characteristics of radio and television.

5. Financial Accountability—Appeals shall be of a bona fide character for legitimate religious purposes and shall be presented in a dignified manner. All donors shall be promptly furnished with receipts and accounting thereof shall be furnished on request to the Board of Directors.

Exhibit 7.4. NRB Financial Accountability Requirements.

- Non-profit members of NRB whose revenue/expenses equals or exceeds $500,000 annually must join and comply with ECFA Standards of Compliance.

- Non-profit members of NRB whose revenue/expenses is less than $500,000 annually will meet NRB's in-house standards established by the NRB's Ethics Committee.

- Denominational and church sponsored broadcasts are exempt from the accountability requirements.

- For-profit members of NRB are exempt but are asked to comply with membership standards as set by the Ethics Committee.

Reports and Other Written Communication

The organization's financial reporting and communications arms—its operating budget, annual report, and other periodic donor mailings and publicity—are necessary not only for organizational survival and prosperity but also to demonstrate accountability.

Having and using a revenue and expense budget should be a basic part of fiscal discipline, yet in my survey of 288 U.S. faith-based organizations, 13 percent did not have a budget. The budget serves a control function by allowing planned allocations to occur. Knowing that an organization has and uses a budget reassures donors and the general public. Further, changes in the budget from one year to the next reveal changed priorities even as they show resources being reallocated. Normally budget specifics are not revealed to individuals beyond the board and officers, but changed priorities are often necessary to maintain mission integrity. On these occasions, shifts in budget funding may need to be communicated to interested publics.

An annual report, which may be mailed to donors, regulatory agencies or offices, the media, members, and select clients and beneficiaries, is another effective accountability tool. In addition to some financial data, it can describe program accomplishments. Demonstrating program outcomes and effects not only verifies that it is accomplishing its mission, but increases donor and grantor support for future funding. The annual report should contain the following information:

- Names of board members and officers, with added information on new board members or officers
- Membership in any certifying organizations
- The results of the strategic planning process, including program redirection or new program initiatives
- Major program accomplishments, including possible testimonials or individual client or beneficiary vignettes
- Major financial statements, including the statement of activities, financial position statement (balance sheet), and statement of cash flows

- Breakdown of revenues by source and expenses by program (pie charts and bar charts are useful here)
- Cost reductions, including information technology investments, or other efficiencies achieved during the past year

This information establishes that the organization is on the stewardship level of the accountability pyramid. It is adhering to its mission and is a good steward of resources entrusted to it. (Organizations that are large or already have compiled the information listed here may decide to go further with the annual report. For helpful information to guide reporting, see Hankin, Seidner, and Zietlow, 1998.)

The public will not assume accountability, so periodic communications with donors, the media, and the general public help provide assurance that the public trust is being safeguarded. Some organizations use a magazine format, although others believe these are not cost-effective—and they may not be if they are looking only at fundraising effects and overlooking the accountability value.

Direct mail letters can be very effective. The key seems to be send information sometimes rather than only asking for donations. Each letter should attempt to meet a spiritual need of readers. A localized service provider, such as a soup kitchen or homeless shelter, probably has a localized donor base. In these instances, newspaper and radio publicity are invaluable. General interest articles in newspapers around the holidays and public service announcements sprinkled throughout the year by local radio stations can tell the organization's story and keep it accountable to the public.

Internal Control Structure

The third major way to demonstrate integrity is through a carefully designed, well-implemented, and fully operational internal control structure. No matter how small an organization, six areas must be covered (PricewaterhouseCoopers, 1982):

Cash receipts. Make sure that cash inflows are received, promptly deposited, properly recorded, reconciled, and adequately secured.

Cash disbursements. Make sure payments made are disbursed only after management authorizes them, are for valid purposes, and are properly recorded.

Petty cash. Safeguard, properly record, and make sure disbursements from petty cash are for approved purposes.

Payroll. Ensure the validity of disbursements (authorized, correct amounts, to actual employees) and proper recording and that withholding taxes are properly remitted on a timely basis to the government.

Grants, gifts, and bequests. Make sure they are received, reported, and managed according to any related restrictions.

Fixed assets. Ensure proper authorization for acquisition and disposal and that they are safeguarded and recorded correctly.

The common elements in this list—authorization, recording, and safeguarding—serve to make and keep the organization accountable. As policies and procedures are set up and established, continuing oversight must provide reasonable assurance of these three elements.

There are five main elements of an effective financial control structure:

- Key policies and procedures manuals
- Segregation of duties
- Record-keeping and information systems
- Financial reporting system
- Budgets

We will look at the key element of that structure—segregation of duties—and then go into detail on the specifics of cash disbursement, probably the area where the organization is most vulnerable to insider or external party fraud.

Segregation of Duties

Ideally all organizations should have a built-in system of checks and balances on financial dealings. Although that is sometimes difficult to accomplish in smaller organizations, the primary tool is to have different people handling related transactions (for example, requiring two signatures on every check). Exhibit 7.5 is a checklist for determining how the organization is doing in this area. An answer of no to any of these questions signals the need to evaluate a potential weakness. There may exist other considerations that mitigate these weaknesses, but it is better to err on the side of caution. You would be surprised how often a trusted veteran employee "who would never do anything like that" did.

Cash Disbursement

Financial fraud, especially check fraud, is reaching epidemic proportions in the United States. Organizations are at risk from both outside parties, such as fictitious vendors, and inside parties, such as the payables clerk, payroll manager, and controller or treasurer.

Exhibit 7.5. Segregating Financial Duties Checklist.

Function	Diagnostic Question
Receipt of cash	Are the cash receiving, processing, recording, and bank reconciliation functions clearly segregated?
Cash disbursement	Are the authorization, processing, check signing, recording, and bank reconciliation functions clearly segregated?
Payroll	Are the personnel authorization, payroll preparation and approval, payroll check distribution, recordkeeping, and bank reconciliation functions clearly segregated?
Billing and receivables	Are the credit authorization, billing, recordkeeping, collection, and cash processing functions clearly segregated?
Accounts payable	Are the authorization, processing, recording, and payment functions clearly segregated?
Inventory	Are the purchasing, custodial (responsibility and safeguarding), processing, and recordkeeping functions clearly segregated?
Fixed assets	Are the authorization, purchasing, custody, and recordkeeping functions clearly segregated?

It is very difficult to prevent all occurrences of fraud, but certain safeguards can go far toward providing reasonable assurances of prevention.

There should be no unauthorized, invalid, unrecorded, or improperly recorded disbursements, and as many of the related functions as possible should be in separate hands. Smaller organizations, with small staffs and some financial work done by volunteers, face difficulty in putting this framework in place. This added risk is partly offset by the fact that the executive director and the financial manager usually have personal knowledge of most major transactions and vendor relationships. Inappropriate transactions are normally prevented or caught quickly because of this familiarity.

In addition to segregation of duties, there are other important cash disbursement controls: authorization and processing, check signing, cash recording, and bank reconciliation.

Authorization and Processing

- Clearly identify who is authorized to disburse funds, and ensure that all disbursements are in fact approved in advance by one of these authorities.
- Ensure that vendor invoices are approved based on verified receipt of goods or services.
- Ensure that expense reimbursements are based on appropriate receipts.
- Communicate policies to all appropriate parties, including volunteers.
- Make disbursements by prenumbered checks, keep a record of cash disbursements (check stubs, check copies, cash disbursements record), and include a listing of disbursement amounts with the checks when given to authorized signatories.
- Investigate a "positive pay" service with the disbursement bank. A checks-issued file is transmitted to the bank when checks are cut, and the bank refuses to honor any checks in which the check number, amount, or signer deviates from the file or preexisting instructions—unless specifically authorized by bank-to-organization communication.

Check Signing

- Place authority at high levels of the organization, with larger checks requiring a higher level of authority.
- Require two signatures on checks, and mail signed checks promptly and directly from the check signer's control.
- Have the check signer review and initial the supporting documentation for checks to ensure completeness and appropriate approval and selectively compare check amounts to the disbursements listing accompanying the checks.

Cash Recording

- Ensure that the person posting disbursements to the cash disbursement journal does not handle check processing, check signing, or check authorization.
- Prior to posting checks, compare the listing of disbursements (initialed by the check signer) to the check processing function's disbursement summary.

Bank Reconciliation

- Ensure that canceled checks and bank statements are received directly and reconciled with disbursement records by someone who does not handle cash authorization, check processing, or check signing.

Demonstrating Stewardship

Stewardship includes everything addressed in the previous sections on demonstrating accountability. Along with those elements, internal financial reviews and budget variance reports, outcome assessments, performance reporting, and board involvement are means of demonstrating stewardship. A strong, well-functioning financial management system is at the heart of such organizations.

Internal Financial Reviews
The following key internal financial reviews are ongoing review needs:

- Reviewing the accountability structure to ensure its adequacy for existing and anticipated programs and operations
- Determination of how well the organization is doing in meeting its primary financial objective
- Progress in meeting budget
- Adequacy of financing for the next three or five years
- The overall financial condition of the organization

Reviews of programs to see if they remain necessary, continue to fit the organizational mission, or are adequately funded also can be undertaken. Determining the need for an external audit or, if audits already are done, their adequacy as well as any additional advisory needs the audit firm can provide, are also important considerations. Everyone in the organization, not just the treasurer or chief financial officer, should have appropriate management qualifications, the time to do their jobs properly, and adequate training.

Budget Variance Reports
Budgets are plans but also control devices that can be used to answer the following questions:

- If spending exceeds budgeted amounts, was the overage due to controllable or uncontrollable causes? If controllable, how can the spending be brought into line with the budget, or what other items can be pared to bring the overall budget into balance? If uncontrollable, what changes should be made now so that the budget serves as an adequate standard for the remainder of the fiscal year?
- What mistakes were made in establishing this year's budget that can be avoided in developing next year's budget?
- What budget ploys were successfully used by program directors (foot in the door, reverence for the past, "make a study," we are the experts) that resulted in unanticipated or undesirable allocations or expenditures?

The fact that such reports are developed and used establishes good stewardship. About the only time there is publicity regarding budget progress is in an end-of-year fundraising letter.

Outcomes Assessment

Some data will be collected on efficiency here, but the main emphasis should be on effectiveness: how many lives were changed, people fed, people sheltered, people taught to read, and so forth. The difficulty is establishing the appropriate outcomes to monitor for an educational or personal development organization. The intangible nature of the service thwarts attempts to develop valuable gauges of accomplishment, but the organization's leaders must do their best to develop outcome measures and explain their relative usefulness to interested publics. One study that supports the strong social service programs of congregations in Greensboro, North Carolina, also found that they evaluated efforts infrequently. One result was an unwitting duplication of services (Wineburg, 1990–1991).

Evaluations usually report good news. The existing data, although not yet conclusive, suggest that charitable services are quite cost-effective. The Alexis de Tocqueville Institution found that the Washington nonprofit homeless shelter CCNV spent only $260 per person (in 1992), while the municipal government spent $11,579 per person to house homeless in government-run shelters. A Progress and Freedom Foundation study determined that government-run drug rehabilitation programs cost $35,000 per addict treated, while two volunteer rehabilitation clinics studied spent 33 cents per addict. (The counselors were reformed addicts who received food for compensation and the volunteer clinics rented their buildings.) This program, Victory Fellowship (San Antonio), run by Reverend Freddie Garcia, has cured 13,000 people of drug and alcohol addiction during the past twenty-five years in its homeless drug abuse and alcohol treatment center (*Investors Business Daily*, 1995).

Performance Reporting

Performance indicators are variables that have a significant effect on the ability of the organization to meet its primary financial objective—for example, the number of clients served or the quality of services provided. These may be process indicators as well as outcomes, and qualitative as well as quantitative ones. Today there is a move toward performance reporting even in financial reports.

Information on outcomes, services rendered, and other results of service provision is vital. This information not only fills out the financial reports to show the programs that gave rise to those financial results, but gives readers an idea of the trends that will affect future financial results.

Board Involvement

Boards interested in and actively involved with financial decisions are a tremendous asset to charities and religious organizations. Strong boards develop as a result of carefully implemented recruitment strategies. Board members should not only have a strong interest in the organization's mission, but be willing to commit to continuous attendance and long-term involvement. (Chapter Four is particularly strong on helping board members to understand their responsibilities to and for the organization.) Although legal requirements vary from state to state (the state's attorney general's office can provide the information), a selected list for a social or human service provider in Minnesota provides a useful illustration:

- Active participation, "including attending meetings, evaluating reports, reading minutes, reviewing the performance of the Executive Director and so on. Persons who do not have the time to participate as required should not agree to be on the board."
- Books and records, including "general knowledge of the books and records of the organization as well as its general operation. Accounting records . . . must be made available to members and directors who wish to inspect them for a proper purpose."
- Accurate record keeping, including the stipulation that the director be familiar with the books and records and ensure that the organization's records and accounts are accurate. This may mean that the director must take steps to require regular audits by an independent certified public accountant. "At the very least, the director should be aware of what the financial records disclose and take appropriate action to make sure there are proper internal controls."
- Trust property, in which the duty is to "protect, preserve, invest and manage the corporation's property and to do so con-

sistent with donor restrictions and legal requirements. Instituting proper internal controls will aid in the protection of assets."

- Investigations, where the duty is to "investigate warnings or reports of officer or employee theft or mismanagement. In some situations a director may have to report misconduct to the appropriate authorities, such as the police or the Attorney General. Where appropriate, a director should consult an attorney or other professional for assistance."

Demonstrating Risk Management and Control

Here all potential threats to the organization's financial viability are monitored and managed. Managers who carefully monitor the organization's financial position and take steps to ensure that it meets its primary financial objective are at this level. Organizations susceptible to high employee turnover, lawsuits, negative publicity, or negative word of mouth from either clients and members or funders often reveal that they have not yet progressed to this level. Threats to the organization's cash position come not only from traditional financial risk factors—interest rate risk, foreign exchange rate risk, and commodity price risk—but insurance coverage, personnel hiring and firing policies and actions, and a possible lack of integrity (especially in fundraising).

There are four keys to risk management. First, brainstorm with the board, employees, and volunteers (and network with officers at similar organizations) to determine the factors that could adversely affect the service provision, cash flows, and overall financial position within the next ten years. For example, if the organization provides a homeless shelter, high interest rates may make housing less affordable and increase the number of homeless. This would create additional demand for the homeless shelter, which probably will not receive additional donations immediately to meet the additional demand.

Second, determine what controllables would help the organization cope with those factors. For example, the organization might become a conduit for housing in the community.

Third, for the factors that are truly uncontrollable, what offsetting measures could the organization engage in? Partnering with a governmental or private employment agency may help otherwise indigent individuals find reasonable employment, thereby enabling them to qualify for some kind of housing. Doing additional fund-raising in anticipation of swelling demand also makes sense.

Fourth, study the joint influence of each force working in the environment. Higher interest rates are a problem here, but what if rising unemployment and a recession compound the problem? These facts increase risk because demand may rise at the same time a weakening economy shrinks donations. The key point is to plan for contingencies, anticipating risk factors and applying faith and wisdom in crafting responses.

The following should be reviewed for this area:

- Hiring, performance review, training, promotion, and termination policies, including due process
- Policies on volunteer entry, safety, involvement, responsibility, and other areas
- Mechanisms for retaining key employees
- Pension plan development or enhancement
- Regulatory compliance, including access for disabled persons
- Withholding tax remittance and electronic submission requirements (this may change as the organization becomes larger)
- Level of involvement by directors and officers
- Insurance coverage, including property and casualty insurance, liability insurance, and directors' and officers' insurance
- Employee benefits, including health insurance
- Retention of qualified legal counsel
- Review of activities to ensure compliance with limitations on political lobbying
- Retention of an auditing firm with nonprofit expertise
- Retention of an outside investment adviser (if there are significant investable amounts)
- Effect of economic changes, including inflation, changing interest rates, and variations in employment
- Cash management study, including rebid of banking services and possible new services
- Working capital management study
- Effect of the business cycle on cash flow

- Establishment of an endowment fund
- Revision of the organization's liquidity position
- Development of an improved cash budget
- Development of a long-range financial plan encompassing the next three or five years
- Development of improved relations with the local media
- Development or improvement of a planned giving program

Steps to Improving Accountability

There are several paths any organization can take to improve accountability. Here are three guiding principles:

1. Achieve level one (integrity) before perfecting levels two and three. Basic integrity in financial dealings and fundraising is the foundation.
2. Make one improvement at a time. Publicize the success of that improvement to employees, volunteers, and board as leverage to move to other steps.
3. Get outside help if necessary.

For the means of developing accountability, the underlying premise is that this should be an ongoing process. An organization never finishes becoming accountable, because the truly accountable organization constantly demonstrates accountability. Three techniques can aid in this process:

- Retreats and workshops, often using an outside facilitator—much like the board development and strategic planning workshops
- Peer networking or learning from a trade association (faith-based homeless shelters are doing this through the International Union of Gospel Missions, headquartered in Kansas City, Missouri) or umbrella organization such as the ECFA or NRB
- Use of an outside consultant

Each technique works to gain buy-in by the officers, other employees, board members, and possibly some key volunteers. There must be an explanation of the what and how of accountability, not just the why. Meetings are important, and not just at the inception of the accountability-building process. Ask employees what they heard after presenting material. Publish an accountability charter, possibly with a listing of frequently asked questions from prior meetings, along with responses. Include an executive summary of the organization's new initiatives. Revisit the document and the entire accountability structure and discuss it annually at a predesignated board meeting, with key employees in attendance for that part of the meeting. If the board is geographically dispersed, invite the chairperson, the finance committee chairperson, and the audit committee or subcommittee chairperson, along with the board treasurer if she or he is not also discharging one of these other responsibilities.

Working with Governments and Foundations

Although financial accountability and control mechanisms would seem to be standard in nonprofit organizations contracting with governmental agencies, such is not the case according to a major study conducted in the mid-1980s (Paige, 1985). It is accurate to say that most of the accountability mechanisms presented in this chapter are appropriate for organizations contracting with governments or foundations and that they will push any organization toward greater accountability.

Financial administration of grants and contracts is the same, except for the fact that contracts call for a product that must be delivered within certain terms and conditions defined in those contracts (Hankin, Seidner, and Zietlow, 1998). Grants are usually given for a specific project or individual's efforts, such as a research grant, but do not require that the grantor receive anything in return for awarding the grant.

The request for proposal (RFP) that announces the availability of funding usually contains the agency or foundation's accountability and reporting requirements. They may require a nonprofit organization to supply a set of its financial policies. The contract or grant award typically spells out policy requirements and exceptions (or additional requirements) that go beyond the standard policies of the grantor or recipient, including matching grants or challenge grants. For example, in 1998, the Shady Grove Missionary Baptist Church of Greenville, Mississippi, received $100,000 from the federal government to run a substance abuse program and was required to match the grant with nonfederal funding and to develop a five-year plan. The recipient organization is responsible for carefully managing and monitoring the funds. The organization commonly places that burden on the chief financial officer or fund manager, who must ensure that all expenditures made based on a contract or grant are appropriate, directly linked to the given project or funding purpose, and reasonable and customary.

Organizations that receive federal funds must meet the minimum policy requirements spelled out by Office of Management and Budget (OMB) Circular A21 and Circular A110. Some federal health and human service awards have additional requirements; publications available from the U.S. Department of Health and Human Services (HHS) detail those requirements. The *Catalog of Federal Domestic Assistance* (CFDA) provides information on all federal grant programs, including HHS programs. This is available online from the GrantsNet information service (http://www.os.dhhs. gov/progorg/grantsnet/index.html).

Government agencies and foundations normally require regular financial reports. These vary by type and frequency, with monthly, quarterly, or annual reports providing a summary of expenditures by budgetary or cost category. Some detailed transaction information may be required as part of these reports or as a separate submission. Often the funder reserves the right to audit financial records pertaining to the grant or contract in order to determine if spending is reasonable and customary. The organization may have to reimburse the funder for spending that eventually is determined to be excessive in the funder's view.

Finally, the same sort of safeguards for cash receipts and disbursements should be applied to grant monies. For example, someone other than the person who oversees cash receipts should record the amount received. Also, grant programs can be monitored by comparing award receipts to award estimates in the operating budget, maintaining separate accounts and avoiding commingling funds, having nonaccounting personnel approve award recipient funds disbursement, documenting and verifying compliance with any award restrictions, and monitoring accounts for nonexpended funds and returning them promptly to the funder if necessary.

Conclusion

Working with governments and foundations pushes organizations to be more accountable. This starts with basic integrity, progresses through more advanced stewardship, and culminates in sophisticated risk management. Although smaller organizations may not be able to pursue all of the steps laid out here, all organizations ought to realize the first level. Religious organizations have a special heritage of accountability and integrity that suits them well in this area. Conscious adoption of a steward mind-set is invaluable. As a closing charge, take John Wesley's words to heart: "When the Possessor of heaven and earth brought you into being and placed you into this world, He placed you here not as an owner but a steward. As such He entrusted you for a season with goods of various kinds—but the sole property of these still rests in Him, nor can ever be alienated from Him. As you yourself are not your own but His, such is likewise all you enjoy."

References
Hankin, Jo Ann, Seidner, Alan, and Zietlow, John. (1998). *Financial Management for Nonprofit Organizations.* New York: Wiley.
Investors Business Daily. (1995). "Micro Charity." May 8.
Paige, Kenneth Lee. (1985). "The Use of Management Accounting Practices by Nonprofit Organizations: An Exploratory Study." Unpublished doctoral dissertation, University of Pittsburgh.
PricewaterhouseCoopers LLP. (1982). *Effective Internal Accounting Control for Nonprofit Organizations: A Guide for Directors and Management.* New York: PricewaterhouseCoopers LLP.
Wineburg, R. J. (1990–1991). "A Community Study on the Ways Religious Congregations Support Individuals and the Human Service Networks." *Journal of Applied Social Sciences, 15,* 51–74.

Additional Readings
Axelrod, Nancy R. (1977). "The Growing Stakes for Good Governance: In the Age of Accountability, How Engaged Is Your Board in Creating an Accountable Association?" *Association Management, 49,* 38–42, 126.

Balda, Janis Bragan. (1994). "The Liability of Nonprofits to Donors." *Nonprofit Management and Leadership, 5,* 67–83.

Bell, Peter D. (1993). *Fulfilling the Public Trust: Ten Ways to Help Nonprofit Boards Maintain Accountability.* Washington, D.C.: National Center for Nonprofit Boards.

Blum, Debra E. (1999). "Leaders of Black Church Call for Increased Accountability in Wake of Scandal." *Chronicle of Philanthropy, 11,* 31.

Bremser, Wayne G. (1994). *Making Public Disclosures.* Washington, D.C.: Accountants for the Public Interest.

Campbell, Bruce. (1998). "Donors Want to Know Where the $$ Goes!" *Fund Raising Management, 29,* 40–42.

Chao, Elaine. (1994). "Accountability That Counts." *Independent Voices,* Spring, pp. 33–34.

Chisolm, Laura B. (1995). "Accountability of Nonprofit Organizations and Those Who Control Them: The Legal Framework." *Nonprofit Management and Leadership, 6,* 141–156.

Clolery, Paul. (1995). "Nonprofits May Be Forced to Return New Era Grants: Bankruptcy Trustee, Judge Will Make the Final Call." *NonProfit Times, 9,* 1, 27.

Glaser, John S. (1994). *The United Way Scandal: An Insider's Account of What Went Wrong and Why.* New York: Wiley.

Greene, Elizabeth, and Williams, Grant. (1995). "Asleep on the Watch?: A Spate of Charity Scandals Raises Questions About the Effectiveness of Government Watchdog Agencies." *Chronicle of Philanthropy,* July 27, pp. 1, 34–36.

Greene, Stephen G. (1995). "Resentment over Board Decisions Started Charity Chief on Decade of Embezzlement." *Chronicle of Philanthropy,* Nov. 16, p. 35.

Gross, Malcom, Larkin, Richard, Bruttomesso, Roger, and McNally, Roger. (1995). *Financial and Accounting Guide for Not-for-Profit Organizations.* New York: Wiley.

Gruber, David A. (1999). "Financial Reporting: Vital Tools for Board Members." *NonProfit Times, 13,* 37, 58.

Hall, Holly, and Williams, Grant. (1997). "Mastermind of New Era Charity Fraud Is Sent to Prison for Twelve Years." *Chronicle of Philanthropy,* Oct. 2, p. 39.

Herman, Melanie L., and White, Leslie T. (1998). *Leaving Nothing to Chance: Achieving Board Accountability Through Risk Management.* Washington, D.C.: National Center for Nonprofit Boards.

"Integrity." (1983). *Christian Leadership Letter.* Monrovia, Calif.: World Vision.

Jeavons, Thomas H. (1994a). "Stewardship Revisited: Secular and Sacred

Views of Governance and Management." *Nonprofit and Voluntary Sector Quarterly, 23,* 107–122.

Jeavons, Thomas H. (1994b). *When the Bottom Line Is Faithfulness: Management of Christian Service Organizations.* Bloomington: Indiana University Press.

Johnson, Sandra L. (1993). *The Audit Committee: A Key to Financial Accountability in Nonprofit Organizations.* Washington, D.C.: National Center for Nonprofit Boards.

Kearns, Kevin P. (1996). *Managing for Accountability: Preserving the Public Trust in Public and Nonprofit Organizations.* San Francisco: Jossey-Bass.

Lilly Endowment Study. (1994). "Organizational Goals and Financial Management in Donative Organizations." Unpublished.

Maryland Association of Nonprofit Organizations. (1998). *Standards for Excellence: An Ethics and Accountability Code for the Nonprofit Sector.* Baltimore: Maryland Association of Nonprofit Organizations.

McIlnay, Dennis P. (1994). *The Privilege of Privacy: A Study of the Public Accountability of Foundations.* Loretto, Penn.: St. Francis College.

Nonprofit Genie. Available at: http://www.supportcenter.org/sf/fmfaq24.html.

Office of Minnesota Attorney General Hubert H. Humphrey III. "Fiduciary Duties of Directors of Charitable Organizations: A Guide for Board Members." Available at: http://www.ag.state.mn.us/consumer/charities/fiduciaryduties.html.

Olson, Layton E. (1996). "Public Disclosure." *Grantsmanship Center Magazine, 30,* 23–24.

Pound, Edward T., Cohen, Gary, and Loeb, Penny. (1995). "Tax Exempt: Many Nonprofits Look and Act Like Normal Companies—Running Businesses, Making Money. So Why Aren't They Paying Uncle Sam?" *U.S. News and World Report,* Oct. 2, pp. 36–51.

Robinson, Maureen K. (1998). *The Chief Executive's Role in Developing the Nonprofit Board.* Washington, D.C.: National Center for Nonprofit Boards.

"What Is an Internal Accounting Control System and How Can We Make Ours Effective?" Financial Management FAQ 24 found at http://www.igc.apc.org/sf/fmfaq24.html. Support Center, San Francisco.

Williams, Kenneth D. (1996). "Financial Statements Prove Accountability." *New Directions for Philanthropic Fundraising, 13,* 99–118.

Young, Dennis R., Bania, Neil, and Bailey, Darlyne. (1996). "Structure and Accountability: A Study of National Nonprofit Associations." *Nonprofit Management and Leadership, 6,* 347–365.

CHAPTER 8

Finding Help and Advice at the School Next Door
Working with Academic Institutions

Arthur Emery Farnsley III

The best way to work with academic institutions is, not surprisingly, the best way to work with any other institution: establish a partnership. Partnerships can produce synergy and economies of scale, but in any relationship both organizations must give up something in the hopes of gaining even more.

Nonacademic organizations generally make two mistakes when they approach universities or colleges for assistance. First, they assume that they are asking for a favor. That is, they are asking to be given something with nothing expected in return. This attitude leads to the second mistake: letting the terms of the arrangement be dictated by the academics. In fact, a successful partnership starts with the assumption that both sides have something to gain and that both sides can negotiate the contours of the relationship.

Why Would They Help Us?

Colleges and universities, especially public universities, are eager to serve their communities. Most stress this service as part of their mission, and they are equally eager to build stronger town-gown relationships.

When universities depend on tax revenues to subsidize their efforts, they are eager to point out the public benefits they provide in return. Historically they have stressed the value of the doctors and lawyers they train or the more general benefit of having a skilled labor force. New factories and new jobs come to places with well-educated workers, after all. Occasionally universities point out that they are themselves major employers. Less often they talk about the cultural and artistic benefits they provide. Increasingly, however, schools have placed greater emphasis on their desire to build partnerships with other local organizations. They want to be seen as active participants in the lives of their communities, not merely training grounds for the individuals who live in them.

This shift in priorities can be traced to at least two sources. One is that the move toward greater privatization of public services (and education is one) has put greater pressure on public universities. Taxpayers see tuition increase annually and hear stories about full professors who are paid six-figure salaries but teach only one or two courses per year. Few taxpayers dispute that having an educated populace is a social good, but many would like to know if that education needs to cost as much as it does. Universities recognize that it is in their interest to show that they provide social benefits that go far beyond the specific training provided to students in nursing, medicine, law, or business.

The other source of the shift in priorities is closely related. The movement toward the privatization and localization of government services—social welfare services are the most obvious example—has prompted funders of all kinds to search for more creative organizational partnerships and alliances. Put most simply, funders do not want to waste their money supporting service organizations that cannot exploit the best available research on practices. Simultaneously, they do not want to support research unlikely to have practical consequences. Both public funds, like community development block grants, and private funds, like those from foundations, increasingly flow toward organizations that form creative partnerships and show the ability to draw on the organizational strengths in their universe. Not surprisingly, colleges and universities want to be involved in those partnerships.

Although colleges and private universities have somewhat different priorities than public universities do, the fact that they do not depend on direct government subsidy does not mean that they are ambivalent about public goodwill. Without access to public monies to offset expenses, private colleges and universities are more dependent on the support of local business and philanthropy. They too have good reasons to build strong community partnerships.

Is Religious Affiliation a Problem?

For a variety of reasons, we are all conditioned to ask this question early and often. Everyone wants to know whether public universities can or will work with congregations or faith-based nonprofit organizations. As with anything else, the answer to the question varies by context. Public universities certainly cannot help with evangelization, and most private universities or colleges would not want to, but that is probably not the help a service organization needs anyway.

Both public and private schools want to be involved in partnerships that lead to community advancement. Both are committed to the well-being of the community, and both could use the potential funding. Public universities have added incentives because they constantly need to convince the broader public of their utility.

Public universities are more constrained because they cannot conduct research for the purpose of advancing religion. Occasionally administrators see these constraints as greater than they are. I know of a university that was told that it should not involve itself in social work practices, or legal issues, or database management because the providers or the recipients of some valuable community service had religious affiliation. Such an extreme position is rare, however, and completely unnecessary, as Chapter Nine explains.

Most public universities want to be involved in advancing the interests of the community. It is their mission. Although public universities cannot always tell religious organizations what, they can tell them how.

Rather than letting the church-state question become a roadblock, the focus instead should be on the more important questions:

- Who in the college or university would be willing to help?
- What kind of help do you need, and what do they offer?
- What is in it for them?

If these questions can be answered effectively, the question of religious involvement generally will take care of itself. There are limits, of course, but not ones that apply to programs simply because they have a religious affiliation.

Who Can Help? Who Wants To?

The fact that colleges and universities would like to be involved does not mean that they always know how. Faith-based nonprofits interested in drawing on the resources available at local schools must recognize that they share responsibility for defining the structure of the relationship.

Some places in the university seem like obvious choices. Urban universities often have schools in applied fields related to social service: social work, public health, public affairs, environmental affairs, law, and so on. These schools have three built-in interests in what the nonprofit organization does. First, a partnership can be a source of funding for them. Whether your organization has a lot of money to pay them or not, grants and contracts can provide support for their activities as they work with you. Second, these schools will be placing their graduates in your field, maybe even in your organization. There will be students and faculty in both interested in your type of organization and its work. The relationship of social work schools to social service may be less lucrative, but the public service schools have an intrinsic interest in your activities. Third, you and your work are potential research subjects. Everything you do could be data—the stuff of observation, analysis, and reports. Never forget that you bring your ideas, your experiences, and the whole of your organization to the table when you enter into an academic-practitioner partnership.

Where to Start?

One of the biggest obstacles to creating a useful partnership with universities is finding the right place and way to enter.

University and college administrators know that public partnerships are important. They recognize the potential for increasing grant funds and highlighting their utility to the larger public. But those administrators are not usually the people with the expertise or programs you need to tap. The people you need are faculty members—the teachers and researchers who make up the disciplinary departments. Unfortunately, their career prospects do not depend on their ability to help you. They are judged and rewarded by their peers on their ability to conduct research and, usually to a lesser degree, to teach. Although many universities increasingly emphasize service as a criterion for promotion and tenure, overall it remains the least important criterion.

It is at least partially for this reason that universities have developed centers and institutes with specific disciplinary or issue-oriented focuses and are designed to bring together related expertise from throughout the university. Where the sociology department may have one faculty member interested in child welfare, the psychology department one such faculty member, and the social work school another, all of whom are working in isolation, an institute dedicated to child welfare provides a place for these people to pursue their work together. Centers and institutes also attract funding that allows them to hire program staff, whose jobs depend primarily on their contribution to practical applications in a particular field. Centers and institutes are often where faculty research links up to resources you can tap more directly.

Some centers specifically exist as conduits between the university and the public. Some exist to analyze and consult. They are interested in intellectual and academic questions, to be sure, but their interest stems directly from the sort of applied questions asked by people who require expert assistance. Like medical schools, centers and institutes link the interests of a public need (say, cancer patients) with scholars doing basic research (say, conducting radiation treatments on mice or creating DNA). Although it is easy, even within the university, to lose sight of the connection between basic research and practical application (everyone has heard stories of pork-barrel research on the sweat glands of arctic wolverines), basic research is the stuff of new knowledge.

Basic research is as central to your field as to any other, but it is not the specific information you need to advance your practices. To get immediately practical information, look for the places that deal in applied research. Geneticists improve our knowledge of birth defects, but you would not go first to the genetics lab with a question about prenatal care. The same is true for social research.

I am familiar with the applied nature of these centers because I work for one. Even if the center you contact does not have exactly what you are seeking, someone there may be able to point you toward the people who do. An employee of a center or institute is likely to be accommodating because he or she knows better than any other arm of the university just how much the center's continued success (read: funding) depends on its relationship to organizations outside the university. Such centers, if they exist in your area and have interests that coincide with your needs, are the best place to locate the kind of help you need.

If you cannot identify such a center or campus office, it is possible to go directly to a department. But be forewarned that receptionists and secretaries often are trained, often unconsciously, to shield faculty members from external distraction. If you call or write to say, "I need some help," do not be surprised when no one comes running. However, if you call to discuss an opportunity that is mutually beneficial—potential opportunities for interns, joint funding ventures, or a proposed data collection effort—then the likelihood of response is higher. The goal is to find the center, office, department, or individual professor who stands to gain the most from a relationship with your organization (gains in visibility and credibility are important too). Once you make the right contact, your chances of tapping into other university expertise increase considerably.

This last piece of advice applies even more strongly to smaller colleges, which are likely to have few, if any, specialized centers, so chances are good that you will need to find exactly the right faculty member. Small colleges often do not have the breadth of faculty necessary to cover every possible area of expertise. Nevertheless, finding whether such a person exists, and then locating that person, is much easier at a smaller college. If a faculty member has an interest in your field, virtually everyone will know.

What Do You Need?

In searching out a partnership with a local college or university it is important to know what it can give. As a rule your local school can provide two major services. They can provide detailed information about your community (contextual information) and knowledge about how to do things (technical expertise).

Contextual Information

Before approaching a school, your organization should be clear on what it thinks it needs from the relationship. If the need is primarily financial, you are going to the wrong place. Schools rarely have the funds to make grants to faith-based, nonprofit services.

There are other important sorts of support that schools offer freely, or at least at prices well below what you would pay for a consultant or even to do the work in-house. Nonprofit organizations—whether social service providers, fraternal groups, or congregations—often have inadequate information about the environment in which they operate. Unless they have a focus on a specific neighborhood or catchment area, they frequently know little about the ages, incomes, races, housing types, or anything else about the people in the community around them. Sometimes they lack this information even when they do serve a specific area. Not every group has to consider market demographics and target audiences in great detail, but familiarity with your surroundings, other programs like yours, and related organizations and interests within your environment undoubtedly will improve your ability to serve.

Schools frequently have U.S. Census or other statistical information about your service area already packaged in some form, and often they have much more. The center I work for collects all kinds of information related to housing, health, human services, education, and many other fields. All of that information can be compared and related to the basic U.S. census information. Since all the information is tied to a geographic information system, it can be displayed visually on maps of the local area. Therefore, we can provide service organizations with a city map that shows, for instance, the census tracts in which births to teenagers are most common. That same map could also show the United Way or religious organizations that offer services to teen parents. It could be overlaid on a map showing levels of poverty or education, or the racial makeup, or whatever other variable is deemed important.

That information is invaluable to an organization that is planning to offer services or thinking about its catchment area. It provides the ability to see a specific vulnerability, the social conditions related to it, and the assets available to address it.

We can also show, as we have done for organizations such as the local libraries, where clients or patrons live. Providers can see their service areas and their client base in relation to the other variables (for example, crime, teen pregnancy, or poverty) that matter to them.

Not every university has such a system, although we are not the only one. The Southern California Studies Center, for example, creates an annual "state of the region" report that covers many topics of regional interest. But even if a local university does not have an integrated database and mapping system, it has access to databases and computer technology that can be provided at low cost. Moreover, universities are full of people who are interpreting and analyzing the information being collected. The presence of someone who can explain the meaning of these data is much less daunting and time-consuming than the prospect of having someone in your organization trying to interpret census data displayed in endless grids.

This sort of technical expertise is by no means the only information that schools have to offer. Universities and colleges are often clearinghouses for information related to a specific field. Sometimes researchers have collected and considered model programs or best practices. Reports on that information, or even informal advice, are often free for a telephone call.

The value of best-practice models should not be overlooked. There are always books and articles that offer insight into what others have done, but frequently the models displayed in those pieces involve organizations and situations that may be unlike yours. If a local university has developed ideas about model programs and practices, they may be more directly linked to local circumstances. There is no guarantee that this will be the case, but the odds are better.

Models provided by case studies of other programs are not the most significant resource universities can offer. What they are more likely to have is access to information about other local groups, coalitions, and partnerships. The question for your organization is never only how you, as a solitary group, can provide services better. The question should always consider the kinds of productive partnerships that can be developed among community organizations, governments, foundations and charities, secular providers, and other religious providers. You may not be in the position to know about all of the possibilities and current practices in detail, but an expert who researches the subject might know exactly that.

Busy service providers often do not know much about other programs in their area. When we conducted a survey of faith-based organizations that offered youth services, we learned that most of these programs think what they are doing is unique, although there were dozens of other programs of a similar nature. Moreover, fewer than 10 percent of respondents could name one other program like their own or provide significant details about it. There often are people at universities whose job is to provide this broader perspective.

Perspective may in fact be the most important thing a university has to offer. People working in a field are often so caught up in the specific needs of their clients or in the dictates of their particular bureaucracies that they have difficulty stepping back to view the big picture. Researchers looking at situations more dispassionately are much more likely to take a broader view.

Perspective is, of course, both a blessing and a curse. On the one hand, no researcher can ever know the details of your organization and its needs the way you do. On the other hand, researchers tend to know more about the broad field than practitioners do. They can see the forest and know about trees in general, which helps you when your time is spent focusing on that one big tree right in front of you.

Any group that expects the wrong thing from partners or consultants is likely to be frustrated. Centers or faculty members should not expect you to know the literature, the typologies, or statistics related to their field. You, after all, are a service provider. Similarly, you should not expect them to offer detailed analyses of your situation in all of its nuances. If you look to them for the perspective they can provide, you will be more often satisfied.

Technical Expertise

Universities, and some colleges, can provide technical, detailed advice on matters in which centers, departments, or individual faculty members have expertise. Although it is true that they are more likely to have expertise about your type of organization than about your specific group, they will know important technical details about other matters that concern you.

One of the greatest needs facing religious nonprofits is expertise in grant seeking and proposal writing. Some faith-based service providers, especially the older ones with developed bureaucracies, are as experienced as any secular provider in the ways of the funding world. But as congregations move rapidly into the sphere of foundation and government funding, they often find themselves stymied by jargon and detail.

The juvenile court judge in our city decided to encourage congregations to provide services to first-time juvenile offenders. His opinion, and this has certainly become a mainstream view, is that a congregation could provide more than counseling or oversight, services he associated with secular caseworkers. A congregation, he believes, can offer a spiritual and moral base, as well as an institutional base of related activities, for its rehabilitative efforts.

About thirty congregations (out of several hundred invited) showed up for the first meeting to discuss the RFP (request for proposals). The judge explained why he was issuing this RFP and his assumptions about the good that churches could do. His assistant then went over the proposal's many details. From my perspective as an observer, the presentation seemed well organized and clear. But when the floor was opened to questions, the first question was, "What is an RFP?" Colleges and universities have individuals with the technical expertise to answer such questions.

Universities have experts who understand the legal and bureaucratic machinations of the social service system. My university has both a School of Public and Environmental Affairs and a Center on Philanthropy. The latter is atypical, to be sure, but something resembling the former exists at many universities, especially public, urban ones. Among the various centers and departments of schools of social work, government, law, and the like are the resources to improve your handling of grant applications and proposal writing.

Sometimes the grant-writing help you need is not all that technical. A new, faith-based service provider may simply need to see examples of successful grants. A congregation just venturing into the world of child welfare services, for instance, may never before have seen a program budget. They may not know what constitutes reasonable charges for administrative overhead or office supplies.

Many different organizations, including universities, can supply this basic need. You, however, have to know (and be willing) to ask. During my stint as an assistant dean in the graduate school, I realized that one of the simplest and most valuable services we offered to students was a file of successful applications to the National Science Foundation or National Endowment for the Humanities. We removed the individual names for privacy, but potential applicants could examine these files to see what proposals had worked.

A related area has to do with program evaluation. Over the past decade or so, both public and private funders have put greater emphasis on a program's ability to chart and measure its effectiveness. Many newer faith-based nonprofit organizations, especially congregations with explicit service missions, have never had to consider how to measure their outcomes. Obviously they hope to do good and have some sense of what constitutes accomplishing that, but they usually have not had to consider how to establish goals and show measurable improvement. When they are funding their own activities, these measures may not be necessary (although even then they might be a good idea). But when they receive funding from elsewhere, these performance indicators become crucial.

Universities can help in two ways on this score. First, a center or institute may be in a position to help organizations design evaluation procedures. Will a simple evaluation form serve your needs, or will you need interviews and focus groups? What are considered acceptable standards of success in your field?

These are important questions to funders. One congregationally based nonprofit, for instance, might think that a 50 percent success rate in keeping truant youngsters in school is fine. Another congregation might think that a 90 percent success rate is a failure. Both need to know the standard for these programs. You should be able to judge your own efforts, and help funders evaluate them as well, by comparison to realistic expectations.

Second, a university or a college may be in a position to conduct an evaluation for you. If there are centers, institutes, or offices related to your field, they probably house experts who could provide the needed judgment, reflection, and constructive criticism. In many fields, one professor with relevant expertise can greatly improve the effectiveness of an evaluation.

Another area in which universities offer support is data management. They can provide information through their own use of databases and other computer technology. But your greatest need may be in managing data about your own organization and its client base; universities, especially under the auspices of centers or institutes dedicated to nonprofit work, may be able to offer advice and support at the lowest cost. The reason is that centers, institutes, and special administrative offices are usually funded by grants or contracts provided by organizations that want to help the community. My own organization houses a program funded by Lilly Endowment, both to study religious groups in Indianapolis and to provide them with useful information and data support. Our services, and the services of other centers, are inexpensive (or sometimes free) because they are subsidized by those funders. Because large foundations or government agencies rarely have the ability to handle innumerable small requests from individual congregations or small nonprofits, they parcel larger sums of money to organizations that can provide services to a specific range of organizations. In some sense, those providers become subsidiaries or field agents for the larger funders.

In many cases, helping you is what these centers and institutes have been paid to do. Although this is not true for every center, your search for help within the university will be much simpler if you ask whose job it is to do this kind of work.

At a college, you are more likely to be trading on the professor's goodwill, which may be a somewhat slimmer commodity since the professor does not get paid specifically to help you. In such cases, it is especially important to look for outcomes that are mutually beneficial, either by opening up funding opportunities for research or by raising the professor's community profile. Beyond that, a professor may be willing to undertake the task for a smaller fee than a consultant because of the intangible benefits to her or his research and higher community visibility.

Language Barriers

One of the greatest obstacles to successful partnerships between universities and service providers is the difference in professional language. Churches speak a jargon, as do synagogues. There are catch phrases, as when evangelicals "have a heart for" or "feel called to" something, that are meaningful and important in the context of the group but confusing to outsiders. Social service providers do the same thing, and no one needs to be told how academics scientize and generalize their work with technical terminology. Academics lecture one another all the time on how important it is to broaden their vocabulary and speak to a broader public. You are welcome to lecture them too. But you are more likely to succeed by taking an active, even aggressive role in the conversation, framing the problems and the dialogue in your own terms. I am not suggesting that you get angry whenever someone uses a different phrase from your own, but only that you hold steadily to your own goals and methods.

Researchers have no right to assume that you will be familiar with their jargon, but neither should you assume that they bear full responsibility for recasting the conversation in your terms. Here as elsewhere, you will succeed to the degree that you can be a contributing partner in a dialogue. Sometimes being a partner means teaching new vocabulary; sometimes it means learning it.

A Working Partnership

To develop a partnership with a university, you must define your own interests and description but also be willing to understand the same from your potential colleagues.

Despite their public service mission and their mandate from funders to provide assistance, university centers and college departments are not usually going to act altogether altruistically. Even if their goal is only and unambiguously to do good, in a world of finite resources, including time, they still must decide what good they will do.

You know from your own efforts to provide services that the process works best when both sides, client and provider, agree on the goals and the methods. In short, a successful outcome usually follows a successful, mutual definition of the situation. In this case you are the client and, like those whom you serve, probably not in a position to command the definition of the situation. (In the for-profit world, clients have more leverage because they are the ones bringing the money.) Here, you are neither an independent consumer nor a passive recipient of charity. This relationship must be a partnership. Be prepared to say what you need and to consider what the university office, center, or faculty member needs from you.

What's in It for Them?

Before you involve yourself in a partnership with a university or college, consider what the university needs from the relationship in return.

Start with money. In what way can a collaborative effort between your organization and the school, or among your two groups and others, bring resources to both? It makes little sense to be unrealistic, of course, but new nonprofits can sometimes be too limited and defined in their thinking. Frequently groups approach a university center or office for information and suggest that they have only a thousand or fifteen hundred dollars to pay for it. They have never considered whether potential funders might take a special interest in this new, cooperative venture. There is likely to be more interest across the board if the proposed partnership is described as an experiment that, if it works, might serve as a model for future collaborative efforts.

It is not easy to picture oneself or one's organization as a model; in fact, it takes a certain amount of vanity to do so. There are great advantages in seeing the potential as well as the mundane effects of what you are doing. This book was undertaken out of the belief that social services are entering uncharted territory. If the nonprofit sector, especially the religious segment of it, is to play a larger role in service provision, then all of us must work to construct the framework in which that activity will take place. The more you can portray your organization as advancing our understanding of that framework (and actually strive to do so), the more attractive your efforts will be to funders and universities.

In addition to positioning yourself as a model, consider how your group stacks up as the public. University offices, centers, and departments benefit when they provide a public service. The more clearly your group addresses a clear and well-understood problem, the more attractive it will be to the university to associate itself with the solution. That is not to say that you should get involved in only

the highest-profile kinds of services. Rather, you should be prepared to explain why your services are a benefit to the wider society, even if they only address the pressing needs of a particular
population.

The last suggestion for collaboration with schools is both the
most important and the one that nonprofit groups are usually least
likely to consider. Your organization is most attractive to a potential educational partner if it is a suitable subject for research. Service providers approach schools all the time with certain needs and
a limited ability to pay. The wise school will recognize where it can
provide the assistance in return for help in conducting research.

This kind of trade-off does not make a school's services free to
you. Being a research subject is a cost to you and your organization. Making time to give interviews or to fill out surveys can be
hard. But those costs on your end can sometimes be the payment
the university most desires.

The matter seems obvious but seldom is. Some people in the
university want to study how organizations such as yours interact
with their environment as they deliver services. You want to know
how your organization can interact more effectively with its environment and better deliver services. There is likely to be a deal in
there somewhere.

Nonprofits that need services for free may best be able to receive them if they are flexible in their request and open to collaboration in research as well as in practice. You must consider just
how flexible you are willing and able to be. Before entering into
such a project, you need to ask certain questions: What is reasonable access to our records? Can our clients be contacted for evaluation and report? How well do we keep our own records, and how
easily can we make them available?

It is reasonable that schools will gravitate toward organizations
that promise the greatest potential for success. The more willing
you are to be both a partner and a research subject, the more interest a school might have. The better your records are (and "better" certainly means "electronically" in this case), the more easily
things will move forward.

The suggestion that you should offer your organization as an
attractive research subject may seem to contradict the suggestion
that you insist on being a dialogue partner. Such is not the case.

You must be a dialogue partner, that is, a colleague, in defining the nature of the relationship. You must make sure that your needs and the needs of the school are met.

One of the school's needs is to conduct applied research. Your availability as a subject may be the most valuable thing you can offer in exchange for the services you need. Half of your collegial role is being a client who must get the services she is paying for. The other half may be as a subject who pays for those services by being a willing research subject.

Conclusion

In the end, a partnership between your organization and a faculty member or branch of the university works when you are both realistic. Neither group is in it only for the money (or they would not be nonprofits), but both need money to survive. Both have noble goals and purposes, but the fact that they are often complementary does not make them identical.

The success of such a partnership depends on both sides' understanding what the other side needs and what it has to offer. If you approach a school hat in hand, do not be surprised to find you are dissatisfied with what you get. But if you approach a school as a potential colleague with knowledge and resources to share, you may find a group of intelligent and committed individuals willing to form a partnership.

CHAPTER 9

Deciding Whether and When to Seek Government Funds

Stephen V. Monsma

Many faith-based agencies accept large amounts of government funds and have done so for years with no apparent constriction of their religious activities; others refuse all government funds based on fears that their religious activities may be severely restricted. Studies have shown a wide variety in the demands placed on faith-based agencies. Some faith-based agencies that engage in prayers, have mandatory religion classes, and use religious art and symbols receive a major portion of their funding from governmental sources; others have been told they must take down a picture of Jesus before receiving government money. Why is this? Why are there such contradictory expectations and experiences in regard to government funding and faith-based agencies? Are there ways faith-based agencies can accept government funds without compromising their religious mission?

This chapter seeks to address these and similar questions. It considers the constitutional and practical issues involved in faith-based organizations receiving public money, and describes the steps a faith-based organization that accepts public funds can take to protect its freedom to pursue fully its religious mission.

Why Accept Government Money?

There are two good reasons for religious service organizations to consider accepting government funds. The first is that in most fields of social service, health, community development, and education, government spending dwarfs both individual and foundation giving. In 1994 total philanthropic giving was $130 billion, with $105 billion coming from individuals, $10 billion from foundations, $7 billion from corporations, and $9 billion from charitable bequests. Meanwhile total government spending—federal, state, and local—in that year came to $2.2 trillion. In health care, total philanthropic giving in 1995 was $13 billion; total government health care spending was $456 billion. In social welfare programs such as public aid and housing, government spending in 1993 was $264 billion, and total philanthropic giving for human service purposes was $13 billion. In 1994 total governmental spending for education on all levels was $386 billion; total philanthropic giving for education was $17 billion (U.S. Department of Commerce, 1997). In summary, although philanthropic giving in the United States amounts to billions of dollars a year, the spending by government—federal, state, and local—far outstrips philanthropic giving by individuals, foundations, and corporations. This means that when a faith-based organization running a program for which government funds are available refuses those funds, it cuts itself off from a source of funds much larger than all its individual, corporate, and foundation sources put together. This is not true of every individual program, but taking government and philanthropic funds as a whole, it certainly is.

For a financially hard-pressed, religiously based agency to deny itself a potential source of funds, there need to be compelling reasons. The agency owes that much to its supporters, employees, and clients. In turning down these funds, it needs to approach its supporters for even more funds, may sometimes need to lay off employees eager to serve those in need, and can serve fewer clients, thereby fulfilling its own adopted mission less fully. New needs will go unfilled, and potential clients will go unhelped.

Another argument that can be made for accepting government money is that in reality government funds originate with those who support faith-based agencies. The government obtains its money from taxes paid by American taxpayers, including the estimated 100 million Americans who attend religious services weekly and the millions of Americans who demonstrate their religious convictions by contributing more than $60 billion a year to religious causes (more than is given by individuals to all other charitable causes put together) (U.S. Department of Commerce, 1997). Thus, when government makes funds available to faith-based agencies that are providing important public services, some of the money funneled to those agencies has been collected from those who are deeply religious and supportive of the religious missions of those agencies. There is a fairness issue here. For the government to collect taxes from all its citizens—religious and nonreligious alike—and then funnel them only to its own agencies and to private nonreligious agencies would be to take funds from all and return them only to some. Every time a faith-based agency turns down government funds for which it is eligible, it perpetuates this unfairness. By accepting government funds, a faith-based organization helps to ensure that the proportion of taxes paid by deeply religious citizens more fully corresponds to the proportion of social service, health, and education spending going to religiously based agencies.

Many would say there are good reasons for faith-based agencies to refuse government funds, despite this unfairness and the availability of such funds. Most of those reasons revolve around the fear that in accepting these funds, a faith-based agency is selling its soul—that with the shekels will come the shackles, as someone has said. Some faith-based organizations under some circumstances may appropriately reach this conclusion, but this is not always the case. Because there are good reasons to accept government funds, an agency should have good reasons for turning them down.

Government Funding Today

Government already funds many faith-based agencies. Lester Salamon (1992) once wrote, "Although government provides most of the funds in many of the key social welfare fields, private institutions deliver most of the services" (p. 105). In a recent year, for example, 65 percent of the Catholic Charities' revenue came from the government, as did 75 percent of the Jewish Board of Family and Children's Services' revenues and 55 percent of the Lutheran

Social Ministries' revenues (Mehegan, 1994; Evangelical Lutheran Church in America, 1996). I found that a majority of faith-based child and family service agencies that I studied reported receiving more than 40 percent of their budgets from government sources (Monsma, 1996). Faith-based international aid and relief agencies also receive large amounts of government funds (Monsma, 1996; Nichols, 1988).

These government funds can take several forms. Perhaps most common is the purchase of service contract; a government agency contracts with a faith-based agency to provide a certain service, such as shelter for the homeless, foster care for an abused child, or counseling for a drug-addicted person. It is a business relationship, with the faith-based agency providing a service and the government paying for it. Receiving more attention recently are vouchers. The government provides vouchers or certificates that the recipients can take to any number of agencies—including faith-based agencies—and redeem them for the services or goods for which they are intended. Some child care programs are of this nature, as was the well-known G.I. Bill following World War II. Government also sometimes makes outright grants to faith-based agencies to assist them in providing services. These can be either cash grants or in-kind grants, such as surplus food supplies or surplus government equipment or property. Finally, government sometimes assists faith-based agencies through low-interest loans or loan guarantees. In short, a significant amount of government money in a variety of forms flows to faith-based agencies.

It is wrong to refer to such funds as "government aid," as is sometimes done. These funds are not gifts, aid, or subsidies. It is much more like a business transaction. The government gives money to the agency for its provision of a service, or so it can provide a public service. The public, through the government, has decided it wants a certain public service: abused children cared for, the homeless sheltered, the drug addicted freed from their addiction, the poor prepared for employment, the sick helped, the elderly cared for, and the uneducated taught. These are public services. Any government funds that go to faith-based groups are not private, pork barrel gifts that benefit the group and its members. Instead, they reimburse the agency for services it provides to the public, thereby enabling it to serve a wider public. With additional funds come additional responsibilities. Thus, the agency is able to do more of what it feels called to do; it can expand its reach. It is not, however, "aided" in the sense of receiving funds with which to increase the wealth or perks of the agency.

Where Is the Wall?

Americans are well acquainted with the metaphor of a wall of separation between church and state, a metaphor first articulated by Thomas Jefferson and later incorporated by the Supreme Court into its interpretations of the First Amendment. In fact, the Supreme Court declared in 1947 in ringing words that "no tax in any amount, large or small, can be levied to support any religious activities or institutions" (*Everson v. Board of Education*). How then can millions, even billions, of tax dollars go to faith-based health, social service, and educational organizations? The answer to that question is largely contained in three legal principles the Supreme Court has articulated. That answer reveals much about the legal position of faith-based organizations that accept government funds.

The first legal principle is the strict separation principle, also sometimes called the no-aid-to-religion principle. This principle says that there must be a wall of separation between church and state and that no government funds may go to support religion. On the basis of this principle, the Supreme Court has declared almost all forms of government funding for religiously based elementary and secondary schools to violate the First Amendment. Similarly, it has used this principle to hold unconstitutional most forms of religious expression in the public schools, such as prayers and Bible readings. These decisions continue to be highly controversial and widely reported in the news media, thereby leading some to assume that it is the only legal principle the Supreme Court has followed in its church-state decisions. But that is not the case.

A second legal principle the Supreme Court has followed is the pervasively sectarian principle: if a faith-based organization is not pervasively sectarian, it is possible for its religious elements to be separated from the nonreligious services it is providing. In the case of such organizations, government can finance or support its nonreligious public services without aiding religion. Its religious elements have been separated out and are privately funded. On this basis, the Supreme Court has approved public funding of religiously based colleges and universities, hospitals, and a teenage pregnancy prevention counseling center (Monsma, 1996).

Various commentators have noted that this legal principle has its difficulties. First, the Supreme Court has never precisely defined what it means by a "pervasively sectarian" agency or institution. In *Roemer v. Maryland Public Works Board* (1976), Justice Harry Blackmun presented the most careful, complete attempt at distinguishing a pervasively sectarian institution from a nonpervasively sectarian institution, yet twelve years later even he admitted that the "pervasively sectarian" standard is "a vaguely defined work of art" (*Bowen v. Kendrick*, 1988, p. 631). The standard attempts to distinguish between organizations in which religion is thoroughly integrated into all aspects of its programming from those where it is a separable aspect. How far and in what ways religious practices can be part of an organization without being found pervasively sectarian remains uncertain. Thus, faith-based organizations may receive government money only if they are not pervasively sectarian, but it is hard to tell in concrete situations which ones fall on which side of the pervasively sectarian dividing line. Thus far, however, the only faith-based organizations that the Supreme Court has found to be pervasively sectarian are elementary and secondary schools. Faith-based organizations other than K–12 schools stand a good chance of being found not pervasively sectarian, even when they integrate a considerable amount of religious practices into their programs.

This conclusion was reinforced by a study I did a few years ago. I found that many religiously based nonprofit organizations received government money even though they took part in a number of religious practices that might appear to make them pervasively sectarian (Monsma, 1996). For example, 38 percent of the faith-based child and family service agencies studied that received public funds took religion into account in making hiring decisions, as did 36 percent of the faith-based international aid agencies studied. Among the faith-based colleges and universities receiving public funds, 25 percent reported they have some required religious exercises and encourage religious commitments by their students. The pervasively sectarian legal principle is crucial for the ability of faith-based agencies to receive public money, yet it remains poorly defined and apparently not often followed in practice.

A third legal principle relevant to the ability of faith-based agencies to receive public funds is the equal access, equal treatment, or neutrality principle (the terminology varies, but all refer to the same concept). This principle says that faith-based organizations may receive public funds as long as they are not given any special position or privilege over their secularly based counterparts. It is a newer principle than the first two and thus is still developing. Thus far, it has been applied by the Supreme Court only in instances where there was also a free speech claim or where the public funds went to the faith-based organization due not to the government's decision but to choices made by individuals. In 1995 the Court decided that since the University of Virginia funded a wide variety of student publications, it could not refuse to fund a Christian student publication (*Rosenberger v. Rector,* 1995). Religious viewpoints, the Court decided, deserve treatment equal to those of secular viewpoints; otherwise government would no longer be neutral between religious and nonreligious viewpoints. But this case also posed freedom of expression claims, since it involved student publications. Thus, unless extended by the Supreme Court in future decisions, it would not apply to a faith-based agency claiming funds equal to those being distributed to similar agencies that are secularly based.

A second example concerns a blind student who wished to attend a Bible college to study for the ministry under Washington State's occupational training program for the disabled. The state of Washington refused, reasoning it would be a violation of church-state separation for state funds to go to a Bible college in support of a student who was studying for a religious career. But the Supreme Court disagreed, saying that the student, not the state, was the one deciding whether the money was going to the college (*Witters v. Washington Department of Services for the Blind,* 1986). Students disabled by blindness were the ones receiving the funds, and they should have the right to take the money where they wish. They should be treated equally or neutrally, whether they wished to pursue religious training in a faith-based college or secular training in a secular college.

In these examples, public money went to faith-based organizations on the basis that they should be treated no differently from their secular counterparts. The decisions did not depend on the ability to separate the religious and secular aspects with only the secular being funded, a separability made possible by their not being pervasively sectarian. Thus, they were decided on a principle distinct from the earlier pervasively sectarian principle.

The Supreme Court has never found the granting of government funds to faith-based organizations unconstitutional, except in the case of elementary and secondary schools. To put it positively, the Supreme Court has found it constitutional for public funds to go to colleges and universities, hospitals, and counseling centers. Indeed, most of the thousands of programs providing public funding for faith-based agencies have never been challenged in court.

I taken this detour through the legal thicket of Supreme Court decisions and legal principles because it is important for any faith-based nonprofit organization contemplating accepting public funds to understand the legal basis on which it would be receiving those funds and the possible legal ramifications of its doing so. Many faith-based institutions have received public funds for years with no constriction of their religious practices. Yet the religious practices they legally may follow and the degree to which they legally may be integrated into their overall programs remain unclear. If religious practices are challenged, there exist few clear legal protections they can fall back on to defend those practices.

The vast majority of public funding programs for faith-based agencies are legally, constitutionally justified under the legal principle that such funds may go only to fund nonreligious programs of agencies that are not pervasively sectarian. Since the term *pervasively sectarian* remains ill defined, the legal position of a faith-based agency accepting public funds is made uncertain. If a government official insists that religious art must be removed, that religious standards may not be used in hiring staff, or that a religious dimension may not be integrated into an agency program, there are few legal bases from which a faith-based agency can mount a legal appeal with confidence. In that sense, it is legally vulnerable, but this is not the entire picture. In practice, many faith-based agencies receive public funds with no constriction of their religious freedom.

Practice Versus Legal Theory

Many faith-based organizations receive large amounts of public money annually. In the light of their legally vulnerable position, a key question for any such agency considering accepting government funds is whether those faith-based agencies accepting public money have been able to do so without compromising their religious missions as they have defined them. Based on a thorough study of this issue I conducted several years ago, the answer is a qualified yes, using an example that focuses on child and family service agencies (Monsma, 1996). Of the 286 child service agencies that returned a written questionnaire, 51 percent, or 137, reported they have a religious orientation or nature. Of these, 82 percent reported receiving some public money. A majority of the faith-based agencies (51 percent) reported receiving at least 40 percent of their revenue from government sources. I divided the agencies into three categories, based on the number and nature of the religious practices in which they reported engaging. Even among those with the most religious practices—such as prayers before meals, informal references to religion by the staff working with the children and their families, and taking religion into account in hiring decisions—two-thirds reported receiving public funds, and 46 percent reported receiving 20 percent or more of their funds from governmental sources. Thus, even the most deeply religious agencies follow the pattern of accepting governmental monies.

Whether they were able to do so without compromising their religious mission is the key question. The faith-based child service agencies receiving public money were asked directly whether their receipt of government money had led to any pressures or requirements that they curtail their religious practices. Of the 122 religious child service agencies that reported receiving government money, 70 percent reported they had experienced no pressures or problems; 30 percent had experienced some difficulties. Even among the agencies that ranked the highest in terms of the religious practices followed, 61 percent reported no problems. But does that mean that almost 40 percent of the agencies pursuing the most religious practices did experience some sort of pressure or problem?

The most frequently cited problem related to the practice followed by a number of the agencies with residential programs of requiring the children or youths in their care to attend Sunday morning worship services. Several comments from the questionnaires reveal the variety of approaches different government officials have taken to this issue. The head of one agency wrote: "In the past, religious services were mandatory, but we can no longer do that. However, we give incentives for attendance and encourage them to attend their own church." This approach was rejected by the officials with whom another agency had to deal: "We used to encourage church attendance by giving children extra free time if they went to church. We had to discontinue the practice. We may encourage church attendance but may not reward for church attendance." A third stated: "[We experience] some informal leaning [on us] that youth should not be required to attend church—they say federal law mandates this, but no on has pushed us or other agencies yet." The variety of approaches to church attendance followed by different officials in different states and localities reveals the uncertainty—some would say the confusion—that marks this issue.

There are many stories—some documented and some not—of agencies that have had their freedom to pursue their religious missions curtailed due to their acceptance of government money. A faith-based homeless shelter was refused a $7,000 grant by the Department of Housing and Urban Development because it had pictures of Jesus in its facility ("Picture of Jesus," 1989); a Salvation Army domestic abuse shelter was told by a federal district court it could not fire a worker who was a follower of the ancient, pagan religion of Wicca (Monsma, 1996). Joe Klein (1997), in a *New Yorker* article, tells the story of Joy of Jesus, a Detroit job-training program that dealt with the hardest to place among the unemployed. The state of Michigan was so impressed with its success that it offered funding, but only on the condition there be no more prayers or Bible studies.

What can one conclude from my study and from a host of newspaper and anecdotal stories of faith-based agencies that either were or were not limited in their freedom to pursue the religious practices they felt important? Does accepting government funds means one's religious freedom will inevitably be sacrificed? There is no simple yes or no, bottom-line answer to the latter question. An agency accepting government funds exists in a legal gray area.

The courts have never spelled out exactly the legal limits for following religiously based practices. The uncertainty is compounded by the fact that some state constitutions and state court decisions insist on a stricter separation of church and state than the federal Constitution and federal court decisions. As a result, a confusion of standards and practices is being followed. In my study, 65 percent of the religiously based child service agencies reported having spoken prayers before meals, but one of the agencies reported that a "county worker removed foster children because foster parents had them saying prayers at meal-time." Sometimes a simple change in names will get an official to back off. The head of a Catholic agency reported, "Our campus ministry activities were originally disallowed by our Department of Social Services but are now allowed because we include them under the auspices of 'values education.'" For the most part faith-based agencies accepting government funds seem to be able to continue most, if not all, of the religious practices to which their faith leads them. There are exceptions. Firmness sometimes is required to protect such practices, and controversy and pressures can arise unexpectedly.

A faith-based agency that accepts government funds increases greatly the number of persons it can help and thereby expands the needs it is meeting, the good it is doing, and the influence it is exerting. Those are major benefits. But it needs to do so with its eyes wide open, realizing the dangers that can arise in accepting government money, and with a self-conscious strategy for avoiding these dangers.

Maintaining Religious Autonomy

There are three basic steps faith-based agencies that decide to accept public money can take to help ensure they can maintain the religious practices they believe are important for their identity and programs.

The first step sounds simple and perhaps insignificant, but it is the most important of all. The agency needs to be clear and in agreement on the nature of its religious mission and what religious practices are and are not negotiable. I have interviewed persons associated with nonprofit, faith-based agencies that receive government funds in three countries: the United States, Germany, and the Netherlands. Some of the agencies with which they were associated were deeply religious and followed many religious practices. Some were nominally religious. I am convinced that the most important factor in enabling those that have preserved their religious mission to do so has been a self-conscious, openly discussed, agreed-on determination that the religious component must be maintained.

The big danger in accepting government funds is not that the agency suddenly will be told it must abandon all religious practices. The danger is incrementalism. Over a period of years and bit by bit, an agency will end up compromising a little here and a little there, only to end up after a period of time with its being—religiously speaking—only a shell of its earlier form. Luis Lugo of the Pew Charitable Trusts often speaks of "preemptive capitulation" as being the policy too many agencies have followed once they accept public funds. Fearing lawsuits or hassles by government officials, they quietly abandon certain religious practices they feel will act as red flags. Even when not engaging in preemptive capitulation, many agencies too quickly accept the pronouncement of some low-level official as the final word and abandon important religious principles. Let no one underestimate the pressures for this to happen, especially once government funds have enabled additional staff to be hired and additional clients to be served. Suddenly the thought of losing those government funds, with staff laid off and clients sent away, appears much worse than the small compromise in religious practices one is being asked to accept. The pressures from staff, board members, and clients to compromise can be great.

I am not saying that all religiously based practices of agencies receiving public dollars must be hung onto with all determination. There are certain practices—such as religious worship services and overt, explicit proselytization—that no agency should expect government money to fund directly. They need to be covered by private donations. Also, there may be religious practices that are not in fact crucial to an agency's mission. On close examination, an agency may conclude that some are counterproductive to its overall religious mission. Every agency accepting government funds must draw its own line beyond which it will not go. That line may not necessarily encompass all current practices, but it is absolutely essential that such a line be drawn thoughtfully.

In drawing that line, the staff, the board, and the top management of the agency all need to be involved. The board will be crucial in this decision, since it will be somewhat insulated from the day-to-day operations of the agency and can take a longer-range perspective. In addition, it is ultimately the board that bears the responsibility for the basic direction and policies of the agency. Where that line is and why it is there need to be topics of ongoing discussion in the agency. Any decision to forgo additional government funds or to stop accepting funds will be difficult, and the temptation to give way can become overwhelming if it is not a truly collective decision. The head of a home for troubled boys that receives government funds once told me that its policy of requiring their youths to attend church services on Sunday morning has periodically been questioned by government officials. He explained that his board has already voted to reject all government funds should those officials ever insist that they may no longer require Sunday church attendance. That is what I mean by drawing a line.

My research also shows that government officials often back down in the light of a resolute agency. Agencies need to realize that they have bargaining strength. They often provide services to the homeless, the drug dependent, the poor, and the abused in society that most other agencies are not interested in providing. At the same time there would be a public outcry if government would no longer deal with these problems. The picture of needy persons not being helped because a government official pushed a faith-based agency too far creates a public relations problem most officials would like to avoid. Also, there are increasing calls in the public policy community for government to run fewer programs itself and turn to private, nonprofit agencies to provide such services. Often a busy, harried government official will find it easier to give way to a faith-based agency that is objecting to the latest directive rather than insist that it be carried out to the letter and run the risk of the agency's dropping out of the program.

A second step agencies that accept government funds can take to protect their religious autonomy is related to the first. Any faith-based agency that decides to accept government funds should continue to maintain additional sources of funding. There is a danger in becoming too dependent on the government for funds. Once governmental funds exceed one-half of an agency's funds, danger flags should start to fly. If nongovernmental funding sources are

firm and long-standing in nature, an agency could allow government funds to creep up to 60 percent or so of its funds. Anything
beyond that greatly increases the danger that the agency will ca-
pitulate to pressures to tone down its religious practices. Two factors are at play here. One is that an agency's threat to reject
government funds becomes less credible as the percentage of total
funds from the government increases. In addition, as the percentage of an agency's budget that originates with the government increases, the pressures to give way to government demands also will
go up.

The second, and less obvious, factor comes into play here as
well. As the percentage of an agency's budget that comes from the
government goes up, government officials will feel more justified
in imposing restrictions on an agency—and agency leaders may
feel a greater obligation to accept those restrictions. This is a sub-
tle, psychological factor, but that does not make it any less real or
powerful. The truth of the old adage, "He who pays the piper calls
the tune," is rooted in economic realities, but it is also rooted in
the right of the payer to call the tune. It is hard to escape the reality that as the proportion of an agency's budget that comes from
government increases, the agency-government relationship will
shift from one of partnership to one of supervisor-subordinate. Any
agency that accepts government funds should, at the outset, place
an upper limit on the proportion of its budget it will accept from
those sources.

A third step for any faith-based agency accepting public funds
to take is to cultivate and maintain good relationships with the
news media and elected officials. When it comes to legal, constitutional protections for the religious practices of faith-based agencies accepting public funds, agencies are not in a strong position.
There is much uncertainty in the law and current judicial interpretations. They are, however, in a very strong position in relation
to the news media and elected officials. Faith-based agencies addressing persistent societal problems tend to be admired. Political
liberals—whether in public office, the news media, or other positions of community leadership—tend to admire and respect faith-
based agencies actually seeking to do something about the
homeless, the hungry, the poor, or those experiencing other needs.
Political conservatives tend to respect the religious commitments

of faith-based agencies and view them as good alternatives to ever more and ever bigger government programs. In terms of public perceptions and attitudes, faith-based agencies are in a strong position and must become more adept at capitalizing on this strength. They can invite the news media to special events such as open houses, dedications of new facilities, or events commemorating success stories (especially if there will be a story the television cameras can capture on videotape). A faith-based agency can invite its local and state officials and its local U.S. representative to visit or to speak at its annual dinners or special events. They can be shown around and introduced to persons helped by the agency's programs.

If such positive relationships have developed over the years, then when some strict church-state separationist group or low-level government bureaucrat decides to challenge an agency's religiously based practices, the agency will have a reservoir of goodwill and sympathetic understanding to draw upon. No outside group or bureaucrat is likely to move against a program if this action is likely to bring adverse publicity and telephone calls from influential elected officials. In short, the legal protections for a faith-based agency may be weak, but the potential political and public relations protections are strong. I do not think I would trade the former for the latter.

In addition to these three steps, Congress has been taking actions that are designed to protect the religious integrity of faith-based agencies that accept public funds. Foremost among these is section 104 of the 1996 act restructuring welfare, which has been dubbed the charitable choice provision. This provision, introduced by Senator John Ashcroft of Missouri, provides, first, that if a state contracts with private agencies to provide services to the needy, it must allow faith-based agencies to compete for those contracts on an equal basis with other agencies. (See Center for Public Justice, 1997.) It further provides that when it contracts with a faith-based agency, that agency may continue to make employment decisions based on religious considerations, it may not be required to take down religious art or symbols, and it may not be required to alter its form of governance or legal structure. General language in the provision seeks to ensure that a faith-based organization will retain its "control over the definition, development, practice, and expression of its religious beliefs" (Public Law 104–193, section 104

[d]). The protections offered faith-based agencies that take part in voucher programs rather than purchase of service contracts are even broader.

The charitable choice provision does have certain restrictions on the use of government funds (they may not be used to fund religious worship, instruction, or proselytization), and agencies may not discriminate against clients on the basis of religion or their refusal to take part in religious activities. Some faith-based agencies may find even these limited restrictions too confining, but for those that do not, charitable choice offers significant new opportunities to receive public funds and protections for their religious nature.

The charitable choice provision, however, has limited legal application. It does not apply to all federally funded social welfare programs, but only to programs under the Personal Responsibility and Work Opportunity Reconciliation Act of 1996, the act that replaced the old Aid to Families with Dependent Children program with the Temporary Assistance to Needy Families program. But it is nonetheless highly significant. It applies to a large number of social welfare programs, the principles and policies it embodies can be applied to areas where legally it now does not apply, and its basic principles and policies can be included in other legislation. In 1998 Senator Ashcroft introduced the Charitable Choice Expansion Act, which would apply the concepts contained in the charitable choice section of the 1996 welfare act to all federal social service programs (S 2046, 105th Congress, 2d Session).

Charitable choice and Senator Ashcroft's 1998 bill stand as examples of the movement toward the equal access or neutrality principle, which says that faith-based agencies are eligible to receive public funds as long as similarly situated or parallel secular agencies are also receiving government funds. Under this approach, the religious integrity of faith-based agencies is in a more secure legal position than under the wall of separation, no-aid-to-religion approach, which required that funding rest on the recipient agencies separating their religious and nonreligious activities and their not being pervasively sectarian.

Conclusion

The title of this chapter, referring to money with (some) strings, captures much of what I have sought to say. Government funds are available to faith-based organizations providing a wide range of public services. Those funds come with some strings, including reporting requirements and standards to be met. For faith-based organizations, the most difficult question concerns whether those funds will lead to a fateful compromise in their religious missions. There is no one, simple answer. The answer differs for different agencies in different situations, and it is rooted in two basic facts: (1) the legal protections for a faith-based agency accepting government funds are weak but have recently been strengthened by "charitable choice," and (2) the public relations position of faith-based agencies is often strong. Therefore, it is crucial for all faith-based agencies accepting government money to be clear, self-conscious, and intentional about their religious missions. If this last observation is followed and if faith-based agencies develop their natural public relations strengths and limit the percentage of their budgets funded by government, I am convinced that they will be able to expand their reach and the good they are doing by taking part in government funding programs for which they are eligible.

References

Bowen v. Kendrick. (1988). 487 U.S. 589.

Center for Public Justice. *Guide to Charitable Choice: The Rules of Section 104 of the 1996 Federal Welfare Law Governing State Cooperation with Faith-based Social-Service Providers.* (1997). Washington, D.C., and Annandale, Va.: Center for Public Justice and Christian Legal Society.

Evangelical Lutheran Church of America. (1996). *Annual Report.* Chicago: Division of Church and Society of the Evangelical Lutheran Church in America.

Everson v. Board of Education. (1947). 330 U.S. 1.

Klein, Joe. (1997). "In God They Trust." *New Yorker,* June 16, pp. 40–48.

Mehegan, Sean. (1994). "The Federal Connection: Nonprofits Are Looking More and More to Washington." *Nonprofit Times, 8.*

Monsma, Stephen V. (1996). *When Sacred and Secular Mix: Religious Nonprofit Organizations and Public Money.* Lanham, Md.: Rowman & Littlefield.

Nichols, J. Bruce. (1988). *The Uneasy Alliance: Religion, Refugee Work, and U.S. Foreign Policy.* New York: Oxford University Press.

"Picture of Jesus Blocks Public Funds for Salvation Army." (1989). *Church and State, 42,* 85.

Roemer v. Maryland Public Works Board. (1976). 426 U.S. 736.

Rosenberger v. Rector. (1995). 515 U.S. 819.

Salamon, Lester M. (1992). *America's Nonprofit Sector: A Primer.* New York: Foundation Center.

U.S. Bureau of the Census. (1997). *Statistical Abstract of the United States: 1997* (117th ed.). Washington, D.C.: U.S. Government Printing Office.

Witters v. Washington Department of Services for the Blind. (1986). 474 U.S. 48.

Additional Readings

Glenn, Charles L. (forthcoming). *The Ambiguous Embrace: Government and Faith-Based Schools and Social Agencies.*

Governor's Advisory Task Force on Faith-Based Community Service Groups. (1996). *Faith in Action: A New Vision for Church-State Cooperation in Texas.* Austin: State of Texas, Dec.

Jeavons, Thomas H. (1994). *When the Bottom Line Is Faithfulness.* Bloomington: University of Indiana Press.

Monsma, Stephen V., and Soper, J. Christopher. (1997). *The Challenge of Pluralism: Church and State in Five Democracies.* Lanham, Md.: Rowman & Littlefield.

CHAPTER 10

Working with Foundations
Edward L. Queen II

There are few other institutions in American life that appear as strange and incomprehensible to most people as foundations. They exist as relatively ubiquitous but shadowy figures. Their workings seem to be shrouded in secrecy, and, undoubtedly most significant, they appear to have piles of money, which they distribute here and there for their chosen purposes.

The combination of seemingly vast sums of money and hidden practices would be more than enough to make foundations the modern equivalent of the Wizard of Oz. This analogy is more apt perhaps than it should be, for also like the Wizard, foundations can bend organizations to their purposes, sometimes to ill effects. Similarly, foundations themselves do very little. They provide the resources for you to do your work, but you have to be clear about what you want to accomplish and not be overly moved by what they suggest simply because they have money. That said, however, it also should be noted that foundations and their staffs also have a wider perspective than your organization. They often know things and can see things that you may be unable to see. Their suggestions about approaches and undertakings often can be productive and helpful and should be taken seriously.

At the coarsest level, foundations are pools of money, the purpose of which is to be given away. These two facts make them particularly anomalous in society. They have resources and they want, indeed are required, to spend them. Foundations, however, are also much more than that. They are places where thoughtful, knowledgeable, and reflective individuals try to determine the best ways to spend money in order to effect the institution's vision of the good. The resources that foundations have are not simply monetary. Even without a grant, your engagement with a foundation can provide you with information, knowledge, and contacts that can be invaluable.

This is important, because despite how much money foundations may have, the amount is finite. It is limited, and the ways in which they grant their monies often are constrained tremendously by their mission and their funding priorities, by considered decisions— beginning with the intent of the donor—designed to make their grant making intelligent and coherent. It is important to realize the relative smallness of foundations' giving on an annual basis. Over the past several years, the basic percentage of giving has been fairly constant. Individual gifts constitute over 80 percent of all donations, with bequests adding another 6 percent from individuals. Foundation grants make up about 7 percent of all philanthropic dollars, with corporations supplying less than 5 percent. These percentages do not include government funding, however, which in the human and social services field, including medical treatment, far outstrips all other funders.

Despite this, the current economy is a particularly good one for foundation funding. The tremendous run-up of the stock market has increased the value of most foundations' assets markedly. The absolute amount that they are giving away has skyrocketed, and it is quite possible that the next several years will show an increase in their percentage against other sources of funds.

For this reason, it might make sense for your organization to consider approaching foundations for money to support your work. Before you do that, however, it is necessary that you understand the nature of foundations, how they work, their limitations, and the pressures placed on organizations that accept foundation money.

Types of Foundations

Different types of foundations have different strengths and different perspectives. Large, private foundations—for example, the Ford Foundation, the Carnegie Endowment, and the Pew Charitable Trusts—are the most familiar. They are distinguishable by their huge assets, their professional staff, and their national, indeed, international reach. Despite their high profile, these foundations probably are not the most likely prospects for support for your organization. Although they should not be dismissed outright, they are not necessarily the place for you to begin. Sights should be set a bit lower as you look for foundations in your community whose funding priorities are most likely to match the mission of your organization. The foundations most likely to fund your organization will be those with a strong commitment to the health of your community. They probably will be small family foundations and local community foundations.

The small family foundation constitutes a potentially important source of funds for faith-based service organizations because most of these foundations focus on the needs of the local community; they are organized and run by people who care about the community and often already have a strong commitment to religion. Some may be members of your congregation. These foundations often tend to be particularly loyal to the projects and organizations that they fund and occasionally prove to be sources of sustained long-term support. In addition, unlike most large foundations, they often take a sincere and hands-on interest in programs that matter to them and can provide useful access to other local funders.

Community foundations, as the name suggests, are directed to the needs and life of the community of which they are a part. To some extent, community foundations are aggregated family foundations, with numerous funds of money designated for particular types of projects or services. Some funds function as mini-family foundations; other create larger pools available for general community needs. Their nature makes them worthy candidates for your consideration and your approach. Their purpose is to care about their community through addressing pressing community needs such as homelessness, hunger, addiction, crime, and vandalism. For this reason, one of your first tasks should be to determine whether your community has such a foundation; the next is to acquaint yourself with its work and funding priorities.

As you and your organization begin to think about how to expand your funding base and decide that seeking foundation support makes sense, the first job is to determine which foundations care about the things your organization cares about. As in all other attempts to raise money, prospect research should be the first step. There are several ways to begin this task, following both formal and informal routes. One of the first is to begin asking people you know—businesspeople, bankers, community leaders. Read the newspapers carefully for announcements about projects supported by local private foundations or the community foundation. Ask, listen, and pay attention, and you will learn about areas you previously were ignorant about.

More formally there are several ways to approach this task. Numerous publications detail foundations and their interests. Some of those that are most relevant to this search are the Foundation Center's *National Guide to Funding in Religion* and its *Grant$ for Religion, Religious Welfare, and Religious Education.* These and similar volumes often are quite expensive and may be beyond the reach of smaller and less well-funded organizations, although the Internet often can save both time and money. Research may have to be undertaken in local libraries, and what you lack in money may have to be made up for in time spent out of the office. This preliminary research may be a job that can be handled by a particularly well-trusted volunteer or board member. In addition, some of the early contacts with the foundation also could be handled by such a volunteer. Substantive discussions, however, must be led by the executive director or the project director and directed by those knowledgeable about the program and the organization.

Approaching Foundations

As you identify who might be interested, you need to begin finding out more about the programs. If it is a formal foundation, as opposed to individual gifts, you should contact its office and request a copy of its program guidelines. If there is a staff, call the office after you have reviewed carefully the foundation program priorities and procedures and talk to the appropriate person. Probe gently and listen carefully. Make sure that you present yourself as seeking information and not as one who has a sense of entitlement. Never start off or end with the question or impression that says, "You funded these guys. Why don't you support us?"

Even if you have more expertise and success than one of the grantees, your task is to demonstrate that fact. You need to help the foundation see why it should support you rather than make the case that it should not have supported someone else. One of the most important components of working with foundations is that of most other fundraising: building relationships. Too many people see dealing with foundations as going in, asking for money, getting a yes or no, and then leaving. This is never the case. Foundations are, to a great extent, no different from other donors, and you need to work to build the same type of relationship with them as you do with all of your other funders.

Like other donors, foundations want to use their monies for purposes that matter to them, and they hope to do so in ways that are intelligent, efficient, and effective. And despite their institutional nature, they are run by people who have concerns, feelings, attitudes, and passions. Although staff members are guided by strong codes of professionalism, especially in the larger foundations, personal relationships matter, for both legitimate reasons and sometimes for others that are less so. Preeminently, foundations are seeking to give money to projects in line with their funding priorities and to individuals and organizations whom they can trust to do the work appropriately. To a great extent, they follow the same rules you would follow if you were going to give large sums of money to someone. They incline toward people and organizations they know, causes that are important to them, and results that they can verify—in other words, organizations they can trust.

Given this fact, your job in working with foundations is to act no differently than you would with any other funder. Primarily you must present your organization and its projects honestly, positively, and compellingly. Be honest about what you are and what you are not. And always be prepared to walk away if necessary.

As in all other relationships, it is important that the way you approach the organization and deal with it be consonant with the organization's culture and ethos. Some foundations are warm and welcoming, others cool and distant. Some foundations welcome meetings and conversations; others simply follow paper procedures. In your preliminary contacts with the foundation and its staff, attend closely to what is said and the way it is said. Be willing to make yourself available for meetings and to offer the foundation staff access to your undertakings where appropriate, but do not force meetings and invitations on them if they appear to be undesired or unwelcome.

After the initial conversation, you need to consider developing a proposal. In doing this, you must first decide whether it makes sense to send that particular funder a proposal. Does your project or program fit within its guidelines? The information you gained in your preliminary conversations should have decided this for you, but if it has not, then a careful review of the printed guidelines, assuming that the foundation has them, should inform you of the extent to which its grant making intersects with the work of your organization. *Intersection* is the key word here. You need to determine where the interests of the funder match the work of your organization. There will be much that you do that will be completely irrelevant to the funder, but there also may be places where your work is central to the foundation's purposes.

In making these determinations, you need to be honest with yourself and with the work of your organization. You should not bend your current work to match funding priorities of foundations. Even more important, you should not establish new programs simply because money might be available for them. The one exception to this rule is if your organization had been seriously considering adding a new program and the availability of foundation funding may make that possible. Even here, you need to be aware that most foundations rarely support programs on a long-term basis, and any new programs you create must include a plan for long-term support.

Preliminary Work

Assuming you have located a funder whose priorities are in line with the work of your organization, the next step is the development of a proposal. Follow the foundation's guidelines carefully, noting deadlines and schedules of proposal reviews. In some foundations, this process can be quite lengthy. Many smaller foundations review proposals only two to four times a year. If you cannot live with these schedules, do not go to the foundation. It is not going to change its structure for your organization, no matter how important you think your project is.

The following components are important to all proposals:

- State precisely and concisely what you are doing and why it is important. Many proposals are weakened by a failure to deal with both of these components.

- Address all the steps in the program, especially if you are initiating a new program or expanding an existing one. The best proposals demonstrate a grasp of all the elements in an undertaking and articulate them clearly and concisely.
- Address the concerns of the foundation. Have you provided all the information it needs and has requested? If the foundation does not have a working knowledge of your organization, supply some background material and evidence that serves to demonstrate your legitimacy and credibility. Do not, however, inundate it with materials and testimonials. Few other things make foundation staff more suspicious than organizations "which protest too much."
- Demonstrate that you can achieve the goals you have outlined in the time allotted. Make sure that your time line makes sense. In addition, show that you have thought through the ways in which you can demonstrate effectiveness and quantify outcomes.
- Explain your plan for evaluation and follow-through. How can both your organization and the foundation learn from this project? If it is to be an ongoing program, how are you going to institutionalize and support it after the end of the grant period?
- Show a strong understanding of the costs of the program and all of its components. Too many applicants worry too much about the total cost of the project, fearing that the higher the amount, the less likely it will be to get funded. While it is true that foundations often will fund some projects at $10,000 or $25,000 that they would not fund at $250,000, the overall total cost of a project is rarely the determinative factor.

Many individuals view proposals as a particularly arcane science akin to alchemy. In fact, proposals are nothing more, or less, than your case for support written to address, usually, one specific component of your work. The writing of a proposal should emerge smoothly and logically out of your case statement. (See Chapter Five.) You may have to adjust certain structures and forms to meet the specific demands of various foundations requirements about how proposals should look, but the content should not have to be adjusted in any serious way.

The body of the proposal should include a short description of your organization and its work, a statement of the issue the project for which you are requesting funding will address, and how you will address it. Always remember that you are explaining to a reader who may be completely unfamiliar with you and your organization and why she or he should put time, effort, and money into supporting your work, especially given the finite nature of resources and the magnitude of need. Your proposal therefore must be substantive. Even as you make your case for why your work is important, the most significant component of the proposal is to show how you are going to accomplish your goals. Foundations are in the business of funding the implementation of ideas.

The proposal also should make it clear to the potential funder why your organization is a good, if not the best, one to undertake this work. A history of successes, strong community support, and experience in undertaking the work should be made clear. Do not disparage or dismiss other organizations working in the same area. Emphasize your distinctiveness, your particular niche, or simply the sheer magnitude of need that demands that several organizations address the same issue.

If you are starting a new program in an area that already seems to have numerous providers, explain why it makes sense to expend the amount of monies necessary for start-up costs rather than just building on existing programs. This will be of particular importance to funders with a local perspective and a sense of what is occurring. If you have something distinctive and important to offer, make that argument.

If you are expanding your work into a new area or initiating a program, you should make sure that you have done your homework and know the community's assets. This knowledge will make your work more successful and may provide powerful opportunities for partnerships and synergies. For example, if you are concerned about providing basic health services for homeless persons and know that there are two shelters and four soup kitchens in your target area, that provides important information as you consider where to site your clinic. But if none of the locations proves viable for whatever reason, you still are able to address that question before it emerges.

These statements may seem relatively straightforward and obvious, but they often go unreflected on and unheeded in our work. Too often in our intense dedication to what we are doing, to doing our work well and keeping programs running, we begin focus too much internally. Our justifiable, we hope, pride in our successes tends to make us think we not only are the only organization doing the work, but the only one that can do it. We must constantly remind ourselves otherwise.

From a funder's perspective, your ability to answer questions they may ask and to acknowledge and address objections, where appropriate, strengthens your credibility, and credibility cannot be overemphasized. In this field we trade in trust, and your reputation as a trustworthy partner will make all of the difference.

Perhaps nowhere else is this element of credibility more at play than in those who work for your organization. Following the body of the proposal it often will be necessary to identify those who will be supervising and undertaking the majority of the work. This may be adjusted depending on the nature of your proposal and program, but even something as simple as a food pantry or clothes closet must have someone who has responsibility. You need to demonstrate that you have sufficient volunteers to keep it open when it is supposed to be open.

You never should write a proposal that sounds as though miracles will happen (although as faith-based organizations we may expect and experience them). Foundations rarely make grants on the basis that the right things always will happen. Indeed, they should not. Their responsibility is to see that their giving has some value. On the other hand, one of the great freedoms of foundations is that they have the opportunity to take risks and be creative, yet they still need to be convinced that the risks make sense. Your job in the proposal is to demonstrate that your organization is a worthy risk, an organization to which it makes sense to make a grant.

Beyond stating what you are doing and why, the proposal also should be relatively clear about how you are going to do it, illustrating that you have thought through the process. This will strengthen your credibility and demonstrate to the potential funder the greater likelihood of your success. Grant periods are usually no more than three years. Anything that may delay your work will decrease the possibility of success or at least limit it. At its best, the proposal process gives you an opportunity to think through everything that needs to be done in the project. For that reason, the proposal needs to be a logical outgrowth of your case statement and your organization's planning. It should function as an action statement of those undertakings you already have considered for your organization rather than an opportunistic response to available monies. This is not to reject the possibility that there may be unanticipated opportunities to which it makes sense for you to respond, but even these situations must still make sense for your organization and its work.

Certainly this is easy advice to give, but for those who are responsible for running an organization and sincerely want to accomplish certain goals, it is hard advice to take. Expansion, more people served, and more success all seem to be reasonable and worthy undertakings, and they are. Here, however, we need to learn from the business world that one of the most destructive business events is overextension. Too much expansion has bankrupted many businesses. This also will happen to you if you attempt to grow programs beyond your ability to sustain and maintain that growth. Supporting the personnel and infrastructure necessary to continue projects is the nonprofit version of servicing debt. It can drain your organization if you do not have a clear vision of why you are doing what you do and how to continue and sustain it.

Money never should be seen as the solution to all your problems. It is a tool that enables you to accomplish your organization's mission. Like all other tools, it will cost you money to get it and maintain it. You have to ensure that the costs are not more than the gain, at least in the long run. Increasing income will cost you in the short run, but such cultivation will pay off. On the other hand, gains in money, especially grants that extend your work, may cost you a great deal in the long run. As you do your work, your thoughts about support and the long-term health of your organization always must be kept in mind.

This conceptual work is part of your job as a manager or board member. It must be done constantly and carefully. (See Chapter Four for more information on this.) Obviously, the daily demands on your time will hinder your chances for doing this, but if you keep it in mind as your major obligation, you will be drawn back to it from time to time. It also will give you a clearer picture of what sense seeking foundation support will make for your organization.

Letter of Inquiry

Usually your first contact with a foundation will be an inquiry of some kind: a personal contact, a telephone call, or a letter. The first formal inquiry, however, almost invariably is a letter because the funder needs a written description of your organization and the project or program you want to have funded.

The writer should rarely send a letter of inquiry without having previously requested the foundation's proposal guidelines and annual report, or at least determined whether there are guidelines. This request can be a telephone call or a simple letter of request stating how you learned about the foundation, a short description of your organization, and the request for an annual report and any application or proposal guidelines.

Read these materials carefully. If the foundation's funding interests look consonant with your work but you are unsure about certain elements, another telephone call may be in order, especially if the foundation has a paid staff. The guidelines should have identified the person most likely to be responsible for programs similar to yours. If a conversation is in order, make it clear to the person that your main concern is whether there is sufficient connection between the foundation's interests and yours to determine whether a letter of inquiry makes sense.

This early connection is an opportunity to listen and learn. It also gives you a chance to connect with a person who can then identify with you and your organization when the letter arrives. Remember to negotiate a fine line between being overly aggressive and working to develop a meaningful and possibly productive relationship.

When it is time to send the letter of inquiry, pay heed to the following points:

- Keep it short (no more than two pages).
- Give a brief description of your organization and its work.
- Explain why you are writing to the foundation.
- Describe the project for which you are interested in receiving support.
- Ask whether the foundation would be willing to consider a more complete proposal.

- Offer to follow up with a telephone call in the next week to ten days (if the structure of the foundation is such that it can handle a follow-up call).

Following the letter of inquiry and assuming you receive an encouraging reply from the foundation, it is time to begin writing the proposal.

The Proposal

In general, proposals should contain the following components:

- A description of your organization and its work
- Evidence of your credibility
- A description of the project or program to be funded
- An explanation as to why this undertaking is important
- A description of how you will accomplish the goals of the project
- The names and credentials of staff and volunteers (where relevant) responsible for the project
- A discussion of how you will evaluate the impact and success of the project or program
- Plans for continuing the project beyond this funding cycle (if needed)
- A budget for the project
- A copy of the letter from the Internal Revenue Services determining your status as a 501(c)(3) organization

Some foundations may require more information about your organization. Often they want to see a list of board members, a copy of the most recent audited financial statement, and the total budget for the organization. Although you might be reluctant to give such information to those whom you perceive as outsiders and strangers, the foundation's staff and board have the same level of fiduciary responsibility as your board. Since they cannot have an intimate knowledge of all the organizations that request funding, they need to gain what information they can from documents in order to make intelligent decisions. If you want to be considered for funding, you need to be willing and able to give proof of your credibility. If you have strong reservations about sharing this information—and there may be legitimate reasons—then withdraw the proposal. Never act as though the foundation is at fault for requesting it. As in all other funding interactions, this is a voluntary relationship. At any time before formal commitments are made, either party can decide that the fit is inappropriate and pull out.

This is not to say that there may be unreasonable demands placed on you or even just bad treatment. When this happens, or when it appears to happen, you need to make some decisions. First, determine whether this is the case. Foundation staff often find themselves under pressures and demands internal to the organization that, for numerous reasons, must remain invisible to you. Often what appears to you to be sheer obstructionism or perversity on the staff member's part might be her or his best efforts to overcome internal objections to funding your project or internal management issues. For this reason, it may make sense to give your program officer the benefit of the doubt. If you are puzzled or disturbed by what is going on, ask. Be tactful, and listen to what is being said and what is not being said. The fact that the program officer is spending the time to work with you on these issues should itself tell you something. If there were no interest in funding your project, it would be much easier simply to tell you, and there are numerous ways to do that and reasons to do so. As a rule of thumb, the willingness of someone from the foundation to work with you on your proposal is a positive sign.

At the same time, you never should become presumptuous. There are too many variables that cannot be controlled. Always remember that foundations, and their representatives, should be treated as you would any other potential funder—respectfully considerately, and seriously. And as with any other funder, it is prudent to end negotiations politely when it becomes obvious that the interests of the two of you are too disparate.

After Approval

After your proposal is approved, you probably will receive an unofficial notification from your program officer, followed by the official notice from the foundation. A letter thanking the program officer working with you undoubtedly is in order. Additionally, the official notification should be read carefully. Sign any items as requested and return them. You also should note carefully all reporting dates, and work the time for making the reports into your organization's schedule.

Although the nature of required reports varies from foundation to foundation, most expect both program and financial reports. When these are due also varies according to the foundation and the length of the grant. If you are unsure of the foundation's specific requirements and needs, ask. Your future relationship with this funder may depend both on how well you fulfill the purpose of the grant and how responsible you are.

Program reports should be honest, straightforward, and fairly detailed; they should not become burdensome reading for the program officer. Financials must be correct, detailed, and easily understandable and organized according to the way in which you structured the proposed budget. Make sure, therefore, that the budget presented with the proposal is aligned with your organization's financial reporting formats.

All reports should be truthful, correct, and submitted in a timely manner. If the project has experienced some difficulties, these should be explained and detailed in the report. Reports should be an honest and substantive relating of what you have accomplished with the foundation's support. Where appropriate, you should explain why certain elements may be lagging, why others have problems, and what you are learning from both your successes and your difficulties.

Although financials are important, they usually are important for reasons other than those that people expect: to prevent fraud and corruption. They are a powerful indicator of an organization's overall administrative health. Indecipherable, incorrect, and inadequate financial reports tell a great deal about how an organization is managed, and although this does not necessarily reflect the power of its work, they can say much about how long the program may be working. Bad financials tell others about the overall health of the organization and need to be treated seriously for that reason.

Communication with the foundation should extend beyond formal, scheduled reports. Certain key events may take place about which your program officer should be informed. Make sure this is done in a timely manner. Where appropriate, provide the opportunity for site visits if the program officer desires them, and make sure that you give her or him sufficient notice. Do not be disturbed if the program officer declines to attend. Similarly, although copies of most newspaper articles, promotional events, and so forth should be included in your reports, a particularly important notice of your work should be sent separately to the program officer for her or his notice.

During the course of the grant period, changes undoubtedly will occur. Budget lines may cost more or less than anticipated, for example, or schedules may move more slowly or quickly. You might need to adjust to these realities. Most foundations have procedures for making such adjustments. Make sure you follow them. You made the budget and wrote the proposal; the foundation did not. It agreed, however, to give you money based on what you said. If you want to change something, request the change in advance, explain why it is necessary, and await the foundation's answer.

Good communication is not the solution to everything, but it can prevent many problems and misunderstandings. In working with foundations, regular and honest communication is imperative. It is much easier to prevent problems than to try to solve them after the fact. You need to demonstrate that you are a responsible and credible partner in all of your interactions. The foundation needs to respect your organization and its mission. If either party fails to meet these obligations, then it is legitimate to withdraw. Such an action, however, must be taken only after careful consideration. Often what you may see as a foundation's disregard for your vision may in fact be a more clear-headed understanding of reality. For this reason, take the negotiations seriously, always remembering that if it does not work this time, there always is another project and another year.

Readings
Blum, Laurie. (1993). *The Complete Guide to Getting a Grant: How to Turn Your Ideas into Dollars.* New York: Poseidon Press.

Brewer, Ernest W. (1998). *Finding Funding: Grantwriting from Start to Finish, Including Project Management and Internet Use.* Thousand Oaks, Calif.: Corwin Press.

Council on Foundations. (1992). *The Inclusive Community: A Handbook for Managing Diversity in Community Foundations.* Washington, D.C.: Council on Foundations.

Ferguson, Jacqueline. (1993). *The Grants Development Kit.* Alexandria, Va.: Capitol Publications.

Foundation Center. (Annual). *The Foundation Directory.* New York: Foundation Center.

Foundation Center. (Annual). *Grant$ for Community Development and Housing.* New York: Foundation Center.

Foundation Center. (Annual). *Grant$ for Religion, Religious Welfare, and Religious Education.* New York: Foundation Center.

Foundation Center. (Annual). *Grant$ for Social Services.* New York: Foundation Center.

Foundation Center. (Annual). *Grant$ for the Homeless.* New York: Foundation Center.

Geever, Jane C. (1993). *The Foundation Center's Guide to Proposal Writing.* New York: Foundation Center.

Gershowitz, Michael V. (1993). *Effective Evaluation: A Systematic Approach for Grantseekers and Project Managers.* Alexandria, Va.: Capitol Publications.

Golden, Susan L. (1997). *Secrets of Successful Grantsmanship: A Guerilla Guide to Raising Money.* San Francisco: Jossey-Bass.

Gray, Sandra Trice (ed.). (1993). *Leadership Is Everyday Ethics: Key Ethical Questions for Grantmakers and Grantseekers.* Washington, D.C.: Independent Sector.

Hartsook, Robert F. (1998). *Closing That Gift: How to Be Successful 99 percent of the Time.* Wichita, Kans.: ASR Philanthropic Publishers.

Magat, Richard (ed.). (1989). *An Agile Servant: Community Leadership by Community Foundations.* New York: Foundation Center.

McIlnay, Dennis P. (1998). *How Foundations Work: What Grantseekers Need to Know About the Many Faces of Foundations.* San Francisco: Jossey-Bass.

New, Cheryl Carter. (1998). *Grantseeker's Toolkit: A Comprehensive Guide to Finding Funding.* New York: Wiley.

Nichols, Judith E. (1995). *Growing from Good to Great: Positioning Your Fundraising Efforts for Big Gains.* Chicago: Bonus Books.

Robinson, Andy. (1996). *Grassroots Grants: An Activists Guide to Proposal Writing.* Berkeley: Chardon Press.

Ruskin, Karen B. (1995). *Grantwriting, Fundraising, and Partnerships: Strategies That Work!* Thousand Oaks, Calif.: Corwin Press.

Sturtevant, William T. (1997). *The Artful Journey: Cultivating and Soliciting the Major Gift.* Chicago: Bonus Books.

Van Rotterdam, Ingrid. (1995). *Building Foundation Partnerships: The Basics of Foundation Fundraising and Proposal Writing.* Toronto: Canadian Centre for Philanthropy.

PART 3

Moving Beyond Basic Needs

PART 7

Moving Beyond
Basic Needs

CHAPTER 11

Community-Based Economic Development

Eric Clay
Elliott Wright

Community development is not a service that can be delivered—by government, church, or any social agency—yet it is one of the most productive means of dealing with hard-core poverty and neighborhood disintegration. Community development is a deliberate process by which the assets of a community and the resources it can attract are marshaled and multiplied in ways that rebuild local economies, provide affordable housing, promote health and wholeness, replace decaying infrastructures, and instill hope within families and individuals on the edge of despair. Both the strength of the concept and the track record of community development attract outside resources, including those of government and business, but community development achieves its potential only when the energy that drives and controls it comes from local residents and institutions. "Community," after all, is the condition of people with common loyalties or location.

The term *community development* has many programmatic applications. In this chapter it primarily means community-based economic development (CED), which, as practiced, includes business and job development, housing development, and the initiation of social programs (such as health, education, and child care) required to ensure a stable community. In this respect, community development embraces social service delivery while projecting a broader vision of community welfare. CED need not be limited to poorer communities. Its strategies work at many economic levels. This chapter, however, focuses on CED in poorer areas because that is where it is most frequently pursued, especially by faith-based developers.

Not all development intended to help a community is community based. Economic policy debates are marked by heady disagreement over the locus of control and the primary players in effective community revitalization. Some partisans would deemphasize local initiative in favor of regional or national policies. Although aware of this controversy, we view community-based CED as a major asset in achieving the goals of broad-based development. (For the policy arguments, see Boston and Ross, 1998.)

Faith-based actors—both individuals and institutions—are among the most productive initiators and managers of sustained community economic development. This often takes the form of congregational action by individuals committed to their communities. From the religious perspective, CED is a form of community ministry distinguished by its inclusivity. It looks beyond a particular religious constituency, encompassing the whole of a specific area; it has no one theology but may profoundly affect the beliefs and actions of individuals and religious groups.

No one knows the extent of faith-based economic development. The number of church- or religion-related community development corporations (CDCs) is in the hundreds, and church-based credit unions exceed the number of CDCs. In addition, religious groups relate to scores of CED operations launched by others.

Examples of Faith-Based Community Development

There are many ways of undertaking faith-based development. The one any organization chooses will depend greatly on its size, gifts, social location, and experience.

Comprehensive, Coordinated Efforts

First African Methodist Episcopal Church (FAME) of Los Angeles, the oldest African American church in the city, chartered in 1872, epitomizes the large urban church—often black—with an aggressive commitment to community development. FAME has created a network of ministries, some are controlled directly by the church and others, with separate but affiliated legal status, are concerned with virtually every social, economic and spiritual dimension of life. The congregation operates under the motto "First to Serve" and expects all 12,500 members to take an active role in one or more of the community efforts. FAME has a clerical staff of twenty-five and numerous lay employees and volunteers, but its success in CED comes from its allegiance to and confidence in an area immediately west of downtown Los Angeles. The CED ministries of FAME touch the lives of thousands of individuals and families.

FAME has a large and varied number of development partners, including local, state, and federal government, corporations, foundations, and other religious organizations. Indeed, partnership is an essential component of community development. The need to find and retain financial partners is a creative challenge to churches, synagogues, and mosques operating in the new global economy, an economy that affects both the rich and the poor. The housing and business development units of FAME constitute community development corporations.

La Casa of Goshen is far smaller than FAME but no less determined to multiply the assets of a once predominantly rural area of northern Indiana. Organized in 1970 by an ecumenical coalition, La Casa's original focus was on housing, especially for former migrant workers who had settled in the vicinity. Today this CDC builds and manages housing, equips persons for home ownership, promotes business development, provides the financial literacy training required for gainful employment, and prepares immigrants for citizenship. It also manages individual development accounts (IDAs), a relatively new financial tool somewhat like the individual retirement account (IRA). Lower-income people contribute to IDAs, held at local financial institutions, and receive matching deposits from private and public sources. IDAs can be used to buy a first home, to capitalize a small business, or for education or job training. La Casa also offers direct social services to a varied constituency, which, between 1991 and 1997, was 60 percent white, 36 percent Hispanic, and 4 percent members of other groups. The thirty-year-old CDC continues to enjoy active support from some twenty churches, which serve as an informal means of communications for its work and provide between $35,000 and $40,000 to its annual core budget. Strong support comes from the Mennonite congregations and institutions in the region.

Frankfort, a community in northeastern Philadelphia, was once a thriving industrial area of single- and two-story row houses, a local business district, and many churches. Economic and demographic changes over a thirty-year period eroded both the financial base and the spirit of Frankfort. Homes and storefronts sagged, "crack houses" moved in, and industrial property stood abandoned. The mid-1980s saw a turnaround sparked by five small to mid-sized United Methodist congregations that banded together to do work they could not accomplish alone. The Frankfort Group Ministry was the catalyst for what is today the Frankfort Plan, an aggressive, interfaith, interracial redevelopment effort sponsored by seventy civic, corporate, and educational groups dedicated to a stable, prosperous community. The Frankfort Plan includes housing rehabilitation, new home construction, mortgage and financial services, business development, and partnerships with local medical, educational, and law enforcement agencies. One priority is keeping the business area clean and inviting, filled with well-stocked stores and necessary community services.

More Discrete Approaches

Faith-based development may address a single issue, such as housing or job training, perhaps on a time-limited or project basis, or an organization may take on a small piece of a larger program. For example, the Downtown Presbyterian Church of Nashville, Tennessee, is an IDA manager. Congregations may band together to undertake a discrete project in collaboration with others. Five churches and a community center in Omaha, Nebraska, worked for seven years to build five duplex units and proved to themselves that they could take on larger tasks. Such innovative, incremental steps can be critical in achieving comprehensive development. Religious organizations often collaborate with secular CDCs on particular projects. The Community Development Corp. of Kansas City has a long history as the builder and financial packager for both faith-based housing and commercial and industrial development in the Missouri city. This CDC recruited the Black Ministers

Union for assistance in raising the initial capital to develop an abandoned property into a commercial shopping center, the first new commercial development in the neighborhood in twenty years. It not only created new jobs but also increased neighborhood pride.

A Movement with Precedents

Community development, as commonly used, names a movement born in the 1960s as localized beachheads of the civil rights campaign. Bolstered but not created by federal war on poverty and Great Society programs, community developers initially sought solutions to acute housing needs in urban and rural areas, along with ways to expand the political capacity of the economically marginal. Some historical accounts see community development since the 1960s in terms of federal policies and programs. That version gets the cart before the horse. Almost forty years ago, William W. Biddle, a clearheaded social analyst, correctly saw that federal programs under the Office of Economic Opportunity, a federal agency, needed the tools and visions of community development. Indeed, he saw the activities of the mid-1960s as the rediscovery of the effectiveness of local initiative (Biddle and Biddle, 1965).

Some religious institutions served as advocates or developers in those years. A groundswell of religious involvement came in the mid-1980s as churches stepped forward to fill the gap created by Reagan administration cutbacks in federal antipoverty funds. Major philanthropic foundations absorbed some of the financial shock and provided assistance in setting up private national and regionalized intermediaries to help local groups finance and professionally manage projects. These intermediaries, such as the Local Initiative Support Corporation (LISC) and the Enterprise Foundation, continue as major funders and as sources of technical assistance for local developers. Another boon to community-based CED in that period was increased implementation of the Community Reinvestment Act (CRA), which requires banks to invest in the areas they serve. This legislation went a long way toward eradicating redlining, the illegal refusal to make loans in certain geographic areas. To their surprise, banks generally have found that equal opportunity lending is good business.

Given the vast number of religious institutions in the United States, the percentage engaged in CED remains small; still, faith-based development is increasingly common and gaining wider recognition. The National Congress for Community Economic Development, a trade association for CDCs, began an emphasis on faith-based projects in the early 1990s and today has a sustained faith-based program engaged in research and training. The Enterprise Foundation has a faith-based component, as does the U.S. Department of Housing and Urban Development (HUD). The Christian Community Development Association (CCDA), which has evangelical Protestant roots, attracts upward of three thousand people to its annual conferences. And some national and regional church agencies have CED desks. Perhaps most significant, faith-based development encompasses the theological and denominational spectrum. Although African American and Roman Catholic institutions predominate, no segment of American religion is absent from the CED scene. Similarly, a variety of social and theological motives propel this broad-based interest.

For generations, especially in times of great spiritual, social, and political transition, religious organizations have intervened in economic affairs on behalf of justice and to reduce the vulnerability of the weakest. In the United States, newly freed slaves, immigrant peoples, and frontier settlers sought community wholeness and formed new economic lives within the contexts of congregations.

Throughout the history of the United States, churches, synagogues, mosques, and temples have helped marginalized people understand changing social and political environments, thereby enabling them to act effectively and faithfully.

African American Church

That African American churches are in the forefront of CED today is hardly surprising. In the aftermath of slavery and subsequent exclusion from the white economy, African Americans formed credit institutions within their churches to strengthen economic control and productivity within their communities. As C. Eric Lincoln and Lawrence H. Mamiya write (1988), "Mutual aid or beneficial societies and churches were among the first social institutions created by black people. They often existed in symbiotic relationship." Some congregations also initiated businesses. In Baltimore following the Civil War, a black church financed a shipyard to counter discrimination and a racist two-tiered wage system in the shipbuilding industry. For more than twenty years, this church-backed shipyard built and sold small ships up and down the East Coast, until it failed in the severe economic depression of the 1890s. Direct business development by the African American Christian churches waned after the 1920s, although Muslim groups persisted in such efforts. Community development through the black church reemerged with the civil rights movement and its attention to economic justice and jobs.

Frontier Churches

Religious congregations reduced the social isolation, violence, and addictions spawned by the rugged life on the American frontier. Churches actively shaped the use of growing wealth and labor resources to promote education and voluntary aid to those in need. Congregations encouraged settlers to rub shoulders regardless of economic status. Ordained and lay leaders promoted the spiritual and material prosperity of their flocks through productive households, strong businesses, and useful education. By the mid-nineteenth century, many one-time frontier congregations found themselves in small cities. In such places, the religious influence shifted from matters of economic production to concern for justice in the distribution of wealth and welfare. In rural areas, progressive, evangelical populists, largely small farm owners, tenant farmers, and sharecroppers, initially both blacks and whites, persisted with an alternative agenda for democratic economic production. In opposition to the monopolies of railroads, local merchants, and large landholders, these farmers promoted producer-owned cooperatives. At odds with urbanization and mainstream modernization, race-baited by conservatives, and politically out-organized, the movement eventually fragmented into defensive localism and religious fundamentalism.

Countercurrent Intentional Communities

Nineteenth-century communes, such as Oneida, Amana, and the Shakers, often combined religious and economic principles. All the economically successful communes of the early and mid-nineteenth century started as cohesive religious communities. Their prosperity came from their ability to adapt social and economic roles to meet the range of caregiving and economic production necessary to sustain the community. Despite their failure in the face of consumer capitalism, their successes are still visible in design and manufactured goods. The legacy of the Amana colony continues to provide health care, services, and pensions for descendants of the original community. More important, these utopian experiments set precedents for an American-style blending of religion and economics.

Immigrant Religious Communities

Prior to and alongside government social services, Jewish, Catholic, and Protestant religious institutions provided funds to assist immigrant resettlement and develop networks for job contacts. They founded independent agencies to provide newcomers with much needed social services and educate them in the language, mores, and skills needed for success in the United States. Religion saw to the widows and the orphans and organized burial societies. Church-based credit unions flourished in many ethnic Catholic parishes beginning in the late nineteenth century. Various Catholic, Jewish, and Lutheran brotherhoods served both social and economic purposes. The introduction of immigration quotas in the 1920s, substantial assimilation, a shift to government services in the 1930s, and post–World War II economic growth reduced the need for many of these efforts. However, with relaxed immigration laws in the 1960s and 1970s, these roles are now played by newer immigrant groups, such as Muslims, Buddhists, and Hindus.

Motives for Faith-Based Development

The reasons for the expansion of faith-based development today are as complex as a housing development package with fifteen funders. Yet the experience of the last thirty years provides insights into motives that can be instructive to those who are considering faith-based CED as a ministry option. Some motives reflect the CED movement in general.

Changing Local Economies

Economic and demographic shifts over the past half-century left many localities vulnerable. Large enterprises merged, closed, or relocated, so that communities no longer could depend on steady employment and local financial commitment. Affluent and middle-class Americans increasingly moved to the suburbs in the 1950s. Jobs became more specialized, leaving poor, often jobless Americans in the inner cities, to be joined by immigrants whose numbers grew again with liberalized immigration policies adopted in the 1960s. More recently, global markets have made economic development decisions less sensitive to community assets and needs as production facilities migrated toward cheaper labor markets. Community development addresses such issues.

Changing Role of Government

A recurrent theme of American public life is the restructuring of government. By the 1960s, old economic patterns supported by government policies no longer worked in many communities, urban and rural, and especially those with large minority populations. In the 1970s, the failure of large governmental assistance programs (such as the war on poverty) to improve communities significantly raised questions about the state's capacity to manage social welfare. Community development is one long-range response to economic crisis, and the issue of the government's role and nonprofit developers has moved to the forefront at the grassroots level.

Governments directly manage fewer community improvement programs than they did in the mid-1980s, but the federal government and the states remain powerful players. Federal, state, and local authorities have become the central policymakers and the monitors of more local actors; millions of tax dollars still go into social service and CDC programs, but increasingly in the form of block grants, tax credits, or subsidies channeled to nonprofit sponsors. Every community development organization, secular or religious, comes into contact with government, often in its role as a funder and always as regulator, in the form of zoning ordinances, construction codes, and service vouchers.

In the 1990s, governments discovered the value and success of faith-based development and cleared away some obstacles to their participation in general funding programs. This is likely a mixed blessing. Dealing with government without being overwhelmed may be a daunting task for many religious institutions with little experience with the state. At the same time, religion has a good history of standing up to secular power and may serve the whole of CED well by offering a constant reminder that community development must be rooted in communities, not in government programs. Faith-based development can help hold government to being just another partner in the CED process.

Competent Private and Nonprofit Actors

The impressive track records of CDCs and similar community-based entities, some pioneered under religious auspices, have encouraged other faith-based developers. All effective CDCs are local organizers and mediators, identifying the resources at hand and using them to leverage broad-based buy-in to a prosperous future for a locality and its residents. CDCs moderate the effects of change and channel community dreams in the following ways:

- Cultivating relationships between community groups and external economic actors
- Fostering mutual understanding and a shared mission among participants
- Promoting community-based ownership or investments in local enterprises
- Encouraging continuous job training and educational options
- Developing community-controlled and owner-occupied housing

A CDC is a particular kind of legal entity. It is a distinct not-for-profit organization, known as a 501(c)(3) corporation in U.S. tax law. A simple majority of the directors are from the community; that is, the whole board cannot consist of the deacons of a church, but nothing prevents community members from having ties to the initial organizer, which could be a congregation. Religious organizations usually do not become CDCs; rather, they organize separate corporations that move both the financial and legal obligations a step away from the parent institution. A church-founded

CDC has its own legal integrity and is subject to various federal and state auditing and reporting requirements generally not applied to churches. For example, a faith-based CDC must file an annual information statement (a Form 990) with the Internal Revenue Service, a requirement from which churches (and some other categories of religious organizations) are exempt.

An Asset Approach

The CED movement has honed effective tools and adopted creative ways for understanding the potential for real community revitalization. The first step is a thorough, realistic look at the community. Who is there? What is the economic picture? The educational picture? What human, financial, and institutional resources can be mobilized?

Communities that wish to remain viable must look searchingly at the resources they may be able to control or influence—for example, their unique geographic location in relation to specific markets, the presence of natural resources, transportation, and the availability of skilled or skill-ready workers. Is the local or regional economic strategy that of mainstreaming the jobless or underemployed into the prevailing system, or is room left for alternative forms of individual or group prosperity, such as cooperative or worker-owned businesses? Are community residents equipped and organized to have a major voice in community planning? If not, how can that be accomplished?

The way in which these questions are asked and answered can make an enormous difference in the success of community development. If community assessment, often called mapping, is only the compiling of small and large needs, the process of development can be short-circuited. Needs assessment too often becomes a list of impossible tasks. The best CED practice begins with asset inventories. Obvious needs call one to the awareness of assets. Mary Nelson tells a story of the early days of Bethel New Life, the Lutheran church-based CDC she heads in Chicago: "We asked ourselves about assets and found that the only thing we had plenty of was garbage. Our first business enterprise, naturally, was recycling."

The Asset Based Community Development Institute at Northwestern University in Evanston, Illinois, has published excellent materials on how to map and assess the assets of particular communities. (See also Chapter Three in this book.)

A Partnerships Perspective

The rhetoric of partnership has come to dominate descriptions of almost all productive or potentially productive relationships—public and private, profit and nonprofit—between any distinct parties regardless of the degrees of equality or inequality. Some of this usage is both glib and faddish. Yet genuine community development cannot be a one-party paradigm, and CED has proved the effectiveness of a collaborative approach, even if partnerships are often tenuous and unequal and sometimes temporary. Not every organization contains all the skills and abilities necessary to undertake a program. Partnerships provide the opportunity to bring in organizations with the necessary skills, especially financial and technical knowledge. For example, numerous cooperating parties are needed to establish a modest housing unit for the disabled or to initiate a job-training program: community groups, government, financiers (maybe a long list of them), auditors, contractors, unions, inspectors, managers, and, most likely, a CDC.

A new faith-based developer needs to start out thinking of partnership as a basic mode of operation, with community-based organizations already at work in the neighborhood the most likely partners. An important first step in starting out should be the identification of other local CED programs, which should be located during the mapping of community assets. A community can have—and some do have—too many CDCs. No would-be faith-based developer should start drafting project plans and contacting potential funders until it understands local and regional development actors. Turf wars rarely add value to the community development agenda. Unique approaches and creative assessment of old issues can renew existing efforts and produce new ones. If no CED programs exist, a congregation or religious organization may have an obligation to become the initiator, especially if it is the only stable and trusted entity in the community.

CED partnerships, however, are not without problems. Tensions flare up, sometimes over who gets the credit or because some partners, such as churches, move slowly in decision making while others, such as business enterprises, move quickly. Monitoring and managing the differences between partners and striving to secure equitable results are essential strategic tasks in community-based economic development. Once religious organizations commit to community development in partnership with their neighbors, they can become substantial voices for realistic, honest partnerships.

Moral and Religious Mandates

One of the key community roles of religious groups is to raise moral issues. The first CDCs in the 1960s quite literally were born in church basements because organized religions were among the first to see and protest injustices and inequalities as population patterns and economic conditions changed. Decent, affordable housing, businesses that contribute to the community, and health and educational programs are moral matters. Knowing a community and its assets, seeing the injustices it suffers, and raising a moral voice can be dangerous to both the complacent and the solicitous. Knowledge and morality introduce accountability, a big issue when a religious institution takes on community development.

Accountability means that religious institutions must assess themselves and their roles in a community and their use of resources. Do members live nearby, or are they commuters? What are their ties—kinship, friendship, culture, business, or community service—with the neighborhood? What economic and material resources does a religious institution have, such as underused space, undeveloped property, and investment portfolios?

A moral stance in community development means keeping the community in mind at every stage of the process. Some faith-based organizations alienate their communities by adopting social service attitudes that treat issues only as problems and people as clients. Some mistakenly think CED will fill empty pews. Others are bedazzled by the possibility of realizing a profit from CED. Some faith-based CED enterprises do make money; sometimes it makes sense for a CED or a congregation to set up a for-profit corporation. However, profitability, if any, usually comes down the road. It cannot and should not be the primary motivation. More creative efforts understand that community-based development is an opportunity to revitalize lives and communities at the grassroots. Neither social services nor community development automatically builds religious membership or fills church bank accounts. There may be an interrelationship between congregational growth and community improvement, but this will unfold slowly, if at all. More important, as religious institutions act as moral partners within their communities, they make their faith more relevant to themselves and others.

Religion addresses the formation of whole persons and whole communities. Its context is unapologetically theological. One challenge for religious organizations setting forth in CED is to maintain a mature approach to faith, to the theological component, as they undertake exciting new activities. Maintaining fidelity to a particular theological tradition and spiritual practice is an obligation that anchors both religious organizations and persons of faith. This means holding onto distinctive forms of worship and celebration, music and singing, study, prayer, and reflection. Religious concerns begin with a person as a member of a household and extend to her or his participation in the cosmos, with attention paid to all intervening steps and structures. Faith is a way of life. Faith-based groups must therefore learn how to form relationships with government and business without relinquishing this special function. (See Chapter Two for further discussion of this issue.)

A parallel obligation, found in most religions, is the need to relate with equity and justice to those who are not like oneself. Community-based development done under the rubric of faith dramatizes the need to balance these obligations in a pluralistic society. We have noted that "being a good neighbor" is the most common theological motivation for faith-based development. Some neighbors may seek God in different ways, or not at all, even as the religious developer works out his or her own faith. At the same time, testimonies by other participants often indicate their own growth in the knowledge of God or a deepening of their particular life commitments through community economic development activities. Persons engage in community issues for a variety of reasons, and that engagement triggers personal growth and discovery, often in unexpected ways.

A Diversity of Goals

The pragmatic goals of faith-based development programs are not always honed in textbook fashion. Over time, specific components, whether comprehensive or discrete, take on particular emphases within the framework of the overall assets and needs of the community. We examine three common sets of goals, some with natural overlaps.

Strengthening Families and Households

This goal especially appeals to religious groups that understand the importance of nurturance and cooperation in domestic life. An emphasis on households and families often animates the concern of faith-based CDCs engaged in child care as an economic enterprise (sometimes forming home child care businesses). CED designed to strengthen families sometimes starts in a social service context. Educational and mentoring programs often pave the way for job training and career development. Faith-based participation in the welfare-to-work efforts mandated by the federal welfare reform law of 1996 is triggered by commitments to productive, secure households.

The first business founded by 12th Street Missionary Baptist Church in Detroit was a preschool and child care program. Success in these enterprises led to confidence in the congregation's ability to address homelessness, housing, and, eventually, real estate and small business development. This expansion does not hide their continuing emphasis on home ownership for families, access to local jobs, and the presence of locally owned businesses to sustain those families. The first director of the preschool program, currently the director of the Michigan Neighborhood Partnership, maintains that "economic development begins with strong families," whether developing a neighborhood or a nation.

Enlarging Community Resources

For other groups, priority may fall on the identification or creation of broadly available community resources. Can housing and commercial property be redeveloped? Can vacant retail space be filled with profitable small businesses—markets, dry cleaners, auto garages—thereby stabilizing the area and bringing services closer to the residents? How can community groups work with banks and other financial institutions to equalize access to financial products for which they may qualify? (The Federal Community Reinvestment

Act provides leverage in this objective.) External links to economic and technical resources can expand greatly the development capacity of any area, but outside assistance is most valuable when community associations help determine how it is deployed.

Congregations may discover they have resources that can serve the wider community. For example, perhaps congregational buildings and land can be developed or redeveloped to serve community educational, housing, or economic purposes. A Lutheran church in Baltimore wondered what to do with a huge old gymnasium it no longer needed or wanted. Today that space houses senior citizens in a beautiful complex of apartments. The vacant lot owned by a Baptist church in Austin, Texas, is now occupied by a community building with a day care center and business incubator. Faith-based CDCs sometimes attract generous donations from landowners holding property they no longer can use productively. Pyramid Corp., a church-founded CDC in Houston, was given an old shopping center, which today is a center for commercial, social service, and community activities.

Expanding Community Control

Another goal may be the promotion of community-controlled institutions and assets. These efforts may produce community-based health care clinics, locally owned and operated businesses and industries, credit unions, community banks and other financial institutions or community-owned, cooperative, or resident-owned housing. A variation on the credit union or community bank is the Collective Banking Group of Prince George's County, Maryland. This ecumenical collaboration (currently with about 130 member churches) began with partnerships with four area banks, which agreed to tailor financial products to the member churches, give the best available rates to people in the collective, and contribute to a scholarship fund. A church-related CDC is the lead agency in bringing the first super-supermarket to the Harlem neighborhood in New York City. Nueva Esperanza, the Philadelphia CDC linked to forty Hispanic churches, owns a youth camp and aims its sights toward the formation of a community-owned senior high school and junior college. Speaking of the large number of high school dropouts in the neighborhood, the Reverend Luis

Cortes, director of Nueva, said, "We need a school for them . . . a place we own and run, so they can get a high school diploma and two years of college, and then finish up at Temple, Drexel and the University of Pennsylvania."

Types of Faith-Based Actors

The primary types of religious actors in community development are congregations, ecumenical and interfaith coalitions, noncongregation religious organizations, religious jurisdictions, and individual religious actors (see Table 11.1). We use the word *actors* here rather than *institutions* or *organizations* because some of the major forces are individuals. In all types, the enthusiastic support of leaders—clergy and lay—is essential, but may not be the force that maintains a CED program.

Congregations

Congregation refers to a church, parish, synagogue, mosque, temple, or any other local unit of the multiplicity of religions found in the United States. These range from huge operations, such as FAME in Los Angeles and Allen Temple AME Church in New York City, to single-project programs, such as those undertaken by a small church in rural Kansas. The assumption is made in CED that any congregation has some degree of interest in the community in which it functions or where its house of worship is located, even if the members are scattered throughout the metropolitan region or commute from the suburbs back into an inner-city neighborhood.

Ecumenical and Interfaith Coalition

These groupings may be formal or informal. Notable examples include the Genesis Fund, a loan program started by a group of small town churches in Maine, and the Ministerial Interfaith Association of Harlem, an association of New York City congregations and clergy that banded together initially for community political organizing and moved on to become a full-service CDC-type of operation. The Michigan Neighborhood Partnership in Detroit is a strong model for how a group of churches banded together,

Table 11.1. Types and Styles of Religious Involvement in Community-Based Development.

Types of Religious Institutions	Congregation	Ecumenical and Interfaith Coalition	Religious Organization (noncongregational)	Religious Jurisdictions	Individual Religious Leader
Styles of Involvement					
Advocate-Convenor					
Enabler-Facilitator					
Community Organizer					
Resource Provider					
Development Partner					
Developer					

Source: Table developed by Elliott Wright and Mark Weinheimer. Some terms were suggested by a report on "Religious Institutions as Actors in Community-Based Development," published in 1988 by SEEDCO.

sought secular partners, and launched an aggressive program that now involves dozens of churches in comprehensive community development.

Noncongregational Religious Organizations

Some of these organizations are community centers, such as Grace Hill Neighborhood, linked to the Episcopal church in St. Louis. Grace Hill is actually more than a single-location center; it has multiple sites engaged in both community development and social service delivery. Bethany House Christian Service Center, a rural Kentucky facility founded by the Glenmary Order of the Roman Catholic church, has played an important role in equipping people for home ownership without itself becoming a builder. Some examples of this type represent religious-secular collaborations, such as a church-labor coalition in Waterbury, Connecticut, which successfully launched a worker-owned health care company.

Regional Religious Jurisdictions

This type includes religious units such as dioceses, associations, synods, presbyteries, and conferences. Some engage directly in CDCs or act as sponsors for grassroots CDC projects. Many diocesan branches of Catholic Charities sponsor CDCs. Religious jurisdictions more often provide financial support, administrative services, or personnel. The Episcopal Diocese of Michigan has an extensive program in community development and economic justice. Several other Episcopal dioceses sponsor CED revolving loan funds, as do some denominations at the national level.

Individuals, Lay and Ordained

Individual initiative can be pivotal to faith-based development. Some CDCs built on faith energy may never have a direct, legal link to religious institutions yet have programmatic ties to many. The New Community Corp. of Newark, New Jersey, is probably the best-known, and perhaps the largest, faith-based CDC in the country, yet is not church related in a formal sense. The founder was Monsignor William Lindner, who started out in a parish but built a program that related to virtually ever church of every denomination and racial group in a large target area. The Reverend Judd Mayfield of Belhaven, North Carolina, played a similar role in the late 1980s in setting up Community Developers of Beaufort-Hyde. Eddie Edwards, founder of Joy of Jesus in Detroit, was a concerned layperson when he began CED work. He later sought ministerial training and ordination and became instrumental in a community partnership among twenty-five churches, mosques, and synagogues. One of the largest programs mentors disadvantaged youth from early childhood through college.

Styles of Engagement

Just as each religious group brings its own theological mandates and expectations for the future to community development, particular religious organizations promote unique habits of mind and select various styles of engagement. These are not necessarily defined by denominational tradition or theology, although polity (church government) can make a difference in the types of projects undertaken. Baptist churches, which have local autonomy, for example, may find it easier than a parish of a highly centralized denomination to negotiate a housing loan.

Decisions to pursue projects may be determined by particular opportunities or crises. A Methodist church in Northport, Alabama, entered a long-term housing partnership with a community action agency and a Baptist congregation because a lay leader serendipitously heard about grants intended to encourage such faith-based development. Several churches in south-central Los Angeles responded to the 1992 riots with community development efforts. Claiming specific roles that fit the faith-based organization's interests and abilities and contribute to the efforts of others is a key step in responsible community development.

Fundamental to the success of any of the styles is a willingness to risk failure and to learn from that failure if it happens. Another necessary risk is that of controversy. Community ministries of all kinds must be willing to hear from the community, even when the message is critical and even strident. The ability to hear and heed "backtalk" is essential in community-based development.

Six styles of CED involvement, neither mutually exclusive nor weighted in terms of their worth to a community, are common among the types of religious institutions: advocate-convener, enabler-facilitator, community organizer, resource provider, development partner, and developer. This arrangement does indicate degree of engagement. An advocate for community development is not as engaged as a developer, for example, although a particular group or individual can become more or less engaged over time. Some groups and individuals are involved in all simultaneously.

Advocate-Convener

These actors become aware of housing or job possibilities and needs, take public stands in favor of CED, and may even bring people or institutions together to pool assets or work on common concerns. Faith groups usually enjoy high credibility in poor and minority communities and can be markedly successful in these roles. Advocacy and convening provide valuable contributions to development even if the involvement of the organization or individual goes no further, although serving as an advocate-convener often leads to a more active role. Communities of Shalom, a community revitalization approach linked to the United Methodist church but ecumenical in many places, begins with the convening of persons over a period of months to look at the assets and potentials of an area. After several weeks of Shalom interaction, a group of business leaders and public officials in Columbia, South Carolina, began to wonder how they could rid the community of an abandoned housing project. Their advocacy and convening of the right people got the job done.

Enabler-Facilitator

Creating the conditions suitable for the development of programs and projects by others is another contribution to CED. This may entail the formation of a community action plan, clearing the barriers to small business development, or providing office space to a new CDC. Without ever getting involved in construction, the Bethany House Christian Center, Olive Hill, Kentucky, prepared two dozen families for home ownership through a state-assisted program carried out by a nonprofit builder. The Naugatuck Valley Project, a coalition of churches and labor unions in Waterbury,

Connecticut, facilitated the start-up of a worker-owned home health care cooperative.

Community Organizer

Organizing equips individuals, families, and communities for major roles in all aspects of their life: social, political, economic, and spiritual. Some organizing is essential for community economic development because it depends in large measure on local initiative. Community organizing can be home grown and casual, such as that followed in the Northport housing collaboration. At kitchen tables, the people themselves defined how the housing rehabilitation project would operate in their community. Community organizing also can be highly structured, multifaceted, often confrontational, and may or may not have community development as a goal. It may be linked to one of several national or regional community organizing networks, such as the Industrial Areas Foundation (IAF) or the Gamaliel Foundation. IAF has become a major producer of housing, usually called Nehemiah Houses (in such places as New York, Philadelphia, Memphis, and Dallas). Because styles differ, formal community organizing and formal community development may have little programmatic overlap. On the day-to-day community level, however, CED will not get far without a foundation in the lives and aspirations of the residents. Given the strong religious connections of many individuals, religious groups are ideally suited for the job of organizing.

Resource Provider

Resources include money, real estate, leadership, and volunteers. In large congregations, such as FAME in Los Angeles, Windsor Village United Methodist in Houston, and Abyssinian Baptist in New York City, much of the money needed to form CDCs came from the members or church-related affiliates. Small- to medium-sized churches in Birmingham, Alabama, and Memphis, Tennessee, banded together to found community development credit unions, which become community assets. Churches sometimes divert money from building or organ funds to assist community development start-ups.

Relatively poor churches may be able to access funds available from regional or national levels of their denominations. Dozens of national religious organizations make alternative investments in community development financial institutions (CDFIs), such as community development loan funds. Orders of Roman Catholic women are especially active in the alternative investment movement. The Roman Catholic Church and Presbyterian Church (USA) have special funds to assist local CED and community organizing, and several Episcopal dioceses have CED revolving loan funds.

Volunteers are valuable resources in some CED projects, but not all. They are essential to the work of Habitat for Humanity, whether in stick construction housing, often built by volunteers and the sweat equity of the eventual owner, or in assembling and erecting modular units. Volunteers may be key to equipping persons for home ownership, providing job mentoring, or drafting business plans for potential entrepreneurs. Volunteers are used less often in housing rehabilitation or construction done by CDCs, but even in these instances, congregational members may help to paint or dig pipelines. Because of construction codes, union rules, and insurance liability, however, some CED builders do not want volunteers on site.

Development Partner

This style may be especially appealing to religious entities because it usually reduces the need for extensive, up-front technical experience in CED. Congregational-CDC partnerships have an impressive track record. The productive collaboration between churches and the Community Development Corporation of Kansas City already has been mentioned. In Cincinnati, more than a dozen African American congregations in the Walnut Hills area joined together with a local CDC to build and rehabilitate houses. The Memphis Leadership Foundation helps a broad range of congregations achieve their goals in affordable housing in their communities. Six congregations in Indianapolis work with the Mapleton–Fall Creek Neighborhood Association to stabilize housing and the general economic picture in an area north of downtown.

Developer

A full-fledged community developer advocates, convenes, enables, organizes, forms partnerships, and undertakes development. It may also manage property or businesses. Faith-based developers are usually one or two legal steps removed from a church or religious institution, usually taking the form of an independent CDC or community housing corporation. As CDCs are technically free-standing nonprofits (called 501(c)(3) organizations in U.S. tax law). This means that all legal and financial records are distinct from those of the originating entity, perhaps a church. (See Chapter Nine for more information.) This separation has historically been required to apply for government funds. It also eases liability concerns and helps ensure community control. It does not remove the faith base or the religious connections in a theological sense. Proposals were heard in the late 1990s to make it easier for religious developers to access government dollars without setting up separate corporations.

Several faith-based, if legally separate, CDCs have been mentioned in this chapter: FAME Renaissance (Los Angeles), New Community Corp. (Newark, New Jersey), Bethel New Life (Chicago), Pyramid (Houston), Abyssinian (New York City), Nueva Esperanza (Philadelphia), La Casa (Goshen, Indiana), 12th Street Baptist (Detroit), and Community Developers of Beaufort-Hyde (North Carolina). None of these (or dozens of others) works in exactly the same way because they serve different communities with different assets. Some manage the housing they build and the businesses they start. Others sell the businesses and entrust real estate to professional managers. A number of faith-based CDCs offer social services; others do not. Their programs are very much determined by the assets and opportunities in the specific place where they operate.

The proliferation of faith-based CDCs is giving rise to a new kind of religious worker: the community development specialist. To some degree, this is one expression of growing CED efforts to identify and equip a new generation of CED professionals, a trend not universally applauded by those who think the best training for community developers lies in actually doing the work. However, the new faith-based specialists are often men and women who come from business, education, or other professions. Often they want to repay the communities that have supported them or to deepen and mature in their particular faith commitments.

While the support and vision of a pastor, rabbi, or imam can be central in convincing a religious institution to venture into community development, few clergy have the time or talent to manage community-based development, at least not alone. The truly visionary congregational leaders turn to professional or volunteer developers to carry the day-to-day responsibilities. They also do not try to contravene the essential community base of the enterprise.

Specialized training for faith-based CED is expanding incrementally as the field grows, and the educational programs, interestingly, are mostly in secular institutions. A few young clergy are staking out careers in faith-based development, but they seldom find experiential or academic training in the ministerial training tracks. Theological education shows only scattered signs of having recognized community development as a form of ministry worthy of sustained attention.

Conclusion

The future of community-based community economic development remains uncertain. The record is strong, champions are many, and opportunities are legion. Still, questions linger about the capacity of CED. Can it mobilize and attract enough assets to make substantial differences in inner cities and poor rural areas in a day of global economics? Will a more highly structured, top-down approach be required to rescue people and communities from economic blight? Answers to such questions depend on many factors, including the general state of the economy, public policy, and the determination of hundreds of communities to carve out a stake for themselves in their own futures.

The issues of capacity and determination will remain only partially answered until thousands more congregations and religious institutions take up the cause of community-based development: bettering the community for the sake of bettering the lives of all people.

If faith-based development is to grow, both established and new practitioners must grapple with tough, recurring challenges, which are not technical so much as attitudinal and functional.

Focusing on the Whole Community

William Biddle was slightly apprehensive in 1964 about promoting religion as a community development actor for two reasons. First, he was mildly worried that religious participants might introduce "partisan denominationalism" into the emerging field. He noted that religion, especially church-related religion, was sometimes authoritarian in a way that would be counterproductive to the goal of community development as benefiting all the people in a locale. Second, and related, he worried that religious workers sometimes did not "trust ordinary people to make ethically good choices." Balancing religious particularism, including truth claims, with overall community welfare is an ongoing challenge to faith-based CED. Biddle urged religious developers to be encouragers, not dominators, of the process and the local initiative it demands. His appeal remains valid.

Acting in Partnerships

Partnership formation entails three challenging steps, each with several questions to be answered. First is the assessment of potential collaborators:

- Who are potential and realistic partners?
- Is there anything in the reputation, the operation, or the objectives of a particular bank or government program inconsistent with the values of a faith-based developer?
- Will the partnership serve the welfare of the community?
- Should certain public association be avoided?

The second step is an awareness that potential partners also evaluate:

- Can the faith-based group articulate its faith in such a way as to be understood by outsiders?
- Does the religious organization have its finances and its organizational house in order?
- Is it comfortable answering questions about its operation style and community linkages?

- Is the faith-based developer willing to listen to the critiques, and sometimes criticisms, of partners?

Finally is the issue of practical and public cooperation:

- Can the partnership operate publicly and with genuine collaboration?
- Can the partners mutually share successes and failures?
- Is the partnership open to additional collaborators? Full partners or limited participants?

Partners need not share theologies, politics, or cultures, but partnerships, once they are formed, must operate in the public eye. Community development partnerships—perhaps all partnerships—are mutual experiences in doing good deals, which is the art of figuring out how to accomplish shared goals in the most effective, honorable manner possible.

Dealing with Money

Money raises three challenges for faith-based development: raising it, spending it, and accounting for it. CED takes money, sometimes huge amounts. Project money—that is, money for housing units or business development—is usually easier to come by than the funds required to keep a CDC or other development organization afloat. Especially difficult to raise are the funds for start-up: for mapping community assets, conducting feasibility studies, and obtaining technical assistance. Religious groups often must bear these initial costs themselves, perhaps borrowing from themselves or tapping denominational sources. Large churches often are able to contribute start-up funds or to raise it from their members. This money can be used to leverage outside project grants, guarantee loans, and build equity. Outside funds, however, may come with strings attached. Good community developers develop keen senses of how to assess, modify, or reject the conditions attached to money. Government and private foundations often provide funds for predetermined programs. What are the implications of such allocations in the light of the community's agenda? A predefined program may or may not fit. Running after money just because it is available is not a good CED practice.

Spending money is a matter of deciding who receives the benefit. In a job training program, does the faith-based developer look for easy cases that can be handled fast and with public fanfare, or does it also look to the hard-core unemployed with little incentive to work? Shall a church-related CDC renovate only housing adjoining the church, or does it also take on a dilapidated building unseen by people coming to worship? Who decides? Is community sentiment a guiding principle? How decisive in CED spending is the question of who is most in need of the assets being used?

Accounting for CED money is a major responsibility—an obligation to both the community and contributors and lenders. Churches and other religious organizations are not exempt from fiscal accountability, and some may wish to obtain professional assistance in complying with both the legal and moral aspects of this duty.

Keeping the Faith

Faith-based CED faces the challenge of retaining its religious foundations. Because community development by definition serves all residents, the possibility is ripe for faith-based developers to drift toward a secular self-definition in order to appear more acceptable to persons of other religions or of no religion, or to seem more attractive to a secular funder. The temptation is strong, and only those strong in faith resist it.

For faith-based community developers to lose their public identity as religious enterprises is deeply regrettable. Religion—faith—is concerned with living toward a vision of well-being for the individual and the community, that is, of our common life. Without the exploration and projection of a vision, families, communities, and societies fall apart. When visions are shared, the possibility exists to transform meager resources into the skills and opportunities required to remake lives and neighborhoods.

Community developments must continuously clarify the vision of community and what each person and institution brings to it. Faith-based community development must honor the faith practices of each particular religious group and person. When a vision of community wholeness begins to be realized, everyone can give thanks for the opportunity to serve and for the benefits earned from working together.

Exhibit 11.1. How to Get Started in Faith-Based Development.

1. Consider and spell out the theological and faith reasons for undertaking community development as a form of ministry.
2. Get any approvals that may be needed to proceed (such as the approval of a congregational administrative board).
3. Select a target area where the work will be done.
4. Organize for community asset assessment:
   Assign tasks.
   Find out what development programs are already under way in that area.
   Find out from public officials whether there is a comprehensive development plan for the city or county and, if so, what implications this may have for development in the target area.
   Research local, regional, and state governmental agencies and private organizations that assist in community development.
5. Understand that community-based development must take its lead from the community will.
6. Assess the community's capacity to undertake CD and attract supportive resources.
7. Take a step-by-step, incremental approach.
8. Clarify the goals of the new program—for example, housing, child care, business development, or job placement.
9. Calculate the financial, technical, and professional resources that will be needed to accomplish a projected task.
10. Consult the relevant specialists in the field of work (for example, housing, business, or child care), and be prepared to pay for expert advice and information.
11. Set up the type of organizational structure most suitable for the objective.
12. Determine how the project will be staffed: new staff, current staff, volunteers, or a combination.
13. Locate partners, realizing that the type of structure may be influenced by the availability and types of partners. (This might come earlier, depending on the situation.)
14. Take action (and pray constantly).
15. Evaluate progress.
16. Publicly celebrate successes and grieve failures.

Exhibit 11.1. How to Get Started in
Faith-Based Development, Cont'd.

What Not to Do

1. Get involved in CED because it seems like a popular thing to do.
2. Expect the effort to be easy or to achieve positive results quickly.
3. Expect it to fill up empty pews or put money in the coffers.
4. Set out without a firm theological understanding of why this project is being undertaken and a keen sense of the community.
5. Promise more than can be achieved. Community development involves the lives of people, and hopes should not be raised without a realistic expectation of attainment.
6. Proceed without adequate financial resources (capitalization) to achieve the objective.
7. Organize a new CDC in a community that already has too many or just enough.
8. Assume financial or technical expertise that is not at hand.
9. Form partnerships that lack mutual trust and respect and cannot be publicly celebrated.
10. Treat community development projects as private fiefdoms unaffected by the community's views and will.
11. Fail to account for in-kind, voluntary, and political commitment, as well financial resources.
12. Ignore the need to remain solvent and to achieve profitability when businesses are launched.

References

Biddle, William. (1964). "Church and Community Development: Introducing a New Concept of Congregational Involvement with Human Problems That Tempers the Element of Conflict," *Christian Century*, Jan. 24, pp. 106–108.

Biddle, William W., and Biddle, Loureide J. (1965). *The Community Development Process: The Rediscovery of Local Initiative*. Austin, Tex.: Holt, Rinehart and Winston.

Boston, Thomas D., and Ross, Catherine L. (1998). *The Inner City: Urban Poverty and Economic Development in the Next Century*. New Brunswick, N.J.: Transaction.

Lincoln, C. Eric, and Mamiya, Lawrence H. (1990). *The Black Church in the African American Experience.* Durham, N.C.: Duke University Press.

Additional Readings

Barry, Brian. (1986). *Strategic Planning Workbook for Nonprofit Organizations.* St. Paul, Minn.: Amherst H. Wilder Foundation.

Blakely, Edward. (1993). *Planning Local Economic Development: Theory and Practice.* (2nd ed.). Thousand Oaks, Calif.: Sage.

Bobo, Kim, Kendall, Jackie, and Max, Steve. (1996). *Organizing for Social Change: A Manual for Activists in the 1990s.* Santa Ana, Calif.: Seven Locks Press.

Brandwein, Robert, and Brandwein, Jennifer. (1996). *Public and Private Financing for CDCs: Funding Sources for Economic Development.* Washington, D.C.: National Congress for Community Economic Development.

Bruner, Charles, and Parachini, Larry (eds.). (n.d.). *Building Community: Exploring New Relationships.* Washington, D.C.: Together We Can. (Contact the Institute for Educational Leadership, 1001 Connecticut Ave., N.W., Washington, D.C., 202–822–8405.)

Clemetson, Robert, and Coats, Roger. (1992). *Restoring Broken Places and Building Communities: A Casebook on African American Church Involvement in Community Economic Development.* Washington, D.C.: National Conference for Community Economic Development.

Division for Church in Society of the Evangelical Lutheran Church in America. (1996). *Give Us This Day Our Daily Bread: Sufficient, Sustainable Livelihood for All.* Chicago: Division for Church and Society.

Dudley, Carl S. (ed). (1996). *Next Steps in Community Ministry: Hands-on Leadership.* Bethesda, Md.: Alban Institute.

Emerson, Jed, and Twersky, Fay. (1996). *New Social Entrepreneurs: The Success, Challenge and Lessons of Non-Profit Enterprise Creation.* San Francisco: Roberts Foundation.

DePriest, Tomika, and Jones, Joyce. (1997). "Economic Deliverance Thru the Church." *Black Enterprise,* Feb., pp. 36–39.

"Faith in the Community." (1996). *Neighborhood Works,* Sept.–Oct., pp. 16–26.

Falicou, Yael. (1995). *Dictionary of Community Economic Development Terms: A Resource Book for Practitioners and Funders.* Oakland, Calif.: California Community Economic Development Association.

Flanagan, Joan. (1982). *The Grass Roots Fundraising Book.* Chicago: Contemporary Books.

Franklin, Robert M. (1997). *Another Day's Journey: Black Churches Confronting the American Crisis.* Minneapolis: Fortress Press.

Freedman, Samuel G. (1993). *Upon This Rock: The Miracles of a Black Church*. New York: HarperCollins.

Fuller, Millard. (1994). *The Theology of the Hammer*. Macon, Ga.: Smyth & Helwys, Publishing.

General Assembly of the Presbyterian Church (USA). (1996). *Hope for a Global Future: Toward Just and Sustainable Human Development*. Louisville, Ky.: Office of the General Assembly.

Gordon, Wayne L. (1995). *Real Hope in Chicago*. Grand Rapids, Mich.: Zondervan.

Harrison, Bennett, and Weiss, Marcus. (1998). *Networking Across Boundaries: New Directions in Community-Based Job Training and Economic Development*. (3 vols.). Boston: Economic Development Assistance Consortium.

Karapin, Roger. (1994). "Community Organizations and Low-Income Citizen Participation in the US: Strategies, Organization, and Power Since the 1960s." [http://data.fas.harvard.edu/cfia/pnscs/s94karp.htm]. Karapin Seminar, Spring.

Kretzmann, John P., and McKnight, John. (1993). *Building Communities from the Inside Out: A Path Toward Finding and Mobilizing a Community's Assets*. Evanston, Ill.: Center for Urban Affairs, Northwestern University.

Kretzmann, John P., and McKnight, John. (1996). *A Guide to Mapping Consumer Expenditures and Mobilizing Consumer Expenditure Capacities*. Evanston, Ill.: Asset-Based Community Development Institute.

Kretzmann, John P., and McKnight, John. (1996). *A Guide to Mapping Local Business Assets and Mobilizing Local Business Capacities*. Evanston, Ill.: Asset-Based Community Development Institute.

Kretzmann, John P., and McKnight, John. (1996). *A Guide to Mapping and Mobilizing the Economic Capacities of Local Residents*. Evanston, Ill.: Asset-Based Community Development Institute.

Kretzmann, John P., and McKnight, John. (1997). *A Guide to Capacity Inventories: Mobilizing the Community Skills of Local Residents*. Evanston, Ill.: Asset-Based Community Development Institute.

Mattessich, Paul W., and Monsey, Barbara R. (1992). *Collaboration: What Makes It Work*. St. Paul, Minn.: Amherst H. Wilder Foundation.

McLean, Mary, and Voytek, Kenneth. (1992). *Understanding Your Economy: Using Analysis to Guide Local Strategic Planning*. (2nd ed.). Chicago: Chicago Planners Press.

Medoff, Peter, and Sklar, Holly. (1994). *Streets of Hope: The Fall and Rise of an Urban Neighborhood*. Boston: South End Press.

National Conference of Catholic Bishops. (1996). *Economic Justice for All: Pastoral Letter on Catholic Social Teaching and the U.S. Economy* (10th anniversary ed.). Washington, D.C.: United States Catholic Conference.

National Council for Urban Economic Development. (1993). *Forces in the New Economy: Implications for Local Economic Development.* Washington, D.C.: NCUED.

Peirce, Neal, and Steinback, Carol. (1987). *Corrective Capitalism: The Rise of America Economic Development Corporations.* New York: Ford Foundation.

Perkins, John. (1993). *Beyond Charity: The Call to Christian Community Development.* Grand Rapids, Mich.: Baker Book House.

Perkins, John (ed.). (1995). *Restoring At-Risk Communities: Doing It Together and Doing It Right.* Grand Rapids, Mich.: Baker Book House.

Reed, Gregory. (1994). *Economic Empowerment Through the Church: A Blueprint for Progressive Community Development.* Grand Rapids, Mich.: Zondervan.

"The Role of the Church in Community Development." (1992). *Agenda: The Alternative Magazine of Critical Issues* (National Center for Neighborhood Enterprise), 2(2), 1–40.

Shabecoff, Alice. (1992). *Rebuilding Our Communities: How Churches Can Provide, Support and Finance Quality Housing for Low-Income Families.* Federal Way, Wash.: World Vision.

Shabecoff, Alice. (1996). *Churches at Work in the Community: Strategies to Improve Local Job Opportunities.* Federal Way, Wash.: World Vision.

Sherraden, Michael. (1991). *Assets and the Poor: A New American Welfare Policy.* Armonk, N.Y.: Sharpe.

Squires, Gregory D. (1994). *Capital and Communities in Black and White.* Albany, N.Y.: State University Press of New York.

Stackhouse, Max L., Berger, Peter, and Meeks, M. Douglas. (1995). *Christian Social Ethics in a Global Perspective.* Nashville, Tenn.: Abingdon Press.

Tholin, Kathryn. (1995). *Lending a Hand: A Congregation's Guide to Community Investing.* Chicago: Woodstock Institute.

Woodson, Robert L., Sr. (1998). *The Triumphs of Joseph: How Today's Community Healers Are Reviving Our Streets and Neighborhoods.* New York: Free Press.

Wright, Elliott (ed.). (1995). *Religious Institutions as Partners in Community-Based Development.* Special issue of *Progressions.* Indianapolis: Lilly Endowment.

Zalent, Kim. (1987). *Economic Home Cookin': An Action Guide for Congregations on Community Economic Development.* Chicago: Community Workshop on Economic Development.

Videos

Block by Block: Building Community in America's Inner Cities. (1997). Virginia Wolf Productions. Washington, D.C.: PBS Video. 57 minutes.

Building Hope: A Film on Community Development Corporations. (1994). Brooklyn, N.Y.: Pratt Institute. 60 minutes.

Faith in Our Neighborhoods. (1996). Washington, D.C.: National Congress for Community Economic Development. 25 minutes.

Magazines and Journals

Neighborhood Works. Bimonthly. Center for Neighborhood Technology, 2125 West North Avenue, Chicago, Ill. 60647, (312) 278–4800. http://www.cnt.org.

Poverty and Race. Bimonthly. Poverty and Race Research Action Council, 1711 Connecticut Avenue, N.W., Suite 207, Washington, D.C. 20009, (202) 387–0764.

Resources. Quarterly. National Congress for Community Economic Development, 11 Dupont Circle, Suite 325, Washington, D.C., 20036(202) 234–5009, http://www.ncced.org.

Shelterforce: The Journal of Affordable Housing and Community Building Strategies. Bimonthly. National Housing Institute, 439 Main Street, Orange, N.J., 07050, (973) 678–9060, http://www.nhi.org.

Interactive Internet Sites

Handsnet: http://www.com. Database on community issues; subscription required for interactive features but some public information at site.

Human Resource Consortium: http://www.hrconsortium. Lists CED training opportunities.

HUDClips: http://hudclips.org. Information for clients of the U.S. Office of Housing and Urban Development.

Religion-Based Organizations Engaged in Research, Training, and Support of CED

Bresse Institute for Urban Training
3401 West Third Street
Los Angeles, Calif. 90020
(213) 387–2822

Campaign for Human Development
U.S. Catholic Conference
1311 Fourth Street, N.E.
Washington, D.C. 20017
(202) 541–3210
http://www.nccbuscc.org/chd

Christian Community Development Association
3827 West Ogden Avenue
Chicago, Ill. 60623
(773) 762–0994
http://www.harambee.org/ccda

Congress of National Black Churches
1225 I Street, N.W., Suite 750
Washington, D.C. 20005
(202) 371–1092

Episcopal Church
Jubilee Program and Peace and Justice Program
815 Second Avenue
New York, N.Y. 10017
(212) 876–8400
http://www.ecusa.anglican.org

Evangelical Lutheran Church in America (units include the Domestic
    Hunger Program and the Division for Church in Society)
8765 West Higgins Road
Chicago, Ill. 60631
(773) 380–2700
http://elca.org

Faith Center for Community Development
99 Park Avenue, 2nd Floor
New York, N.Y. 10016

Habitat for Humanity International
121 Habitat Street
Americus, Ga. 31709
(912) 924–6935
http://205.142.155.71

Interfaith Center on Corporate Responsibility (ICCR)
475 Riverside Drive, Room 550
New York, N.Y. 10015
(212) 870–2295

Mennonite Economic Development Associates
1821 Oregon Pike, Suite 201
Lancaster, Pa. 17601
(717) 560–6546
http://www.meda.org

Presbyterian Church (USA) (several programs concerned with community development, including Self-Development of People, the
Hunger Program, and the Office of Urban Ministries)
100 Witherspoon Street
Louisville, Ky. 40202–1396
(502) 569–5000
http://www.pcusa.org

Unitarian Universalist Affordable Housing Corp.
2201 P Street, N.W.
Washington, D.C. 20037
(202) 588–1010
http://www.uuahc.org

United Methodist General Board of Global Ministries (CED-related programs include Shalom and the Unit on Community and Institutional Ministries)
475 Riverside Drive, 15th Floor
New York, N.Y. 10115
(212) 870–3600
http://gbgm-umc.org

World Vision
P.O. Box 9716
Federal Way, Wash. 98063–9716
(206) 815–1000
http:///www.worldvision.org

Yachad: The Jewish Community Housing Development Corp. of Greater
Washington
2027 Massachusetts Avenue, N.W.
Washington, D.C. 20036
(202) 667–6924

General CED Organizations: Research, Training, Publications, and Technical Assistance

Some of these organizations have special programs in faith-based development. Contact the individual organizations for annual and regional
conference or specialized seminars.

American Association of Enterprise Communities
1620 I Street, N.W., Suite 300
Washington, D.C. 20006

Asset-Based Community Development Institute
Center for Urban Affairs and Policy Research
Northwestern University
2040 Sheridan Road
Evanston, Ill. 60208–4100
(847) 491–3741
http://www.nwu.edu/IPR/abcd/html
To order publications, contact ACTA Publications, 4848 North Clark
     Street, Chicago, Ill. 60604, (800) 397–2282.

Association for Enterprise Opportunity
70 East Lake Street, Suite 620
Chicago, Ill. 60601–5907
(312) 357–0177
http://www.cdfi.org/cdfi/aeo.html

Center for Community Change
1000 Wisconsin Avenue, N.W.
Washington, D.C. 10017
(202) 562–5020

Community Information Exchange
1029 Vermont Avenue, N.W.
Washington, D.C. 20005
(202) 628–2981
http://www.comminfoexch.org

Community Workshop on Economic Development
100 South Morgan Street
Chicago, Ill. 60607
(312) 243–0249

Corporation for Enterprise Development
777 North Capital Street, N.E., Suite 410
Washington, D.C. 20002
(202) 408–9788
http://www.cfed.org

Council for Urban Economic Development
1730 K Street, N.W., Suite 700
Washington, D.C. 20006
(202) 223–4725
http://CUED.org

Development Training Institute
2500 Maryland Avenue
Baltimore, Md. 21218
(410) 338–2512
http://www.ncl.org/anr/partners/devtrin.htm

Economic Development Assistance Consortium
One Fanueil Hall Marketplace
Boston, Mass. 02109
(617) 742–4481
http://www.ncced.org./edac.html

Housing Assistance Council
1025 Vermont Avenue, N.W.
Washington, D.C. 20005
(202) 842–8600
http://www.ruralhome.org

Institute for Community Economics
57 School Street
Springfield, Mass. 01105–1331
(413) 746–8660
http://www.ic.org

Jewish Council on Urban Affairs
618 South Michigan Avenue, Suite 700
Chicago, Ill. 69605
(312) 663–0960
http://ans-www.uchicago.edu/~bitko/index.html#home.top

National Association of Community Action Agencies
1875 Connecticut Avenue, N.W., Suite 416
Washington, D.C. 20009
(202) 265–7546
http://www.nacaa.org

National Congress for Community Economic Development
Faith-Based Program
1020 15th Street, N.W., Suite 325
Washington, D.C. 20005
(202) 289–9020
www.ncced.org

National Economic Development and Law Center
2201 Broadway
Oakland, Calif. 94612
(510) 251–1600

National Neighborhood Coalition
1875 Connecticut Avenue, Suite 710
Washington, D.C. 20009
(202) 986–2096
http://www.comminfoexch.org/nnc.htm

Neighborhood Reinvestment Corporation
1325 G Street, N.W.
Washington, D.C. 20006
(202) 376–2400
http://www.ncl.org

Seedco
915 Broadway, Suite 1703
New York, N.Y. 10010
(212) 473–0255

Sustainable America
350 Fifth Avenue, Room 3112
New York, N.Y. 10118–3199
(212) 239–4221
http://www.sanework.org

Urban Institute
2100 M Street, N.W.
Washington, D.C. 20037
(202) 833–7200
http://www.urban.org

Women's Institute for Housing and Economic Development
179 South Street
Boston, Mass. 02111
(617) 423–2296
http://www.bostonwomen.com/orgs/wihed/1.html

Woodstock Institute
407 South Dearborn Street
Chicago, Ill. 60604
(312) 427–8070
http://www.nonprofit.net/woodstock

Intermediaries and Community Development Financial Institutions

These groups make loans and grants, and they often, provide technical assistance.

Enterprise Foundation
American City Building
Columbia, Md. 21044
(410) 964–1230
http://www.enterprisefoundation.org

Local Initiative Support Corporation
733 Third Avenue
New York, N.Y. 10017
(212) 455–9800
www.liscnet.org

McAuley Institute
8300 Colesville Road
Silver Spring, Md. 20910
http://www.housinglink.com/mcauley.htm

National Community Capital Association
(formerly Association of Community Development Loan Funds)
924 Cherry Street
Philadelphia, Pa. 19107
(215) 923–4754
http://www.nacdlf.org

National Federation of Community Development Credit Unions
120 Wall Street, 10th Floor
New York, N.Y. 10005
(21?) 809–1530
http://www.natfed.org

RuralLISC
1825 K Street, N.W.
Washington, D.C. 20006
(202) 785–2908
http://www.rurallisc.org

Other Funders

The funders of faith-based community development range from free-will offerings in Sunday school classes to large grants from the federal government. Other types of funders include the following groups:

Local, regional, and national denominational or other religious grant and loan programs

Private foundations: national, state and local

Community development loan funds and other community development financial institutions

Intermediaries

Corporate community programs

Banks

The Foundation Center publishes directories that can guide local groups to private funders. Its publications can be purchased or used at hundreds of libraries across the country. For a list of its publications and ordering information, consult the center's Internet site: http:// fdncenter.org.

Government Support of CED

The federal government alone funds more than twelve hundred programs in domestic assistance, including many in community economic development. In addition, state and local governments fund CED, sometimes in partnership with federal support. Lists of government programs and how to access them are efforts in futility because they change too often. The federal government, most states, and some local governments now provide up-to-date, user-friendly information on the Internet.

The Catalog of Federal Domestic Assistance (CFDA) is located at http://aspe.os.dhhs.gov/cfda. This interactive site lets the user search the nine federal departments and fifteen independent agencies. Virtually every federal department, including Justice and Defense, have CED programs. The best known are under the Departments of Housing and Urban Development (HUD) and Commerce. HUD is the source of Community Development Block Grants (CDBG), expended in concert with states and local governments. Faith-based CDCs may apply for these funds, as they can for most other government programs, as long as the local housing or economic venture is open to all residents in an area. The Department of Commerce sponsors the Economic Development Agency, the Office of Community Services, and the Minority Business Development Agency, which has regional and district offices across the country. Most federal departments operate on regional or district levels, so a local developer will want to find out how to contact the nearest office rather than calling Washington directly. CFDA maintains a current directory of regional and district offices.

Some important Internet sites for program information include:

HUD: http://www.hud.gov.

Department of Commerce: Economic Development Agency, http://www.doc.gov/eda; Minority Business Development Agency, http://www.doc.gov.mbda

Agriculture: http://rurdevl.usda.gov

Health and Human Services: Office of Community Services, http://www.os.dhhr.gov

Several independent agencies support community development. These include:

Environmental Protection Agency: http://epa.gov.

Small Business Administration: http//www.sba.gov

Some federally chartered financial organizations that operate in an autonomous manner encourage and support community development. These include the Federal National Mortgage Association (Fannie Mae), the Federal Home Loan Mortgage Corporation (Freddie Mac), and the Federal Home Loan Bank Corporation.

State and local governments often have CED structures similar to that of the federal government, but they may go by different names from place to place. Internet sites that link to the relevant agencies can usually be found on the Internet.

Academic Programs in Faith-Based
Community Development (Master's Level)

Eastern College, M.A. in community economic development with a faith emphasis. Contact: Eastern College, 10 Fairview Drive, St. Davids, Penn. 19087–3696, (215) 341–5847.

New Hampshire College. M.S. in community economic development; can elect emphasis in faith-based. Contact: Woullard Lett, New Hampshire College, 2500 North River Road, Hooksett, N.H. 03106, (603) 644–3102.

North Park University, in collaboration with the Seminary Consortium for Pastoral Education. M.A. in community development. Contact: Edward J. Lamm, North Park University, 3225 West Foster Avenue, Chicago, Ill. 60625–4895, (773) 244–5516.

Community Organizing Networks and Organizations

Association of Community Organizations for Reform Now
National Office
739 8th Street, S.E.
Washington, D.C. 20903
http://www.acorn.org/community

Center for Third World Organizing
1218 East 21st Street
Oakland, Calif. 94606
(510) 533–7582
http://ww.ctwo.org/ctwo

Direct Action and Research Training Center
314 Northeast 26 Terrace
Miami, Fla. 33137–0791
(305) 576–8020
http://www.fiu.edu/~dart

Gamaliel Foundation
203 North Wabash Avenue, Suite 808
Chicago, Ill. 60601
(312) 357–2639
http://www.gamaliel.org

Industrial Areas Foundation
220 West Kenzie, 5th Floor
Chicago, Ill. 60610
(312) 464–1802

Organize Training Center
422-A Vicksburg
San Francisco, Calif. 94114
(415) 821–6180

Organizing Leadership Training Center
25 West Street, 3rd Floor
Boston, Mass. 02111
(617) 247–3373

Pacific Institute for Community Organization
171 Santa Rosa Avenue
Oakland, Calif. 94610
(510) 655–2801

CHAPTER 12

Congregations and the Delivery of Health Care Services

Sandra C. Burgener

The health of all persons and the delivery of traditional health care has been a major concern of most of the world's faith traditions, and they have often taken the lead in the provision of care to the ill and infirm. This history provides a strong basis for today's continuing efforts. In the Christian tradition, the roots of this involvement are in the biblical support for the relationship between spiritual care and health, including reference to the healing acts of Jesus (Fahey, 1997). The first documented founding of a hospital under Christian auspices dates to 372 C.E., providing a strong historical precedent for the church's involvement in health care. In addition, religions have long been committed to the ideal that all persons have the right to health care adequate to meet basic human needs and have acted on this conviction in differing ways. An examination of the three great monotheistic religions provides a clear indication of the bases for and scope of varying religions' commitment to healing the sick, injured, and infirm.

The Catholic church, for example, has had a history of establishing hospitals and care centers within its religious orders. These orders met the health care needs of the local community by using the members of the order as professional leaders within the health care facility (Fahey, 1997; Sullivan, 1996). The organizing body or diocese assumed financial support and management of the facility, actualizing the church's concern for justice in the provision of health care. Lest one think this is only of historical importance, a recent report from the National Convocation of Catholic Health-care Leaders indicates that the Catholic church currently has 622 hospitals in forty-eight states, 714 long-term care facilities in forty-seven states, and thousands of community-based health programs. These hospitals account for nearly one-sixth of all U.S. community hospital admissions annually (Fahey, 1997).

Although the Catholic church may present the largest and most systematized example, other denominations and religious organizations mobilize significant resources to address health care needs in underserved areas in both the United States and abroad (Fahey, 1997).

The Jewish perspective on health care and the importance of accessibility of health care for all is based on several principles that underlie Jewish history and literature. These include the infinite value of each individual, the moral laws of justice, and the understanding that a just and merciful God rules the world (Wechsler, 1997). Within the Jewish tradition, accessibility to health care services is viewed as essential to fulfill the principle of equal rights and a respect for the human dignity of each person. Jewish principles would dictate that health care should be available despite the financial costs, considering the human costs involved and the basic need for these services. Accessible health care is considered to be more than a good; it is demanded by justice (Wechsler, 1997). Jewish-supported and -sponsored hospitals and long-term care facilities are found throughout the United States, speaking to the commitment within Jewish traditions to health care provision.

Examples of Protestant-supported health care facilities are found in practically every large city and town in the United States, with this effort also being carried out around the world through well-established missional efforts to chronically underserved areas or countries having short-term health care needs. These efforts are grounded in the biblical assertion that "what you do for the least of these you do to the one you consider the greatest" (Forbes, 1997). Within the Protestant perspective is the reality that today's health care delivery systems and the biblical mandate for equality are in tension, with many persons omitted or excluded from health care systems. To address this conflict, the Protestant perspective requires a willingness to commit the needed resources to provide the morally and ethically required services, while broadening the view of health beyond treatment for physical illnesses to include disease prevention and health promotion.

Collectively, these perspectives provide a significant view of the religious mandates for the involvement of both local congregations and larger denominational agencies and bodies in the delivery of health care. In addition, mounting evidence based on systematic research suggests a strong link between an individual's religious and spiritual well-being and health outcomes for all ages (Idler and Kasl, 1997a, 1997b; Kutter and McDermott, 1997). This is particularly notable among older adults, many of whom become more involved religiously as they age (Krause, 1997).

The link between religion and health, coupled with escalating health care costs and constricting health service delivery mechanisms, makes this an appropriate time to examine innovative collaborations and outreach mechanisms between religious and secular organizations as a partial solution to the growing health care crisis (Krause, 1997). The involvement at the level of the local congregation is particularly useful in addressing certain chronic problems. Examples of the commitment at this level provide guidance and direction to smaller efforts at meeting the health care needs of diverse populations. Although I use the terms *congregation* and *church* in this chapter, these examples apply to a variety of faith-based communities, including outreach services implemented within parachurch organizations, interfaith ministries, or among collaborating congregations.

Congregational Considerations in Developing a Health Care Program

Prior to committing resources to the development of effective health care ministries, congregations must undertake a careful process of assessment. First, a determination must be made whether the focus will be on the congregation's members or the wider community and information gathered about the health needs of that population. This knowledge will be the basis for the structure and focus of the health ministry. Too often congregations act on perceptions of local health care needs and often ignore actual needs, which, in fact, are often quite different from the perceived need.

Although this chapter is not intended to be a primer on health or community assessments (see Chapter Three), it is a good place to emphasize that the assessment of need should include the perspective of the major stakeholders in the program: the recipients of care, the health professionals providing the health services, and any funding sources. Other stakeholders are central community or congregation leaders, especially persons with health-related expertise. Community-setting stakeholders would be local pharmacists; practicing health care providers; leaders of community services agencies, such as Women, Infants and Children programs or food banks; and major local employers who may be supporting a major portion of health care costs. Table 12.1 provides an overview of relevant stakeholders by group.

Within the congregation, relevant stakeholders include persons responsible for outreach ministries, financial management, and program development. If the project or program requires ongoing or even temporary support from the larger organizational body, such as the diocese or regional conference, an assessment of that entity's goals and funding priorities should also be conducted. (Chapter Six explains more completely the importance of stakeholder analysis and the ways in which it should be undertaken.)

A careful needs and resources assessment will help ensure that a health care service will be needed, used, and supported. Recent research suggests that assessments undertaken by faith communities provide richer and more textured information than those obtained from the results-oriented approach of traditional health care organizations and managed care entities (Cook, 1997). To facilitate the development of a complete and meaningful assessment, it is best to develop an assessment guide listing questions directed toward meeting identified community needs and supported by resources. For example, if the health ministry is directed toward meeting the chronic health care needs of older adults, questions should focus on identifying gaps in existing health care provision, characteristics of the targeted group, existing health care services, other available resources, barriers to health care access and utilization (such as a lack of public transportation), and disease statistics for the target group to determine the most prevalent chronic

Table 12.1. Potential Health Care Stakeholders.

Congregation	Local Businesses	Local Health Care Professionals	Community Organizations
• Supporting professional staff (clergy, education directors) • Health and Outreach committees • Supporting congregation members • Health professionals • Financial management and support persons • Building and facilities committee	• Food stores • Pharmacies • Employers of potential care recipients • Laboratories • Public transportation providers • Service centers • Employment agencies	• Pharmacists • Community-based health care providers • Dentists • Ophthalmologists and Optometrists • Community clinics and service centers (for example, Planned Parenthood, WIC programs, March of Dimes) • Parish nursing centers • Diagnostic centers	• Youth organizations (for example, YMCA, YWCA, Boys/Girls Clubs) • Laboratories • Churches • Service groups (for example Rotary, Lions Club, Optimist Club, Women's Leagues) • Council for Aging • Food and clothing banks

Collaborators	Program Funders	Local Residents/ Recipients of Care
• University health schools • Other local congregations, faith-based groups • Local health providers • Regional dioceses or church conferences • Local health departments	• Private and public foundations • Health departments • Federal and state health-related funding agencies • Local philanthropic groups (i.e., service organizations) • Individual contributors	• Persons living in the target geographic area • Congregation members • Family members of persons living in the target area

Note: This listing is illustrative, not exhaustive. Stakeholders vary with the context.

illnesses. Once the assessment tool has been developed, face-to-face or telephone interviews with stakeholders will provide the most complete information. When time and personnel permit, such interviews are far more successful than mailing out an assessment questionnaire and asking the stakeholder to complete and return it. The interview format also allows individuals to raise issues and questions not initially considered, further enriching the information collected. Another benefit of direct contact is that it initiates the development of linkages with key community individuals and organizations, helping to foster a spirit of familiarity and cooperation.

A second consideration in the development of an effective health care service is the assurance of the congregation's full endorsement for the program. Congregational ownership of the health service is of particular importance for long-term programs, such as primary care or parish nursing services, while mere congregational endorsement may be all that is required for a limited or focused program, such as educational or screening services. Many older, established congregations reside within changing inner-city neighborhoods or older rural settings. In the former instance, many members now live outside the church's immediate neighborhood. In the latter, many younger families have moved to more populated areas, leaving the community and the church populated by older rural residents. In the case of the inner-city congregation, members residing in or close to the neighborhood may be more committed to serving that neighborhood or using any developed health service than those residing outside. In rural settings, while older congregation members may benefit from the services offered, they may lack the resources required to support it.

In any of these situations, it is essential that the congregation as a whole develop a commitment to the program. Too often a small, nonrepresentative committee or action group within the congregation takes leadership and responsibility for developing and initiating a program. Then, without having received congregational approval or commitment beforehand, it later expects or demands ongoing support from the larger congregation. While volunteer efforts and philosophies within a congregation represent a rich resource, when these responsibilities fall on a small number of persons, the likelihood of continued support and success decreases.

A third consideration prior to developing a health care service is the sustainability of the service. Especially in poor inner-city communities, services often are started with special federal or state health initiative monies, only to disappear when the funding is no longer available, although the targeted health problem remains. Temporary or stop-gap measures often leave care recipients distrustful of health care providers. These temporary programs also contribute to the fragmentation of care, as local residents who have established a relationship with the provider within the temporary program face the task of transferring their care to another accessible and accepting provider, a task that becomes increasingly difficult and complex within the current managed care environment. If the health service requires substantial volunteer efforts or funding, it is especially important that these human and monetary resources be evaluated carefully prior to implementation to help ensure that the health service will remain available to the target population as long as the need exists.

These considerations and the important questions listed in Exhibit 12.1 should not discourage local congregations from establishing a health service program; rather, they are intended to assist congregations in understanding the responsibility undertaken when developing and supporting these valuable, and often essential, programs. Fully understanding and attending to these issues not only increases the likelihood of the program's success, but also decreases the likelihood of conflict within the congregation or loss of confidence by the local community.

Care Delivery Models

The rich traditions of religious concern for the health of all individuals offer numerous approaches to approaching a health-

---

**Exhibit 12.1. Considerations in Planning
and Developing a Health Care Ministry.**

What are the health care needs of the local congregation and community?

Are the needed resources and expertise available to conduct a thorough health needs assessment?

What are the goals and funding priorities of supportive groups (such as the local conference or diocese) and organizations?

What is the level of congregational support and endorsement for a health care service or ministry?

How will the health care service or ministry be financially supported and sustained?

Is the needed expertise (volunteer and paid) available to fully support an ongoing health care service or ministry?

---

focused program. There also exist many studies documenting the various outcomes of the different approaches to local congregational health care outreach ministry. This chapter examines the traditional parish nurse model, health center/local congregation collaborative models, and the local congregation as a site for delivery of health promotion or screening programs.

These care delivery models have the advantage of increasing accessibility to health care services. Regardless of region or location, whether rural or urban, churches and synagogues are present in the local community even if formalized health care services are not. Even in the most rural settings, where the closest health care provider may be in a middle-sized town miles away, congregations can be found serving the needs of people. In impoverished, inner-city areas, congregations often are the most stable community organization, offering sanctuary from the stresses of living in an area beset with violence, poverty, limited choices, and barriers to resources. And because disadvantaged persons often have had negative experiences with traditional health care providers, including long waiting times, service denial, and extensive interrogation about finances and personal habits, they often distrust them and fail to seek out necessary care. By locating key health services in the more comfortable setting of a congregation, much of this distrust can be alleviated. Since local congregations often provide other services, such as food pantries or clothes closets, some residents already are accustomed to receiving services there.

The prevalence and familiarity of congregations make them a particularly good place to locate community health services. When combined with the general commitment of religious traditions to the physical, mental, and spiritual well-being of all, the use of congregations as supporters, deliverers, and housers of health services constitutes an important response to the lack of affordable and accessible health care.

Parish Nurse

One of the most widespread models for congregational delivery of health services is the parish nurse. Philosophically, religious institutions and nurses share a commitment to help individuals achieve their highest capacity for functioning. Both view the individual from a holistic perspective, recognizing the interaction between the individual's spiritual, physical, social, and psychological needs and life outcomes (Weis, Matheus, and Schank, 1997).

The parish nurse model was developed and instituted in the United States in the 1980s, although it has had a long history in Europe, Australia, New Zealand, Canada, and, most recently, Korea (Simington, Olson, and Douglass, 1996). In the United States, this model was a response to the governmental challenge of finding more effective ways for delivering health-promoting services at the community level. Such a location for community nursing also provides an excellent location for the use of advanced-practice nurses. These nurses, prepared at the master's level, have the knowledge and skills to deliver health care services similar to those provided by the typical community-based physician. They treat and manage illnesses and can prescribe medications. More important, they are adept at providing preventive and screening services, including immunizations and cancer examinations and delivering health promotion programs.

Parish nurse models share a concern for increasing the health of the local community, while acting as advocates for social justice. Such programs are easily structured to avoid duplicating existing service. Their flexibility allows them to complement existing services by offering programs and services not readily available locally, thereby enhancing health care delivery. Typical parish nurse programs are health education; disease prevention focused on diseases common to the target population; wellness programs, such as exercise and relaxation; counseling services; and referrals. Parish nurses visit congregation or community members with physical, emotional, or spiritual needs in their home, nursing homes, or the hospital, supplementing the supportive visiting offered by clergy. In addition to health programming, parish nurses typically have regular office hours during which people can receive services.

Parish nurses are particularly adept at providing health information. They can disseminate this information through congregational newsletters, community newspapers, or specialized bulletins. They also can advocate for those needing more advanced services, facilitating their interactions with the larger health care system (Weis, Matheus, and Schank, 1997). Although the educational requirement for a parish nurse is a bachelor's degree in nursing with three to twenty years of general experience, many parish nurses are master's or doctorally prepared. This background enables them to interpret the latest medical and health-related information, including the success of new drugs or surgical procedures, for the target community (Simington, Olson, and Douglass, 1996; Weis, Matheus, and Schank, 1997). Exhibit 12.2 summarizes common activities of parish nurses.

Structurally, parish nurse programs fall into four categories, depending on support mechanisms and the relationship with the sponsoring church. In one model, the program is directed by a local health center or hospital, with the practicing nurses being employees of the hospital. The health facility assumes responsibility

Exhibit 12.2. Example Activities and Responsibilities of Parish Nurses.

Activities/Responsibilities:

- Direct care for clients with acute and chronic illnesses
- Program planning
- Networking with community agencies, including other health care providers
- Meeting with congregation support and planning groups
- Health education for individuals and groups
- Development and implementation of disease prevention and wellness programs such as exercise, nutrition, stress management, and smoking cessation
- Community assessment
- Collaboration with key stakeholders and community health organizations
- Referral resource for clients
- Client advocate
- Assisting with fundraising/grant writing
- Program and service evaluation
- Visiting clients in the home, nursing homes, or hospitals, as needed
- Health screening
- Local health information resource
- Financial management
- Preparation of reports and outcome evaluations for local congregation, funding agencies, and relevant stakeholders

for the program's development, implementation, and evaluation. Program goals, by necessity, are congruent with the health center's or hospital's. The health center or hospital benefits by having a direct community link and a feeder system of clients into the center, and by instituting local health promotion programs that decrease costly emergency or in-hospital care. This also assists the center in meeting its mission goals, since many for-profit health institutions are required to return a percentage of all profits to the community served. This model requires less financial and operational commitment from the local supporting congregation, but it also affords it less input into and control over the delivery of services (Simington, Olson, and Douglass, 1996).

A second model represents a more typical structure for parish nursing. Here the nurse, often a member of the local congregation, is hired directly by the local congregation (Simington, Olson, and Douglass, 1996). The adoption of this model usually represents the congregation's commitment to serve the health care needs of both its own members and those of the surrounding community. The nurse generally works directly with an internal advisory committee, often consisting of church members with a special interest or expertise in health care. Together they undertake the assessment of the congregation's needs, plan appropriate health care programs, and evaluate the program's effectiveness.

Adoption of this model usually emerges from evidenced congregational needs. These often include those of a growing elderly population requiring health promotion and screening services not available locally or the desire to facilitate overall wellness of members through the convenience and accessibility of congregationally based programs. Although these models generally have a limited scope, they nevertheless require a thoughtful commitment to long-term financial and institutional support. Experience has shown that it is important to continue a health service program once congregational members become accustomed to using it to meet a major portion of their health care needs.

The remaining models involve networks structures that extend beyond the local congregation. The first is the extension of the parish nurse model to a judicatory level. Here the nursing services are formulated and directed from a regional level, such as district, diocese, synod, or conference board. Although programs are delivered locally, the direction for content is generally mandated at the regional level, resulting in similar programming offered within a defined area or district.

The fourth model, the coalition model, also has a broader structure, developed collaboratively among local congregations in conjunction with local social organizations and health and educational institutions. The result is a network of parish nurses (Simington, Olson, and Douglass, 1996). This structure has the advantage of the strengths inherent in any collaborative relationship. The cooperating parties bring a variety of expertise to the development and implementation of the project and a diverse funding base. Another advantage is that it affords the parish nurses an opportunity to interact with and receive support from others who are addressing similar problems and needs. This professional support can help prevent burnout since parish nurses often find themselves working in highly stressful and demanding positions without the presence of supportive colleagues.

Both of these models, however, have the disadvantage of removing the program from the direct oversight of the local congregation. An individual congregation also will have less direct input into the types of programming offered. Programming may not therefore be as congregation or neighborhood specific as some may desire. Several readily available publications offer detailed guidelines for the development of parish nurse services (Djupe, Olson, Ryan, and Lantz, 1994; Striepe, 1989; Westberg, 1990; Westberg and Westberg, 1987).

Primary Care Services Within a Local Congregation

A second model for health care delivery is the establishment of a full primary care center or office within the congregational setting. In this model, the organizing group, usually a local health center, community action group, or educational institution, identifies a need for health care services in an underserved area and then initiates a relationship with a local congregation to facilitate the delivery of health care services. The designation "medically underserved area" indicates that there is an inadequate supply of health providers to meet the health care needs of the local population. This designation is most common in rural or inner-city areas that cannot financially support formal primary care services. The congregation's involvement in this relationship requires different support mechanisms, since the community-based health service typically would try to meet most of the acute and chronic health care needs of the target population. This requires offering a variety of services and an ongoing stable presence in the community.

Although the structure for the collaborative relationship necessary to support a primary care service varies depending on congregational assets and commitment, local needs, and the level of commitment of the collaborative health service, some basic considerations and supports are consistent. The congregation must consider whether it is able and willing to sustain the collaboration for at least five to ten years. Because formal leadership may change during that length of time, it is important that the entire congregation accept this undertaking as central to its mission and be willing to commit the resources necessary for the collaboration to succeed, despite changes in leadership. Also, some way must be found to educate new members about the value of and importance of the health program and to ensure that incoming clergy are also committed to its continuation and success.

To facilitate this working relationship, the congregation must establish a committee to work consistently with the health care organization in the design, implementation, and delivery of the health service. Where possible, it should include members of the local community or target population to ensure that the developed services remain consistent with community needs. This advisory group represents a means for allocating congregational resources, receiving ongoing feedback from the community, and establishing clear lines of communication between and among all stakeholders. Formal tasks delegated to this group may vary depending on circumstances, polity, and abilities. It may serve primarily a communication and facilitation function or be empowered to make major decisions for the primary care service, including hiring decisions, overseeing financial management, and undertaking policy development. These decisions, along with the extent of its ability to make decisions affecting congregation resources, need to be made after careful reflection and discussion. Once made, they need to be stated as explicitly and in as much detail as possible. Precision and clarity will minimize the likelihood of conflicts that may threaten the program.

In addition to the effort and resources of the advisory group, the congregation generally commits physical space within its building for the service's operation. This is particularly key in rural settings, where centrally located and accessible buildings are scarce.

Space decisions must be made carefully and with attention to the specific needs of the program. The following considerations must be addressed when designating a space for a health facility:

- The space must be one that can be dedicated to health center use (although the space may be available on weekends for congregational use, since most health centers operate through the weekdays only).
- There must be some secure space within the health center with limited access. This is a necessity given issues of confidentiality of health records and the presence of medications on location.
- The space must be handicapped accessible.
- There must be lavatory and toilet facilities.
- Utilities must be adequate to the demands of the health program.

When committing to the designation of a physical space, the congregation usually provides utilities, although the health center will require a separate telephone line and may support these costs separately. Building modifications may be necessary as well. As part of its commitment to the program, these costs may be borne by the congregation.

The congregation's ability and willingness to bear these costs and any additional support for the primary care center should be determined early and set out in the agreement with the sponsoring health center or educational institution. The congregation may commit to facilitate the health center's work through volunteer efforts, recruiting, training, and coordinating volunteers to assist with the center's functioning. Ongoing financial support may be another way to aid the health center. In some congregations, the health center may be designated as part of its mission work, receiving a portion of the usual congregational giving to missions. Since the health center usually serves congregational members as well as the local community, especially in rural settings, it will be offering a valued service to all. Categories of required support for a primary health care service are outlined in Exhibit 12.3.

Exhibit 12.3. Required Support for Housing Primary Care Services Within a Church or Synagogue.

- Ability to sustain the primary care service for at least five to ten years
- Provision of an internal advisory group or board to facilitate communication and collaboration between the congregation and health professionals or health care organization
- Commitment of physical space within the church or synagogue building to contain health service, including locked areas for client records and medications, accessible running water and bathroom facilities, and handicapped-accessible spaces
- Tolerance for continual traffic within the building by community residents accessing the health service
- Support by volunteers within the congregation for the health care service
- Financial support by the congregation as part of its own commitment to outreach missions

The benefits of this type of collaboration include extending the congregation's involvement with the local community without requiring it to manage or support the health care effort. Since the local health organization or educational institution takes the major responsibility for offering the health service—including ensuring compliance with all regulatory requirements—the congregation can use existing resources (such as physical space and volunteers) to aid the program and address an existing community need without extending itself into unfamiliar areas. In a medically underserved area, the congregation is providing a particularly important service.

The more negative aspects of this type of collaboration include the requirement of a long-term commitment and the shared control of the service with the sponsoring health facility or educational institution. Since this collaboration requires the cooperating health organization to be responsible for the health center's day-to-day operation, the congregation loses some control. For example, it is unable to limit or control traffic through the building in the ways it has in the past. This loss of control, along with the long-term commitment required, demand careful consideration and planning prior to entering this type of collaboration.

Local Congregation-Based Health Promotion and Screening Programs

A report from the Princeton Religion Research Center (1994) indicates that 43 percent of all adults surveyed claimed they had attended worship services at least once during the past week, and 69 percent of all adults claim to belong to a church, synagogue, or other religious community. These statistics demonstrate the importance of religion in the lives of most of the adult population in the United States. This widespread contact and affiliation with a faith community have made congregations increasingly important sites for health promotion and illness prevention programs. The intensity of involvement varies from program to program. In some, the congregation serves as a site for offering health promotion programs (Smith, Merritt, and Patel, 1995). Others involve congregations in intensive programs where leaders and members take an active part in delivery of a health promotion intervention (Voorhees and others, 1996).

In an excellent description of congregationally based community health programs, Reverend Edwin Sanders (1997) provides important guidelines for congregations and their leaders in determining their roles in offering health programs. He states that the credibility of the program among those using it is key to its acceptance and success. Credibility is essential to building trust among the program's recipients. Viewing health issues in a holistic fashion, rather than compartmentalizing health issues such as hypertension, heart disease, or diabetes, also is important to a program's acceptance and use. Since all illnesses or diseases affect the whole person—behaviorally, psychologically, and spiritually—it is essential to recognize the multifaceted effects of disease within any faith-based health promotion program.

Sanders also believes that congregations need to interact with the health professions in a meaningful way. To do this effectively, medical professionals need to adopt a common language free from exclusive medical terminology. Simultaneously, the congregation needs to attempt to understand the particular needs and perceptions of the medical professionals.

Sanders's experiences in creating programs addressing major health concerns, including HIV/AIDS, within his congregation have demonstrated the importance of the congregation's total involvement in offering health promotion programs. Without this commitment and involvement, congregational members often begin to feel exploited by the health care agency. There are several ways to facilitate full involvement. These include identifying and using people within the church to assist in the delivery of the health care program. These resource people may possess distinctive program-related expertise or may be trained in basic skills (such as blood pressure monitoring) necessary to assisting with the program's offering. Advisory boards or groups can be formed by the congregation to work with the health profession's team in order to establish input at every level, including program development and resource utilization. Each level of involvement increases the congregation's sense of ownership in the project or program, thereby increasing the likelihood of a successful outcome.

Finally, Sanders notes the importance of the program's emphasizing healthy living rather than a fear of dying. Since health issues often are framed with statistics about deaths from certain diseases, the concern for an early or preventable death often is the emphasis that health professionals take in arguing for lifestyle changes. Religious communities, while spending time on equipping or preparing congregation members for death's inevitability, seem to prefer to align themselves with professionals and programs that emphasize healthy living or improving the quality of life in ways that reflect a commitment to the whole individual. These programs more readily affect the participant's life positively rather than simply furthering the research agenda of the health provider or institution (Sanders, 1997). Sanders's lessons from the field offer important guidance to any congregation considering participation in a health promotion program. At the same time, they give health providers and researchers insights into how to approach partnerships with congregations in mutually beneficial ways.

Health promotion programs requiring intensive involvement from the congregation were studied by Voorhees and colleagues (1996) among churches throughout the Baltimore area. Twenty-two African American churches participated and were randomly assigned either an intensive, culturally specific intervention for smoking cessation or a minimal self-help intervention. In the intensive-intervention churches, active participation and leadership was required for delivery of the intervention. This included one to four pastoral sermons on smoking, testimony by participants going through the cessation process during church services, the training of lay volunteers to act as smoking-cessation counselors, and sponsoring two health fairs. Results tended to be positive. The authors found that participants in the intensive-intervention churches were significantly more likely to make progress toward smoking cessation than those in the self-help intervention. The commitment required of the local congregation, including lay and professional leaders, in the actual delivery of the health promotion program remains the biggest obstacle. If this can be overcome, and Chapter Two in this book suggests ways of ensuring long-term congregational commitment to congregational social services, the successes seem to be great. Congregations willing to make the commitment can obtain guidelines for developing such programs from federal health agencies (U.S. Department of Health and Human Services, 1987).

Continuing Considerations

Several areas of general concern must be addressed when developing and supporting all health care programs, especially those requiring a long-term commitment. While congregationally based or faith-based programs end for myriad reasons, most fail due to lack of funding. In a 1997 article, Mark Hager and colleagues described the reasons for the termination of several health care programs in the Minneapolis–St. Paul area. The two main reasons for ending the programs were loss of income and reduction of client base. Given the competitive climate of managed care and shifting revenue streams supporting health care programs for indigent populations, small health care services unconnected to a larger health care system are particularly vulnerable to financial loss. Because most managed care contracts are awarded to large, multisite health care centers, small, independent providers are excluded from funds based on managed care contracts. This limits the sources of steady revenue. In addition, many persons requiring health care are the working uninsured. They do not qualify for Medicaid services yet lack the money to pay for care. Few options are available to support services for this group, making managed care contracts designed to include the working poor the only payment source for this potentially large consumer group. The small size of congregationally based health care services, the lack of a formal connection to a larger health care provider system, and limited secure revenue streams demand the design of innovative sources of revenue, such as endowments and incorporation of the health service into the congregation's budget.

The second major reason for cessation of health services is declining use by the target population (Hager, Pins, and Jorgensen, 1997). This results from changing demographics, increasing health care service options, or the resolution of the health problem addressed. If the health care service was designed to address one particular health problem, such as high infant mortality, and the desired result was achieved, the decline in need should be both anticipated and celebrated by the congregation. If the health service is designed to meet a variety of health care needs and another provider enters the same target area, the congregation may need to establish a cooperative relationship with the new provider in order to prevent fragmentation of care for the target population. Through a cooperative relationship, provider groups can work together to meet diverse and pressing health care needs, while choosing to focus on different, less prevalent problems, such as mental health needs or substance abuse. Anticipating changing conditions and demands can aid the congregation in planning its own health service delivery priorities and cooperative relationships. The presence of a new provider may also mean that the services delivered by the congregation are no longer necessary. If that proves to be the case, the congregation should be willing to close up shop. An exit strategy should be part of the planning process, with an articulated means of shutting down the service over a period of time or of shifting its focus in the light of new realities.

If the congregation offers only short-term programs, such as the education or research intervention programs, the exit issues should focus on how to assist participants, including congregation members, in maintaining the gains realized during the program. Because short-term programs generally have adequate up-front funding, financial support is less of an issue. What remains a concern, however, is transferring the care or treatment received through the short-term program to a more permanent source, especially if the treatment was nontraditional or experimental. Health interventions such as exercise, diet therapies, or education may not require continuing support for patient participation, since they usually can be transferred easily to the home setting and the educational program should be completed prior to termination. More complex health programs, such as multilevel interventions combining counseling services and support programs or therapeutic interventions necessitating a team approach, generally cannot be transferred easily to another source or replicated in the community. Some arrangement may need to be made with the health organization to ensure that participants will have continuing access to the programs.

Conclusion

The decision to address community health care needs requires a congregation to give thoughtful consideration to the factors discussed throughout this chapter, which highlight the elements necessary to facilitate successful development and implementation of a health care delivery program. The empirical evidence for the effectiveness of faith-based health service programs should encourage local congregations about the benefits of such an undertaking (Krause, 1997; Simington, Olson, and Douglass, 1996; Voorhees and others, 1996). This discussion should serve to inform local congregations of the possible scope of any venture into the delivery of health care services and the possible variety of tested structures in which these services can be facilitated. Actualizing the historical and missional precedents for a health care ministry can yield multiple benefits for the target community or population, while enriching the congregation's experience with its own tradition of faith and service to others.

References
Cook, C. (1997). "Faith-Based Health Needs Assessment: Implications for Empowerment of the Faith Community." *Journal of Health Care for the Poor and Underserved, 8*(3), 300–302.

Djupe, A. M., Olson, H., Ryan, J. A., and Lantz, J. (1994). *Reaching Out: Parish Nursing Services.* (2nd ed.). Park Ridge, Ill.: Lutheran General Health System.

Fahey, M. C. (1997). "Religious Perspective on Access to Health Care: A Catholic Perspective." *Mount Sinai Journal of Medicine, 64*(2), 80–83.

Forbes, J. A. (1997). "Religious Perspectives on Access to Health Care: A Protestant Perspective." *Mount Sinai Journal of Medicine,* 64 (2), 75–79.

Hager, M., Pins, J. J., and Jorgenson, C. A. (1997). "Unto Thy Maker: The Fate of Church-Based Nonprofit Clinics in a Turbulent Health Care Environment." *Nonprofit and Voluntary Sector Quarterly, 26,* 85–100.

Idler, E., and Kasl, S. (1997a). "Religion Among Disabled and Non-disabled Persons I: Cross-Sectional Patterns in Health Practices, Social Activities, and Well-Being." *Journal of Gerontology: Social Sciences, 52B*(6), 294–305.

Idler, E., and Kasl, S. (1997b). "Religion Among Disabled and Non-disabled Persons II: Attendance at Religious Services as a Predictor of the Course of Disability." *Journal of Gerontology: Social Sciences, 52B*(6), 306–316.

Krause, N. (1997). "Religion, Aging, and Health: Current Status and Future Prospects." *Journal of Gerontology: Social Sciences, 52B*(6), 291–293.

Kutter, C. J., and McDermott, D. S. (1997). "The Role of the Church in Adolescent Drug Education." *Journal of Drug Education, 27*(3), 293–305.

Princeton Religion Research Center. (1994). "Importance of Religion Climbing Again." *Emerging Trends, 16,* 1–4.

Sanders, E. C. (1997). "New Insights and Interventions: Churches Uniting to Reach the African American Community with Health Information." *Journal of Health Care for the Poor and Underserved, 8*(3), 373–376.

Simington, J., Olson, J., and Douglass, L. (1996). "Promoting Well-Being Within a Parish." *Canadian Nurse,* pp. 20–24.

Smith, E. D., Merritt, S. L., and Patel, M. K. (1997). "Church-Based Education: An Outreach Program for African Americans with Hypertension." *Ethnicity and Health, 2*(3), 243–253.

Striepe, J. (1989). *Nurses in Churches: A Manual for Developing Parish Nurse Services and Networks.* (2nd ed.). Park Ridge, Ill.: Parish Nurse Resource Center.

Sullivan, J. (1996). "A Journey of Community." *Health Progress,* pp. 39–42.

U.S. Department of Health and Human Services. (1987). *Churches as an Avenue to High Blood Pressure Control.* Bethesda, Md.: National Institutes of Health.

Voorhees, C., and others. (1996). "Heart, Body, and Soul: Impact of Church-Based Smoking Cessation Interventions on Readiness to Quit." *Preventive Medicine, 25*(3), 277–285.

Wechsler, H. J. (1997). "Religious Perspectives on Access to Health Care: A Jewish Perspective." *Mount Sinai Journal of Medicine, 64*(2), 84–89.

Weis, D., Matheus, R., and Schank, M. J. (1997). "Health Care Delivery in Faith Communities: The Parish Nurse Model." *Public Health Nursing, 14*(6), 368–372.

Westberg, G. E. (1990). *The Parish Nurse.* Minneapolis, Minn.: Augsburg Fortress Press.

Westberg, G. E., and Westberg, J. M. (1987). *The Parish Nurse: How to Start a Parish Nurse Program in Your Church.* Park Ridge, Ill.: National Parish Nurse Resource Center, 1987.

CHAPTER 13

Faith-Based Initiatives with High-Risk Youth

Harold Dean Trulear

Urban churches in general and African American churches in particular have often been cited for their strategic, central role in their communities. Historically, many urban churches have functioned as what Carl Dudley and Sally Johnson have referred to as "pillar churches," congregations that have served as veritable thermostats of community vitality and neighborhood health (Dudley and Johnson, 1993). Many who studied the history of African American churches reached similar conclusions. The first social-scientific study of black communities, performed by W. E. B. Du Bois in the last decade of the nineteenth century, clearly demonstrated the role of black churches in the development of community infrastructure (Du Bois, 1967). This conclusion has been echoed by successive studies undertaken by Horace Cayton and St. Clair Drake (1962), Benjamin Mays and Joseph Nicholson (1933), Charles S. Johnson (1967), and even black church critic E. Franklin Frazier (1963). Similar conclusions are found in the recent literature, from local studies conducted by Jeremy White and Mary deMarcellus (1998) to the massive national survey of black churches conducted by C. Eric Lincoln and Lawrence Mamiya during the 1980s (1990).

At the same time, these churches have not been unaffected by the increased social stratification of urban centers, the outward migration of first white and now black residents, and the recent appearance of the so-called underclass. Drastically underchronicled but easily observable, urban churches have increasingly become commuter churches, especially those larger churches that tend to dominate the social landscape when the community asset maps are drawn. Ida Rouseau Mukenge analyzes this phenomenon in a case study of the First Baptist Church of Richmond, California, and the changes it experienced as members moved to Bay Area suburbs (1983). Mukenge notes a drastic shift in the congregation's understanding of social outreach. She attributes this to the membership's growing isolation and alienation from its surrounding community, a community of need. When the church was the center of the community, its outreach was to "us"—church members who were community residents, friends, and neighbors. Elsewhere I have added to Mukenge's case study with ethnographic material from other congregations that have seen similar shifts (Trulear, 1991).

In addition to shifts in residence and social attitude, one must also note the increasing complexity of community problems and the social malaise that accompanied social stratification in the black community. Issues once clearly defined by racial convention are now complicated by the shifting tide in economic relations within the black community and the extent to which black communities seem to have turned in on themselves through the escalation of gang violence, drug trafficking, youth crime, and other problematic behavior. These are not problems easily addressed through the appropriation of Gandhian nonviolent strategies, labor union sit-ins, or marches from Selma to Montgomery. Complex analyses must now buttress attempts to be truly prophetic in a world where there are no "white only" signs.

Finally, the black middle class, many of them churchgoers, is awakening to the fact that their integration of the American system was fundamentally uncritical, subjecting them (quite willingly I would argue) to forms of tribalism and consumerism that fifty years ago combined with arcane racial conventions to keep blacks out of that same mainstream. W. E. B. Du Bois put the case thus: "The Negro has asked for a seat at the front of the bus for so long, he has forgotten to ask where the bus is going."

Such a shift in social convention has led me to seek solace in James Russell Lowell's maxim, oft cited by Martin Luther King himself: "New occasions teach new duties, time makes ancient good uncouth. He must upward still and onward who would keep abreast of truth." Urban church work, what we now refer to by the euphemism "faith-based initiatives," is reinventing itself in the light of the bus's destination. Indeed, contemporary problems among urban youth mirror the worst of consumerist, hedonist, and perverted self-interested dynamics of the larger society: crucial elements of the destination. This fact has forced congregations to rethink their ministries with that population even as they readjust to the concerns and issues of the larger society. Yet the forms that such consumerism, hedonism, and self-interest take in urban youth culture reflect a greater structural alienation from the mainstream of American society. Therefore, religious leaders must find ways in which their institutions can be better positioned to deal with a population from which it is increasingly alienated, often as a direct result of the upward flight of urban church members in general and black congregants in particular.

Defining Characteristics

It should surprise no one that the most innovative strategies in addressing youth problems in the 'hood are being employed by congregations that:

- Resist the tendencies toward uncritical upward mobility.
- Challenge social service agencies that usurp community empowerment and erase community memory of problem solving.
- Concentrate on strategies that build community infrastructure.
- Affirm and emphasize moral virtue and altruism.
- Reconnect persons and institutions within their own environment.

Interdenominational Theological Center ethicist Riggins Earl has called this process "reneighboring the 'hood."

To discover successful ways of achieving this goal, the Ford Foundation supported a study of thirty theological educational programs serving African American ministers and churches. This revealed a number of creative strategies by small to midsize (membership under five hundred) congregations. By targeting nondegree educational programs, it hoped to identify practices more characteristic of churches whose leadership was formed outside the mainstream of formal theological study and within a cultural and institutional context more clearly related to grassroots social and political associations and organizations (Trulear and Carnes, 1997). The Ford Foundation, led by program officer Robert Franklin, was rightly concerned that much of the vibrant activity of inner-city churches was overlooked because most social observers were prone to look at the historic, established churches and to calibrate the health of urban ministry based on their activity. In talking with the students, the research team that the foundation employed sought to get at ministry practices of churches not normally considered in the modeling process for community-based ministry.

This research, conducted in 1996 and 1997, coincided with the discovery by Princeton political scientist John DiIulio (1997a, 1997b, 1999; DiIulio and Walker, 1997) and others that faith-based strategies were among the most successful in reaching the most at-risk youth in urban communities. The demonstrable, and high-profile, success of the ministry of the Ten Point Coalition in Boston, Massachusetts, became a catalyst for growing interest in the work of small to midsize congregations in inner-city neighborhoods ("Savior of the Streets," 1998). In Boston, congregations such as the Azusa Christian Community with a membership of under one hundred took the lead in reducing juvenile crime and violence. They developed innovative partnerships with law enforcement and juvenile justice; neighborhood patrols and street presence; community-based programming in education, personal skills, and job readiness; and neighborhood advocacy on behalf of the poor and disenfranchised of their communities. The oft-repeated statistic of no juvenile gun-related homicide in Boston from July 1995 to November 1997 is only one of a number of indicators documenting the successes of congregations such as Azusa.

This success led to extended observation of such churches across the country in preparation for an upcoming research demonstration project by Public/Private Ventures on the work of faith-based institutions with high-risk youth. Also, preliminary research by Jeremy White and Mary deMarcellus (1998) reveals that such innovation is more common than one might suppose. While some may argue that if there is such innovative ministry going on in inner cities, why do its problems persist, I would side with DiIulio, whose observation of these tendencies has led him to ask the converse: "How much worse off would our cities be if such congregations did not exist?"

From my conversations with church leaders and observations of church programming in inner cities, it became clear that at least four significant strategies characterize successful church initiatives with the most alienated and troubled at-risk youth:

- Focused leadership
- Targeting high-risk population (as distinguished from a general focus on at-risk populations)
- Recruiting, training, and mobilizing committed, caring, and faithful adults as volunteers
- Developing a ministry of advocacy

Indeed, these principles appear to be transferable to a variety of urban ministries, and not applicable to youth ministry alone.

The first two components, focused leadership and targeting the high-risk population, reflect the orientation of programs successful in concentrating and mobilizing limited but important resources toward the problems of high-risk youth and their communities. The second two, recruiting, training, and mobilizing caring, faith-motivated adults as volunteers—the majority of them community residents—and developing a ministry of advocacy, speak to the individuals best recruited in and supported for the labor-intensive work of ministering to high-risk youth. They also point to the important issue of building and sustaining community infrastructure, resisting the tendencies of communities to become overly dependent on external, often commodified (services for sale), resources. This point, emphasized repeatedly throughout this book, is highlighted significantly in Chapter Three.

Focused Leadership

Congregations in distressed urban communities are often called on to meet a variety of needs. The historic role of African American churches as centers of neighborhood and community life reflects a similar dynamic. Pastors, ministers, and other church leaders respond to numerous community concerns, evidencing the myriad expectations placed on them by neighborhood residents.

Sometimes the needs are personal. Ministers serve as the primary sources of counseling in their neighborhoods as residents seek psychological and spiritual help amid the real pressures of living in distressed communities. Congregations and their leadership often receive requests for food, clothing, and shelter from the poor in their midst. Congregations also respond on an emergency basis to the needs of working members and friends who are experiencing layoffs, income shortfalls, and other temporary crises in their lives. Many congregations have emergency funds, soup kitchens, diaconates, and benevolence committees charged with responding to the variety of needs requests that come before the congregations (Cohen and Jaeger, 1997; Printz, 1999). It is not difficult for those needs to become the driving force behind community service. Need itself becomes a veritable idol consuming most, if not all, of a congregation's human service capacity.

When governed by the tyranny of need, congregations become fragmented in their approach to service, stretched to the limits of resources, and unsystematic in the development of their delivery systems. At times, faith-based organizations responding to the immediacy of crises before them allocate resources in ways that create shortfalls in other areas, weaken the ongoing infrastructure of the congregation's community service system, and lead to burnout among congregational leadership in general and pastors in particular. Smaller congregations with larger percentages of resident memberships are particularly vulnerable to such fragmentation and burnout, drawing from a smaller pool of human, financial, and other resources. Programs that manage to avoid fragmentation and burnout tend to be characterized by what we call focused leadership: pastors and congregational leaders who have determined that they will be driven by specific initiatives rather than general needs.

Congregations and faith-based organizations must develop the ability to say no to some demands in order to have the capacity to address significant problems that mandate responses requiring depth of analysis and intensity of labor. At one level, this requires resistance to the theological tendency to portray God or Jesus (and therefore the congregations who minister in God's name) as one who meets all needs at all times. "Jesus met the needs of everyone he came in contact with" is a familiar mantra chanted by the leadership of urban congregations. Yet persons such as Jude Tiersma have noted that following God's lead does not require meeting every need in urban congregational work (Tiersma, 1994).

Once freed from the tyranny of need, congregations can become proactive and strategic about the ministries they develop and the specific initiatives they employ. Those that focus on high-risk youth often do so at the expense of casting a broad net in community service. They do not attempt to be all things to all people. This is a difficult decision, given the intensity and extent of needs in inner-city communities of the poor. Yet the very intensity of need mandates the mobilization of concentrated resources on behalf of targeted populations, especially for congregations with limited resources and smaller memberships. In the case of some congregations, this means filtering all ministries through a lens that focuses on the particular need being addressed. In the East New York neighborhood of Brooklyn, the heralded congregation of St. Paul's Community Baptist Church decided to focus on youth ministries expressed by the church policy that they are "youth centered, adult led, and elder ruled." The congregation subjects all church programs, existing and proposed, to the litmus test of relevance for youth in general and neighborhood youth in particular (Freedman, 1994). This focus, dating back to the 1980s, predates Kansas City's important civic campaign, "Is it good for Kids?" where public and social policy and decision making were subject to similar examination.

Focused congregational leadership enables congregational members to target the issue at hand. In the Azusa Christian Community and its Ella J. Baker House in the Dorchester section of Boston, pastor Eugene Rivers has successfully directed the energies of his congregation to work and witness among youth. Though relatively small in membership, Azusa congregants understand that their energies in mission and community outreach are contextualized by the church's commitment to placing caring adults in the lives of every youth in the neighborhood. All Azusa programming uses this goal as the underpinning of the congregation's work. Azusa, through its decision to target the community's high-risk youth, developed a clear focus that kept congregational energy from being diffused by the myriad needs and concerns in the community. Indeed, working with youth and their families became the lens through which all community problems were viewed.

When the congregation gets involved in economic development, through the work of church member Eva Thorne, who holds the doctorate in political science from MIT, it is with the express focus of how community development and policy benefit the lives of youth and their families in the neighborhood. Azusa members virtually all live in or relocate to the Dorchester neighborhood to symbolize and actualize the focus of their attention on the youth of the community and to be present for them in the midst of distressing conditions.

One thing that helps smaller, focused congregations with their work is a willingness to collaborate with other congregations as well as community organizations, law enforcement, and educational institutions. When a religious organization decides to do one thing well, it must be in relationships with both the agencies that help it do that focused task and those that can help it with the other tasks of ministry that cannot be neglected. Cooperation with law enforcement and probation and parole requires that faith-based institutions know both the operations of juvenile justice in their communities and the players. Often clergy are seen as adversaries to law enforcement because of ongoing prophetic activity. But as Rivers noted, "At one point, I had to drop the Father Flanagan routine and recognize that there are some bad kids who need to be locked up. Once I admitted that to the police, we had some grounds for conversation."

Similarly, law enforcement officials noted the need for community programs, educational opportunities, and jobs. Police officer Paul Joyce regularly visits the office buildings in downtown Boston to arrange summer and regular jobs for youth as alternatives to life on the streets. Also, the juvenile probation department has developed the Fatherhood Program, which places young men on probation in a twelve-week group seminar led by clergy, probation officers, and court psychologists that focuses on issues of responsible fatherhood and challenges those young men who are fathers to play an active, nurturing role in their children's lives. By using cooperative strategies, the small, focused congregation multiplies resources and develops relationships that enable it to maximize its efficiency in delivering services to high-risk youth.

Targeting Population

Targeting community populations is a corollary of focused leadership. Many inner-city ministries target neighborhoods in their outreach. The churches rightly reflect a parish approach to urban ministry, focusing on communities as the primary repository of social and community life. Many congregations feel a sense of responsibility for community wholeness and well-being, regardless of whether they have significant resident membership or are essentially commuter congregations. In the former category, congregations consist of members from the neighborhood and therefore have a genuine existential interest in the welfare of the community. In the latter category, black and other urban middle-class congregations physically located in the inner city but whose membership commutes from the suburbs or "better" neighborhoods, consistently admonish congregants to have a sense of responsibility for the old neighborhood. Churches and other faith-based institutions often develop ministries and programs that reflect this parish idea, focusing on the needs of the entire neighborhood or community.

When it comes to working with high-risk youth, such programs often fall short precisely because of the strategy of addressing a broad spectrum of needs or a broad, geographically based constituency. Youth programs and ministries that target neighborhoods cast a broad net, saying, in the words of the Bible, "Whosoever will, let them come."

When churches and agencies offer such a general invitation, however, they tend to attract the youth already looking for guidance or a safe haven from the distressing elements of life in their communities. Many times, targeting a community's youth without specifying a strategy that addresses the identification and recruitment of high-risk youth leads to programs that work with "the good kids in a bad neighborhood." Such work is necessary and noble, and it is critical to the development of those at-risk youth who need love, support, and resources for their development and for successful and meaningful lives. Yet often faith-based institutions (and nonsectarian institutions for that matter) are assumed to be working with the most difficult youth in the community, when this simply is not the case.

The error lies in the failure to distinguish between at-risk and high-risk youth. Youth and other community leaders declare that "all of our youth are at-risk youth," as they reflect on the myriad challenges facing youth in disadvantaged communities. However, some youth are more at risk than others. Indeed, if one were to interrogate the language concerning at-risk youth issues, one can assume that to be at risk is to be at risk of becoming something—in this case, something negative, presumably something profoundly antisocial, even criminal or violent. Some youth, however, are not at risk of such behavior; they already are engaged in it. This population does not normally respond to the "whosoever" call mentioned above. Congregations and faith-based agencies that hope to reach high-risk youth successfully must develop specific strategies targeting that population. Such targeting normally comes in one of three forms: referral from juvenile justice, referral from public education, and street intelligence.

Churches that receive referrals from juvenile justice do so in a variety of ways. Many faith-based institutions take advantage of diversion programs in their cities. These programs enable community organizations and agencies to have youth assigned to their charge. Youth receive mentoring from church members and often perform some form of community service. By linking young people with persons in the community, churches mobilize human capital in the community to support youth in such programs. In Oakland, California, Oakland Police and Clergy Together (OPACT) diverts nonviolent first offenders into mentoring relationships with church laypersons as an alternative to adjudication or incarceration. Adolescent Resource Management, a faith-based nonprofit, developed a similar program for the churches in Atlantic City, New Jersey.

Other congregations and faith-based institutions begin their intersection with high-risk youth while they are incarcerated. Many congregations go to juvenile detention facilities to provide worship services and counseling; others use their access to youth in detention centers to build relationships with youth from their communities and then continue those relationships when they are released. Shiloh Baptist Church of Washington, D.C., piloted such a program with adult offenders in the Lorton Correction Facility. Parishioners were concerned that churches, while fairly visible and active with persons during their incarceration, seemed wholly absent as these men made the difficult transition back to their old neighborhoods. The church began to establish relationships with the men at Lorton at least six months prior to their release, providing them with a support system for their transition back to the community. Other churches support incarcerated youth, providing them with a network of caring adults when they return to their communities. This network assists the youth in making the transition from the structured environment of detention back to the neighborhoods where they got into trouble.

In Paterson, New Jersey, Women on the Move for Christ received a list of every youth in the Passaic County Juvenile Detention Center who had not received a visit. They visited the youth, built relationships with them, and were waiting for them on release. The organization visited their families to determine what the impediments were to visiting their incarcerated adolescent. If the family needed transportation to the facility, Women on the Move for Christ arranged it, even providing rides from Paterson to the facility. If the family did not visit because of shame, resentment, or anger toward the youth, the church women worked to facilitate reconciliation between the youth and his or her family.

The San Francisco Foundation's Foundation Alliance Interfaith to Heal Society (FAITHS) has placed a chaplain in the county juvenile hall who links incarcerated youth with religious institutions in their communities, an interesting challenge in such a religiously diverse city. In Chicago, Reverend Harold Bailey began the Probation Challenge program in 1979. The program works with youth under court supervision, house arrest, probation, or parole by providing them with tutoring, counseling, and rap sessions. Probation Challenge, located on the campus of Olivet-Harvey College, has served over eighty thousand youth, with a recidivism rate of only 7 percent among program graduates (Merida, 1996). In Austin, Texas, a city whose local government has been a leader in developing diversionary programs, African American and Latino congregations have begun to network with juvenile justice officials to participate in such programs. One such program involves the planting and tending of community vegetable and flower gardens. This initiative not only teaches the youth planning, responsibility, and maintenance—all under the watchful eye of caring adults— but also helps to beautify the neighborhood. In fact, the youth display so much pride in their gardens that they vigorously (though now nonviolently) defend them against vandalism. The sense of accomplishment and responsibility helped make neighborhood beautification and neighborhood pride major issues for these inner-city youth.

School referrals demand a process of building relationships with education officials such as principals, guidance counselors, and others who have significant intelligence on which youth are in the most difficulty, academic and otherwise. In Boston, Eugene Rivers led a group of Ten Point Coalition preachers in an antigang initiative that relied on school officials to supply them with the names of active and suspected gang leaders. Clergy and police then visited the homes and schools of gang youth, offering alternative programs, job opportunities, and the promise of a "no-tolerance" policy on gang activity. East End Cooperative Ministries (EECM), a social agency wholly owned by over fifty congregations in Pittsburgh, holds the contract for the federal government's Communities and Schools initiative, which provides community support for youth in public schools. Through this initiative, EECM staff and volunteers (including a cadre of AmeriCorps volunteers) work with some of the most difficult young people in local schools. Although careful to avoid improper breaches of the wall between church and state, school officials express significant gratitude for the presence of religiously motivated persons from the community in their schools.

In New York City, the Urban Youth Alliance, a parachurch organization that sponsors and supports Bible clubs attached to local high schools and colleges, entered into a collaborative relationship with the Latino Pastoral Action Center and the Love Gospel Assembly to target students at Taft High School whom school staff deemed to be "the one hundred most at-risk youth" entering the ninth grade. With their partners, the alliance received the list during the summer before the school year. Volunteer and paid staff went door to door through the South Bronx, asking youth and their families to participate in a special after-school program of tutoring and life skill development. Fully a quarter of the families responded to the invitation, and twenty youth remained with the program during its first year. In addition to providing tutoring, the alliance supplied mentors recruited from graduates of their Bible clubs in other inner-city high schools. They also identified job internships at local colleges and businesses where the youth were able to apply skills developed in the program. The regular ministries of the Latino Pastoral Action Center and the Love Gospel Assembly offered additional support services.

In Memphis, Tennessee, the Memphis Leadership Foundation (MLF) raised money to support the salaries of several guidance counselors for the public school system. Although they are careful not to proselytize, these counselors do build relationships with nearby churches that provide support, programs, and advocacy for the neighborhood school and its most difficult-to-reach children. MLF founder Larry Lloyd, along with MLF youth director Rudy Howard, also trains youth ministers for service in local churches, then works with the congregations to build relationships with neighborhood schools using the youth ministers as primary liaisons.

Street intelligence requires developing a presence in the neighborhood sufficient to identify high-risk youth and win their trust. While all youth in a neighborhood may be considered at risk, youth actively engaged in criminal behavior constitute a smaller percentage of young people in a distressed community. Even if the oft-cited, almost apocryphal, statement that approximately 30 percent of African American males under the age of thirty are either incarcerated, on probation, or on parole is true, it still means that the majority of young black males are not under court supervision. Even among those who have been adjudicated, it is important to distinguish between those guilty of nonviolent offenses and those who are truly menaces to society. Finally, one should note that the overwhelming majority of youth who are arrested once are never arrested again. When a youth worker at a gathering of church leaders in Pittsburgh suggested that interventions ought to be targeted at first offenders because of the potential recidivism, Allegheny Family Court justice Cheryl Craig replied, "Of the first time offenders that come before me in my courtroom, eighty percent never come back." Indeed, Craig's experience is more common than popularly imagined.

Building relationships with youth and young adults in urban neighborhoods enables church workers to identify the truly high-risk youth in a community. But such presence requires time—time on the streets and on the playgrounds—with youth, enough time to enable the young people to understand that there is someone who really cares about them and the communities in which they live. This creates trust, a scarce resource in African American communities in particular (Fukuyama, 1996), which becomes the basis for significant relationship building with at-risk youth.

Developing trust cannot be underestimated as part of a strategy for gaining knowledge of who's who in the community in general and among the urban youth subculture in particular. Reverend Ray Hammond of the Ten Point Coalition in Boston recounted how drug dealers responded to local clergy's initial attempts to build relationships with youth on the streets of Boston. He noted that the young men were cynical about the presence of the ministers and church workers out on night patrols and spending time in parks and playgrounds where youth hung out. Several dealers thought that the ministers were just out for publicity and that their initiative would be short-lived. "Actually," offered one, "I don't see much difference between me and you preachers. I drive a nice car, you drive a nice car. I wear nice clothes and jewelry and so do you. I got lots of women and I know you preachers do too. If you're still here six months from now, I'll believe you're for real." Trust is in short supply in urban neighborhoods, and troubled youth often reflect the lowest amounts of trust, especially toward adult authority figures.

In Boston, Ten Point Coalition leader Eugene Rivers speaks candidly about learning the lesson of presence on the street. Shortly after moving to the Dorchester section of Boston, he befriended a young drug dealer, Selvin Brown, who over time came to trust Rivers as being deeply concerned about and committed to the community. In one conversation, Rivers asked Brown why he thought that drug dealers were more successful at reaching youth in the streets than the church. Brown replied that "when Johnny goes past my corner on the way to school, I'm there, you're not. When he comes home from school, I'm there, you're not. When he goes to the corner store for a loaf of bread, I'm there you're not. When he leaves to take it home, I'm there, you're not. I win, you lose."

Rivers took that lesson to mean that the church would have to establish a presence on the streets in order to gain the trust of area youth. He, along with other ministers and church leaders, went on weekly Friday night street patrols. While many saw this as a move to strengthen neighborhood safety through the presence of religious men "taking back the streets," Reverend Jeffrey Brown of Union Baptist Church in Cambridge, Massachusetts, insists that relationship building was a key part of the patrol strategy. "For the first six months," said Brown (no relation to the drug dealer), "very few people talked to us. They had to get to know us." When asked what they talked about with the street youth and drug dealers when they did have conversations, the pastor noted that the street patrol did not preach to them; rather they asked how they, as churches and church leaders, could be of service to them—offering counsel, job and educational opportunities, and a variety of sound alternatives to life on the streets. Rivers wryly noted, "These kids want jobs, real jobs—they'll even work at McDonald's if they don't have to wear those funny hats. The key is that when we offer them help, we have to be able to deliver. The jobs have to be there for the young men."

In Washington, D.C., the Alliance of Concerned Men brought their skills as gang interventionists to the Benning Terrace housing projects in the southeastern part of that city. There, through sharing tough love, faith, and direction, they brokered a truce that brought gang violence to a virtual halt. These men, all former gang members themselves, knew that jobs were an important concern for the youth of that neighborhood and began to broker employment opportunities for former gang members there. The alliance understands that "faith without works is dead" and that jobs were an important deliverable in the battle to win trust among urban youth.

Detroit's Alex Montaner operates a job training program for former gang members called the Gang Retirement and Continuing Education and Employment (GRACE). GRACE began when Montaner, just released from prison, went to his priest at St. Ann's parish and told of his desire to turn his life over to God and begin a new life. His priest suggested that his early release from prison was God's act of grace and that Montaner should extend that grace to others.

In response, Montaner developed a program that would offer local youth an alternative to gang life. With the help of the parish, he negotiated a truce among the neighborhood gangs. The gang leaders told him that if he were to take young people out of the gangs, they would have to be offered something better: education and employment. And these gang leaders insisted that the employment opportunities be good-paying jobs with health benefits. As of early 1999, GRACE had served close to 250 youth and young adults, with no episodes of recidivism and a better than 90 percent job retention rate. GRACE's ability to deliver helps Montaner and other women and men of faith who work the streets earn trust with neighborhood youth.

Much like the youth and young adults Alex Montaner works with in Detroit, the young people of Boston were eager to find good work when it was available. If Montaner, Rivers, and others working the neighborhoods cannot deliver, however, they lose the trust that enables street intelligence to be an effective strategy in targeting high-risk youth.

The Right Staff: Faith-Motivated Caring Residents

John DiIulio's study (1990) of effective programs in the nation's prisons led him to conclude that the right personnel make programming more effective than program content. The reality of the difference that caring adults make in the lives of young people has been documented through studies of a variety of mentoring programs, as well as the work of such important organizations as Big Brothers and Big Sisters (Tierney and Grossman, 1995). Ministries such as those discussed all bear out such findings. The approaches vary, targeting strategies differ, and program content and curricula are tailored to local constituencies, but one element they all share is a commitment to mobilize adults to mentor, disciple, and befriend youth in need of caring adults in their lives. For high-risk-youth ministry, the work is particularly labor intensive. Program volunteers find themselves called on at all hours of the day and night. This is one reason that many congregations either require that their volunteers be residents of the community—what John Perkins (1976) has referred to as "relocation"—or recruit their volunteers from among the membership that lives within the community. Having a strong resident membership builds relationships with and community infrastructure for high-risk youth. If the volunteers who work with them live in the neighborhood, the likelihood is that they will see them not only during the formal hours of a program initiative but also on the streets and in local stores, community gathering spaces such as parks or community centers, even the barber shop. Many police departments and district attorney's offices recognize the wisdom of mobilizing community residents to work with troubled youth, often staging police district–based hearings for juveniles with minor offenses, to be "adjudicated" by a community board that then "sentences" the youth to community service with a neighborhood organization. Churches in such neighborhoods often serve as venues for these diversion programs.

When staff and volunteers are community residents, they are available to build relationships during "off-hours." It is another variation on Selvin Brown's "I'm there, you're not" theme that Rivers and his cohorts sing so well. Youth pastor Ed Glover of the Allegheny Center Christian and Missionary Alliance Church in Pittsburgh attributes much of the success of his ministry with difficult youth to his residence in the community. While many of the activities, such as sports leagues, trips, and athletic clinics, seem to be draws in and of themselves, many hard-to-reach youth would not go to such programs if they were offered by other organizations. It is the trust capital earned by Glover's decade of living in the inner city that has enabled him to attract high-risk youth to his church programs.

Many of the volunteers from Love Gospel Assembly in the Bronx are not only community residents; they are also well acquainted with the ways of the streets. According to Pastor Ron Bailey, many of the congregation's members are former gang members, drug dealers, or users. Their ability to relate to the struggles of community youth is enhanced by their own biographies. Similarly, they are less likely to be taken in by street cons or feel inappropriate sympathy that lets youth off the hook for irresponsible behavior.

Because of the intensity of the work, those who minister to high-risk youth require training and care themselves. Burnout is always a danger, and volunteers who leave a program after a short period of time can damage a youth's sense of trust in adults in general and authority figures in particular. In discussing mentoring relationships, Jean Grossman (1999) notes that "volunteers typically come to mentoring programs because they want to help youth. Without establishing trust, however, mentors can never truly support the youth with whom they interact. Learning to trust, especially for youth who have been let down before, requires time" (p. 15).

This means that ministries that use volunteers for work with high-risk youth must invest in the care of the volunteer base as well as the youth themselves. Congregations must screen volunteers to ensure that they have recruited persons who, given proper support, are willing and able to invest time and energy over the long haul to build trust and strengthen relationships. Metro Youth for Christ of New Jersey, which worked in Eastside High School in Paterson, New Jersey, while Joe Clark was principal, accepted no volunteers unwilling to sign a written pledge committing themselves to at least six months of service. Reverends Arturo Lewis and Michael McDuffie held regular meetings and retreats among themselves and their volunteers in order to gain strength and support for their work in Paterson. Their motto was, "Ministry flows from community." This was their statement that support for each other was as critical as their support for the young people. William Myers, in *Theological Themes for Youth Ministry* (1987), makes the point that unless those who work with youth are aware of their own limitations and shortcomings, they will work them out through their work with the youth themselves. This is especially true in the labor-intensive work with high-risk youth, and congregations must support volunteers in these efforts.

Here the motivation of faith looms large. When volunteers are asked why they engage in such intensive work, they point to a sense of calling: "This is what Jesus would do." "The Lord told me to go to the hedges and the highways." "This is Allah's work." Faith-motivated volunteers draw strength from their sense of mission, even when program goals do not press for youth to find faith themselves. For these volunteers, faith enables them to do the difficult work of ministering to underserved youth, take the time required to build relationships of trust and accountability, and endure the struggles and setbacks that inevitably come when youth fall away or become recidivists.

Joel Van Dyke, a midwesterner who came to Philadelphia to attend Westminster Seminary, became a youth pastor in that city's hardscrabble Kensington. There he works the streets, building relationships with area youth, including drug dealers and gang members. His faith led him to relocate to the neighborhood—a far cry from his native surroundings—and to offer faith to others. His church, Bethel Tabernacle, has become a place where the faith of its youth workers is particularly strong, in large measure because they are products of the streets themselves and know how a life of

faith provides hope in a despairing community. Former gang leaders work the drug corners offering faith as an alternative to the un-
derground economy. They built a weight room to attract young
men from the neighborhood and the local middle school. Bethel
also operates a recording studio where neighborhood youth can
make their own recordings, and their first CD, "Street Psalms," has
been produced. Regular youth worship services, called "Off the
Hook," attract scores of community youth who sing and rap their
faith in praise to God. A look around the sanctuary shows clearly
that while the youth workers and their charges may not have
changed their clothing, they clearly, through faith, have changed
the direction of their lives.

Some worry that the faith factor in volunteers may be abused
through overzealous preaching at youth, the proffering of narrow
bigotry and prejudice often associated with more conservative religious groups, and a refusal to cooperate with others because of
theological or doctrinal concerns. Interestingly, most religious alliances that work with high-risk youth are able to bracket doctrinal
concerns for the larger goal of reaching youth and changing their
behavior and circumstances. When Eastern Baptist Theological
Seminary began offering courses for inmates in the county prison
system in Philadelphia, they discovered a strong degree of cooperation between Islamic and Christian groups working in the jail.
They had joined forces, despite clear religious differences, because
of their common goal of reaching the younger generation of inmates, eighteen to twenty-five years old, who were seen as extremely high risk. "There are two types of people in here," offered
one inmate who was studying to be an imam, "people with God
consciousness and those without it. Our job, the Christians and the
Moslems, is to develop God consciousness among those that don't,
so that when they hit the streets, they won't do the things that will
bring them back here."

Such cooperation is evident in high-risk-youth initiatives sponsored by Clergy United for Juvenile Justice in Cleveland, where an
alliance of Baptist and Islamic clergy has targeted youth in the Fifth
Police District, the Michigan Neighborhood Partnership where
Protestant, Catholics, Jews, and Muslims work together. In the Ten
Point Coalition, the support of the Jewish community has been in-
dispensable in mobilizing suburban resources for inner-city young

people. The lesson seems to be that when the stakes are high, the mission difficult, and the labor intense, doctrinal concerns take a back seat to results.

Similarly, while evangelism is central to many initiatives, it often takes forms less direct than the overzealous preaching about which some worry. Both Amy Sherman (1999) and Heidi Unruh (1999) have shown how the most important dimensions of evangelism have been the presence of clear sets of moral values contained in the offering of faith perspectives to people in distressed communities. Consistent with the notion that people need some meaning system to navigate life's journey, an evangelistic component within the faith-based initiative offers a moral compass to high-risk youth. The methods therefore have more to do with the caring adult sharing her or his faith with youth than some hard-sell rally-for-God approach that calls for confessions of faith in a large meeting. Evangelism, then, becomes an activity whose efficacy is directly linked to the presence of "the right staff."

Advocacy Ministries

Faith-based initiatives that are successful with high-risk youth understand that those youth are, in the words of missions specialist Harvey Conn (1992), not only "sinners, but sinned against." Programs that only "fix kids" are subject, philosophically, to charges of "blaming the victim" in that they do not address the exigencies of context. One can refer to the case of the youth minister who, on being asked by a parent to work with a child failing school, talks with the youngster only about his failure without questioning the role that a particular teacher, the school itself, the school system, or something else in his life may have played in the youth's struggle. Successful programs understand that they have a responsibility to address those structures that "sin against" youth, as well as the sin of the weak, violent, or criminal young person.

Luis Lugo, in his essay "Equal Partners: The Welfare Responsibility of Government and Churches" (1998), notes that churches that enter into collaborative relationships with public agencies must retain their autonomy in order to remain effective. Faith-based institutions need that autonomy in order to maintain their prophetic voice in addressing the ills of society in general and the complicity of government in particular. Just as government must be granted a certain sense of experience that gives it a right to offer its perspective on how projects might be formed, so too must congregations be respected for their experience. Only a respectful, clearly defined autonomy can offer such hope. Churches must be free to speak to government, business, social organizations, and other groups about the perspectives of faith that deem certain practices of those agencies wrong. And those agencies must be free to offer knowledge to faith-based initiatives.

But from the faith-based perspective, the problem looms large. Indeed, many inner-city pastors have rejected partnerships with government and business on theological or philosophical grounds. "I don't want any of pharaoh's money," declares the pastor wary of the strings attached to the pretense of government largesse. But the biblical models of persons such as Nehemiah suggest a role for governmental funding for faith-based initiatives that gives those communities full voice in their critique of the problems that confront the powerless of today's Jerusalem (Trulear, 1999). In Boston, the Ten Point Coalition is clear that their cooperation with law enforcement is not a blanket endorsement of everything a police officer does in the black community. That is why they hold award ceremonies and prayer meetings for police: to encourage and recognize good works among law enforcement officials and, by implication, to critique the work of those not concerned about the residents of the community. Black Clergy of Philadelphia and its social service agency, African American Interdenominational Ministries, work diligently at developing an independent stance that holds government accountable and seeks to work with government at points of mutual interest. Indeed, it is in establishing such points with government officials that AAIM, Ten Point, and others have found the need for a great expenditure of energy.

At a more basic level, advocacy means being there for youth when they come up against the system. Rivers and others speak of how often they are called on to be present with young men when they come before the courts. Often the presence of a clergyperson can mean the difference between a long sentence and a diversion into community service. This is effective only when the church is willing to be responsible for monitoring the young person during the time of diversion, as in Austin, Texas, and in Pittsburgh through the Christian Life Skills Center.

But the larger context of advocacy ministry remains the church's ability to stand outside any relationships of partnership and patronage and speak clearly to those in power when they are wrong. High-risk youth know when they have been "sinned against," and trust is built through a mutual recognition of the external factors that contribute to youth violence and criminality.

Conclusion

Much of what we learn about faith-based initiatives with high-risk youth continues to evolve from the efforts of organizations such as the Ten Point Coalition of Boston, the Urban Youth Alliance of New York City, the Michigan Neighborhood Partnership of Detroit, Los Angeles Metropolitan Churches, and the Regional Council of Neighborhood Organizations in southeastern Pennsylvania. In the early years of the new millennium, we should be able to make more informed judgments about extent, efficacy, capacity, and replicability of such efforts. For now, it is sufficient to state that preliminary findings clearly point to the importance of faith-based initiatives in working with high-risk youth and the need for all concerned to take a closer look at the potential for bringing to scale the relatively small efforts that such congregational efforts represent.

References

Cayton, Horace, and Drake, St. Clair. (1962). *Black Metropolis*. New York: HarperCollins.

Cohen, Diane, and Jaeger, Robert. (1997). *Sacred Places at Risk: New Evidence on How Endangered Older Churches and Synagogues Serve Communities*. Philadelphia: Partners for Sacred Places.

Conn, Harvey. (1992). *Evangelism: Preaching Grace and Doing Justice*. Phillipsburg, N.J.: Presbyterian and Reformed Publishing House.

DiIulio, John. (1990). "Getting Prisons Straight." *American Prospect*, Fall, pp. 54–64.

DiIulio, John. (1997a). "The Church and Civil Society." *Brookings Review*, Fall, pp. 27–31.

DiIulio, John. (1997b). "Jeremiah's Call: Inner City Churches Are Saving At-Risk Youth and They Deserve Our Support." *Prism*, 5(3), 18–23, 31–34.

DiIulio, John. (1999). "Supporting Black Churches." *Brookings Review*, Spring, pp. 42–45.

DiIulio, John, and Walker, Gary. (1997). "The Four M's of Fighting Crime." *Philadelphia Inquirer,* Mar. 10, 1997, p. A11.

Du Bois, W.E.B. (1967). *The Philadelphia Negro.* New York: Schocken.

Dudley, Carl, and Johnson, Sally. (1993). *Energizing the Congregation: Images That Shape Your Church's Ministry.* Louisville, Ky.: Westminster/John Knox.

Frazier, E. Franklin. (1963). *The Negro Church in America.* New York: Schocken.

Freedman, Samuel. (1994). *Upon This Rock: The Miracles of a Black Church.* New York: HarperCollins.

Fukuyama, Francis. (1996). *Trust: The Social Virtues and the Creation of Prosperity.* New York: Free Press.

Grossman, Jean. (1999). *Contemporary Issues in Mentoring.* Philadelphia: Public/Private Ventures.

Johnson, Charles S. (1967). *Growing Up in the Black Belt.* New York: Schocken.

Lincoln, C. Eric, and Mamiya, Lawrence. (1990). *The Black Church in the African American Experience.* Durham, N.C.: Duke University Press.

Lugo, Luis. (1998). *The Welfare Responsibility of Governments and Churches.* Annapolis, Md.: Center for Public Justice.

Mays, Benjamin, and Nicholson, Joseph. (1933). *The Negro's Church.* New York: Institute of Social and Religious Research.

Merida, Kevin. (1996). "Proposals Push to Try Juveniles as Adults." *Emerge,* Nov., pp. 26ff.

Mukenge, Ida R. (1983). *The Black Church in Urban America: A Case Study in Political Economy.* Lanham, Md.: University Press of America.

Myers, William. (1987). *Theological Themes for Youth Ministry.* New York: Pilgrim.

Perkins, John. (1976). *A Quiet Revolution.* Waco, Tex.: Word Publishers.

Printz, Tobi Jennifer. (1999). *Faith Based Service Providers in the Nation's Capital: Can They Do More?* Washington, D.C.: Urban Institute.

Rivers, Eugene, Hammond, Ray, and Brown, Jeffrey. (1996). *A Ten Point Plan to Save Our Youth.* Boston: National Ten Point Leadership Foundation.

"Savior of the Streets." *Newsweek,* June 1, 1998, pp. 20–24.

Sherman, Amy. (1997). *Restorers of Hope: Reaching the Poor in Your Community with Church Based Ministries That Work.* N.p.: Crossways.

Sherman, Amy. (1999)."The Response of the Churches to Welfare Reform." Brookings Institution/Civitas Conference, Jan.

Tierney, Joseph, and Grossman, Jean. (1995). *Making a Difference: An Impact Study of Big Brothers Big Sisters.* Philadelphia: Public/Private Ventures.

Tiersma, Jude. (1994). "What Does It Mean to Be Incarnational When We Are Not the Messiah." In Jude Tiersma and Charles Van Engen (eds.), *God So Loved the City: Seeking a Theology for Urban Mission.* Monrovia: MARC.

Trulear, Harold Dean. (1991). "The Black Middle Class Church and the Quest for Community." *Drew Gateway, 61*(1), 44–59.

Trulear, Harold Dean. (1999). "The African American Church and Welfare Reform: Toward a New Prophetic Perspective." Annapolis: Center for Public Justice.

Trulear, Harold Dean, and Carnes, Tony. (1997). "A Study of the Social Service Dimension of Theological Education Certificate Programs." Report prepared for the Ford Foundation.

Unruh, Heidi. (1999) "Using the 'E' Word: Evangelism, Church-Based Community Services and Social Transformation." Brookings Institution/Civitas Conference, Jan.

White, Jeremy, and deMarcellus, Mary. (1998). *Faith-Based Outreach to At-Risk Youth in Washington, D.C.* Washington, D.C.: Center for Civic Innovation.

Conclusion
Using God's Gifts in Service
Edward L. Queen II

Writing a conclusion for a book may be necessary, but it can often strike the author as a pointless endeavor. After the richness and detail of the chapters, what can a conclusion offer? It appears about as exciting as a one-hour monologue by the ringmaster following the three rings of the circus. The audience already has been thrilled; it is now time to let them go on about their business.

Still, the need to bring about some closure, to give the appearance of completeness, is important. That is what the conclusion does. All of the previous chapters have spoken knowledgeably and seriously about the various tasks and obligations that lay before those who manage and work in faith-based human and social service organizations. The various chapters share four major themes:

- Work from and maintain your faith commitment.
- Build on strengths.
- Maintain your ethical integrity.
- Be willing to work with all in serving those in need.

Faith Commitment

An underlying presumption of all the chapters is that human and social service organizations that are driven by a faith commitment provide something special that exists beyond the mere significance of their numbers and the amount of service they deliver. It assumes that the activity of faith-driven individuals provides some added value to service delivery. This value may not be quantifiable, but it is there. Its presence is noted even by those who do not approach this work from a faith perspective. The chapters by John Kretzmann, Eric Clay and Elliott Wright, and Harold Dean Trulear make this point explicitly. In many communities and for many individuals, churches, mosques, synagogues, and temples provide one of the few integrating and trustworthy institutions around.

Institutions of faith have this privileged position because they are institutions of faith and retain that position only so long as they remain faithful. While James Lemler and Carl Dudley may be the only authors who mention it explicitly, the activities of worship, prayer, and faithfulness are key components to ensuring that the distinctiveness that gives faith-based workers strength and privilege is maintained.

Certainly the nature and form of such explicitly religious activities will be conditioned by the composition of an organization. Indeed, the struggle to find and maintain a powerful, communal religious life in complex and pluralistic organizations will mirror the complexity of living and working together. The undertaking should not be shunned because it may be difficult. Neither should it be short-circuited by some vapid minimalism. If our strength lies in serving others out of our strong faith commitments, then we must find ways to maintain that strength and build on it. Only in that way are we true to our faiths and the claim of offering something that other service agencies do not.

Build on Strengths

One of the strengths on which we should build is our faith; we are driven to serve others because of our religious commitment and the accompanying view that service to others is divinely mandated. Such a position separates us from other service agencies; in our work, we must find ways to maintain that source of our power and to strengthen it.

In our relationships with others, the religious dimension also provides us with many privileges and powers that we should use appropriately. The ability to function as an honest broker, a community convener, and a trusted mediator devolves on us because we are viewed as, and expected to be, driven by higher motives and to act accordingly. The result is that faith-based organizations can accomplish things other agencies cannot. This strength should be used wisely and prudently. By existing in this privileged position, we can leverage much and should do so. This privilege, however, exists only to the extent that we continue to be deserving. If we begin to look no different from any other interest group, just one more player, the privilege will disappear, as perhaps it should. It is only by maintaining our distinctiveness through our emphasis on worship, in its broadest sense, and our integrity that our organizations truly can realize their highest potential. Faith commitment is a gift to that organization which provides you with resources to place in the service of those in need. Do not waste it.

The strengths on which we need to build are not only those internal to the organization but those that are external, located in the community. This point, constantly repeated throughout the book, bears repeating here. Our communities are places of power, wealth, and skills waiting to be used for good. One of our obligations in undertaking this work is to ensure that we build on existing community strengths and community assets.

This realization constitutes an important strength. Like Jesus' feeding of the multitude with the little boy's lunch of loaves and fishes, by building on the myriad gifts held by individuals and associations in our community, much can be done.

But first we must be willing to see those gifts. Here again, faith will serve well. Our theological stance that each individual is a child of God, that all sentient beings have worth, should make it easier for us to seek out and recognize those gifts and call individuals to realize that which is best within them.

The ability to recognize the giftedness of others also comes from religion's continued value on community, on living our lives with and for one another. Religious traditions retain the view that life is with people. Recognizing that life is not, or ought not to be, simply one of struggling against others and grasping for goods, faith traditions remain the one strong locus for community. We know that it is not good "for man to be alone." That sense of community, of living with and for others, is a powerful strength that faith-based organizations have.

It is just that strength that drives many individuals into acts of solidarity with their communities, even when congregations are composed of commuters. Even more important, it causes many individuals of faith to in-migrate, to live in communities that are economically distressed and torn by crime and violence.

While we may not all be called to that, religions know the strength of that divine demand. Whether Jonah must go to Nineveh, Paul to the ends of the earth, the early Buddhist monks to Tibet and Sri Lanka (the examples could be multiplied): that is perhaps the greatest strength that faith-based organizations have, their compulsion to be responsive to divine commands and not merely to human caprice.

Integrity

The assumption that religious organizations answer ultimately to a higher authority makes the discussion of integrity richer and more complex. While many assume automatically that religious organizations are more honest than others, they simultaneously demand a higher level of integrity from those organizations than they would from secular organizations.

Both of these have their roots in the same place. Religious organizations are not merely presumed to be different from secular organizations; they *are* (or ought to be) different. Their entire ethos emerges from a connection with ultimate things that separates them radically from their secular counterparts. By explicitly recognizing their accountability to some transcendental judgment, they must struggle to realize the mandates of the tradition. From the way they keep their books, treat staff and those they serve, to their interactions with donors and the wider public, religious organizations ought to function differently. At the very least, they ought to believe they should act differently and struggle to do so.

Failures on our part at any level are not merely violations of fixed rules but offend against entire sets of values. Incompetence prevents us from doing our work well, hurting those in need, stealing from donors, and violating our own personhood in many ways.

These are heavy burdens. Fortunately religion is not only judgment but forgiveness as well. Knowing our weaknesses and failings, although striving to overcome them, enables us to struggle and work with others despite differences. This is the last major theme of this book: working with others.

Working with Others Serving Those in Need

Our work to serve those in need is our work to express, to live out our religious values. We have our obligations in doing this, and the work ought not to be instrumental to some other purpose. The focus must be our service to the other, to helping children of God.

If this is what we are about, then coming together with others to fulfill that obligation should be encouraged. Anything that helps those and does not violate our principles cannot be dismissed or ignored. If our focus is on serving, anything that enables us to effect that ought to be welcomed and encouraged. This outward focus means we need not only work with the pure and the perfect. Indeed, honesty about ourselves should remind us that the search for such perfection is a vain and fallacious task.

Our struggle is to serve the weak and helpless, and where we share that goal with others, we should work with them. Where we can recognize the dignity and value of individuals, we should do so. Where the spirit of God manifests itself, regardless in whatever shape, we should recognize it. The United States today is a place of variety and complexity. To meet the pressing needs of so many of our communities by using the strengths of those communities requires not only a recognition of that complexity but also the vision to see it as a gift.

Ultimately that is the power religious organizations bring to serving others, the scriptural and theological traditions that recognize the power and value of divine gifts. They have the knowledge that God's ways are mysterious and often emerge from that which the world has disparaged. Our communities are places of such gifts. Our obligation is to find them, honor them, and use them well.

Index